INCLUSIVE GROWTH IN GLOBALISED INDIA
Challenges and Options

INCLUSIVE GROWTH IN GLOBALISED INDIA
Challenges and Options

Edited by

P. JEGADISH GANDHI
Director
Vellore Institute of Development Studies (VIDS)
Vellore

DEEP & DEEP PUBLICATIONS PVT. LTD.
F-159, Rajouri Garden, New Delhi - 110 027

INCLUSIVE GROWTH IN GLOBALISED INDIA
Challenges and Options

ISBN 978-81-8450-057-8

Typeset by RAHUL COMPOSERS
358, Pocket-B, Phase-II, Sector-16B, Dwarka, New Delhi - 110 075

Printed in India at MAYUR ENTERPRISES
WZ Plot No. 3, Gujjar Market, Tihar Village, New Delhi - 110 018

Published by DEEP & DEEP PUBLICATIONS PVT. LTD.,
F-159, Rajouri Garden, New Delhi - 110 027 • Phone : 25435369, 25440916
E-mail : ddpubs@gmail.com • ddpbooks@yahoo.co.in
Showroom :
2/13, Ansari Road, Daryaganj, New Delhi - 110 002 • Telefax : 23245122

Dedicated To

The Living God who has blessed me with a new lease of life to carry out missions in the world.

Dr. Sunil Thomas Chandy and Dr. Roy John Korúla, Christian Medical College & Hospital, Vellore for their medical support during my critical hospitalization.

My wife Sugirtham, daughters Mary Shanthini Isaac, Shobhana J. Devaraj and Deepa and grandson Joe for their moral scaffolding at times of physical crisis.

Contents

Part III

ISSUES IN INCLUSIVE GROWTH

Preface

Ever since the Planning Commission (June 14, 2006) styled its Approach Paper to the Eleventh Five Year Plan (2007-12) with a caption, *Towards Faster and More Inclusive Growth,* the phrase "Inclusive Growth" has assumed greater significance in plan paradigm shift discussions at different levels all over the country and abroad.

Inclusive growth is a welcome shift in emphasis in Plan Approach Paper, but will it mean better distribution? This appears to be the genuine reasons for the dissatisfaction expressed by some experts on the four alternative growth targets ranging from 7 percent to 9 percent envisaged in plan strategy. This compendium carries analytical papers on challenges and options confronting inclusive growth dream in the globalised India.

I record my sincere thanks to Professors: M.R. Aggarwal (Panjab University), G.M. Bhat (The University of Kashmir), A. Ranga Reddy (S.V. University), I. John Mohan Razu (The United Theological College), S. Iyyampillai (Bharathidasan University), V. Mohanasundaram (PSG College of Arts and Science), Sherly Kurien (Avinashilingam University for Women) and R. Christopher Rajkumar (The Rural Theological Institute of Tamil Nadu Theological Seminary) and, the research scholars, G. Narasimha Raghavan, M. Sampth Kumar Raju and Shabir Ahmad Padder for their invited papers.

Apart from academics, I have compiled published materials from leading newspapers and economic journals in India and important speeches given by eminent economists and policy-makers. My grateful thanks are due to all of them in a special way.

Thanks are due to Prof. S. Thiagukumar, Voorhees College for the help in language work of the manuscript and Mr. L. Pradeep Kumar and Ms. S. Sasikala SLN Xerox, Sathuvachari, Vellore and Mr. Nataraju, Communication Centre, ECC, Bangalore for their computerized work.

I personally thank Mr. G.S. Bhatia, Managing Director, Deep and Deep Publications Pvt. Ltd., New Delhi for his continued support in printing and publishing my books.

P. JEGADISH GANDHI

Acknowledgements

Special thanks are due to the Editor of *The Economic Times* for reproducing Prof. Joseph E. Stiglitz's article on *Promise of Globalization* published on 1st January 2007.

The following addresses of the eminent persons were reproduced with great thanks: Dr. A.P.J. Abdul Kalam, *Farewell Thanks giving Speech,* 24, July, 2007, Dr. Manmohan Singh, *Speech at the University of Cambridge,* 11 October, 2006, Dr. Montek S. Ahluwalia, *Twenty-seventh Jawaharal Nehru Memorial Lecture,* London, 10 April, 2005 and Dr. T.S. Papola, *Inaugural Address at the National Seminar* on "Making Growth Inclusive with special reference to Imbalances in Regional Development", Department of Economics, University of Jammu, Jammu, 12-13 March 2007.

Some of the materials in this volume have already been published in *The Hindu* and *The Hindu Business Line,* Chennai. I am thankful to the editors of those leading newspapers.

P. JEGADISH GANDHI

List of Contributors

Dr. A.P.J. Abdul Kalam, Former President of India.

Mr. Aditya Puri, Managing Director, HDFC Bank.

Dr. M.R. Aggarwal, Professor of Economics, Panjab University, Chandigarh.

Dr. Bhanoji Rao, Professor Emeritus, GITAM Institute of Foreign Trade, Visakhapatnam, Andhra Pradesh.

Dr. G.M. Bhat, Head, PG Deptt. of Economics, The University of Kashmir, Hazratbal, Srinagar.

Dr. Branco Milanovic, Economist, The Carnegie Endowment for International Peace and World Bank.

Dr. C.P. Chandrasekhar, Jawaharlal Nehru University, New Delhi.

Mr. R. Christopher Rajkumar, Director, The Rural Theological Institute of Tamil Nadu, Theological Seminary (TTC), Madurai.

Dr. P.V. Indiresan, Former Director, Indian Institute of Technology, Chennai.

Dr. S. Iyyampillai, Professor of Economics, Bharathidasan University, Thiruchirapalli.

Mr. V. Jagan Mohan, Managing Director, Coastal Local Area Bank Ltd., Vijayawada, Andhra Pradesh.

Dr. Jayati Ghosh, Jawaharlal Nehru University, New Delhi.

Dr. P. Jegadish Gandhi, Editor of the Book.

Dr. I. John Mohan Razu, Professor of Christian Social Ethics, The United Theological College, Bangalore.

Dr. Joseph E. Stiglitz, The 2001 Winner of Nobel Prize in Economics.

Mr. T.B. Kapali, Freelance Journalist, *The Hindu—Business Line*, Chennai.

Dr. M.Y. Khan, Former Economic Advisor, Securities and Exchange Board of India (SEBI).

Dr. V. Mohanasundaram, Reader in Economics, PSG College of Arts and Science, Coimbatore.

Dr. Manmohan Singh, Prime Minister of India.

Dr. Montek Singh Ahluwalia, Deputy Chairman, Planning Commission, Govt. of India.

Mr. G. Narasimha Raghavan, Project Fellow, Department of Economics, PSG College of Arts and Science, Coimbatore.

Dr. T.S. Papola, Past President, Indian Economic Association.

Mr. C.J. Punnathara, Columnist, *The Hindu—Business Line*, Chennai.

Mr. Ranabir Ray Choudhury, Senior Editor, *The Hindu—Business Line*, Chennai.

Dr. A. Ranga Reddy, Professor of Economics, Sri Venkateswara University, Tirupati.

Mr. Sampath Kumar Raju, Research Scholar, Sri Venkateswara University, Tirupati.

Dr. Sherly Kurien, Reader in Economics, Avinashilingam University for Women, Coimbatore.

Mr. Shabir Ahmad Padder, Research Fellow, PG Deptt. of Economics, The University of Kashmir, Srinagar.

Introduction

The spread of globalization is universal, but its distribution is partial in society. The Prime Minister, Manmohan Singh has openly acknowledged that "the gap between the rich and the poor is widening. This coupled with the inability of the public sector to provide adequate and quality services in health and education, and caters to the needs of the poor, is causing resentment and alienation. This is nurturing divisive forces and putting pressure on the practice of democracy. . . . *We need to work for inclusive globalization*. This calls for a new global vision". The Planning Commission has approved the Approach Paper to the 11th Plan rooting for a growth rate of 10 per cent in the final years of the plan in order to be in the front ranks of fast growing developing countries "with faster and more inclusive growth".

To be genuinely inclusive, the plan must have a goal of providing food security to all Indians, that is universal food security. This will require a focus on much more than a higher rate of economic growth. Growth is undoubtedly important, but not at any cost. Since independence, we have operated in the belief that equity and growth constitute a win-lose game; we can have either one or the other but not both at the same time. Equity and growth is a win-win game, provided we are good managers. The market-driven experiences of the 15-year old (1991-2006) Economic Reforms regime in India has shown asymmetrical growth especially in social sector (health, education, housing and welfare of the poor) development.

This edited book, *Inclusive Growth in the Globalised India: Challenges and Options* is an attempt to focus on various ongoing debates and discussions on the new paradigm shift in planning strategy. The book is divided into three parts. Part I analyses the dynamics of economic globalization and its impact on major sectors of growth in India.

President *Abdul Kalam* in his Farewell Thanksgiving speech to the Nation on 24th July 2007 referred to the question, "Why India cannot become a developed nation before the year 2020?" It is possible to realize the vision if we work resolutely with the following 10-point distinctive profile: (a) A Nation where the rural and urban divide has reduced to a thin line. (b) A Nation where there is an equitable distribution and adequate access to energy and quality water. (c) A Nation where agriculture, industry and service sector work together in symphony. (d) A Nation where education with value system is not denied to meritorious candidates because of societal or economic discrimination. (e) A Nation which is the best destination for the most talented scholars, scientists, and investors. (f) A Nation where the best of health care is available to all. (g) A Nation where the governance is responsive, transparent and corruption free. (h) A Nation where poverty has been totally eradicated, illiteracy removed and crimes against women and children are absent and none in the society feels alienated. (i) A Nation that is prosperous, healthy, secure, peaceful and happy and continues with a sustainable growth path. (j) A Nation that is one of the best places to live in and is proud of its leadership.

To *Joseph E Stiglitz*, globalization has been a double-edged weapon. With some reforms, globalization has a chance of living upto its promises and potential of improving standards of the rich and the poor, in both the developing and developed worlds. Successful countries have managed globalization on their own terms; take a pragmatic course, eschewing ideologies and market fundamentalism. Therefore, the problem is not with globalization, but with the way globalization has been managed. In his incisive analysis, "Globalization in Trouble", *Branco Milanovic* explored the growing resentment, as only a few poor countries adjust to globalisation. China and India compete globally, and yet only a fraction of their citizens prosper. Forty of the poorest nations, many in Africa, have had zero growth during the past 20 years. For the world's poor, globalization has resulted in a loss of self-respect and hope.

Manmohan Singh forthrightly pointed that globalization has not removed personal and regional income disparities. The gap between the rich and the poor is widening. We need a new global vision-inclusive globalization—that ensures the gains from globalization are more widely shared. To convince people in poor countries about the benefits of globalization, we must take a more enlightened view liberalizing trade in service and labour-intensive manufactures, in which developing counties are competitive. *Montek S. Ahluwalia* elaborately analysed how India could grapple with the challenges posed by globalisation and chart out solutions to these challenges within the framework of democratic polity. He identified three priority areas to move towards more inclusive growth in the globalised India. They are health and education levels especially in rural areas, revival of momentum in agriculture and improving the quality of infrastructure. There is no reason to fear that globalisation will hurt India's growth prospects considering it's a vast resource availability, adaptable economic policies and strong institutional support.

M.R. Aggarwal made a detailed study of globalisation, growth, its pattern and structural changes in India in the post-reform period. The final success of the policies of globalisation and market-friendly reforms will to a great extent depend on the global framework of cooperation and not on confrontation. Domestically, India has to create a favourable climate for "good governance". In their joint paper *A. Ranga Reddy* and *M. Sampath Kumar Raju* highlighted the macro changes of globalisation on Indian agriculture. Infact, Indian agriculture is not so advanced during the reforms regime. It has to improve its nature and extent through corporate farms, agri-business agri-industry, ecological protection, bio-village development so that it can remove rural poverty and promote employment opportunities. *I. John Mohan Razu* in his analytical study interrogated empirically the relation between "inclusive growth" "food security" when we talk about food security, we need to take into account bio-safety. Unless and until we protect our agrarian economy as against the onslaught of market economy crisis would escalate wherein the farmers resorting to suicides would increase. Therefore, we need to think about public-private partnership for farm ar ' non-employment. If both are well developed, inclusion becomes possible because the diverse groups in the rural sector can compete for better incomes. He also raised a question: would the private sector driven by profit motive be committed to social corporate responsibility? *T.B. Kapali* predicted that financial globalization gathers momentum in India. The RBI in its road map released in 2005, laid out a graduated scaling up of foreign bank activity in order to enable Indian banks to better prepare themselves for global competition. Indian banks might have to reckon with newer dimensions of competition as foreign players create niches on both leading and funding sides.

Part II focuses on various dimensions of inclusive growth. In their explanatory study, *C.P. Chandrasekhar* and *Jayati Ghosh* lamented over the Approach Paper of the Eleventh Plan for it did not even attempt to provide a clear statement of goals and mechanisms. Instead, it adopted an uncritical "trickle down" approach to economic growth, by making the basic objective the achievement of a creation targeted annual GDP growth figure. The most critical aspect of growth that determines whether it is more inclusive is the extent to which it generates productive employment. But there is no mention about employment generation at the start of the plan document.

P.V. Indiresan, in his characteristic way, rued that the Eleventh Plan Approach Paper has been accused of departing from conventional wisdom. But it has not departed enough. The critical issues it lists are all chronic sores that innovation, not conventional wisdom, could solve. But the Approach has no answer. Our poor are disillusioned not because they are getting poorer, but because the rich are getting richer, faster, because the rich-poor disparity is increasing. Unlike SEZs that are overloaded with capital and commercial experts but short on local content, PURA includes social development and multiple classes of services cater to both rich and poor. PURA is inclusive without being altruistic.

Aditya Puri opined that India has transitioned to a 7 per cent—plus growth, and one contributor is the emerging marked-led consumerism. But the imperative is an "inclusive" model of development with focus on the poor. The broadening and deepening of consumer support, consequent to inclusive policies, should shift the GDP dynamic and ensure robust growth.

P. Jegadish Gandhi traced the growth strategies from the First Five Year Plan to the Eleventh Plan in a historical way and found out that the concept of "inclusiveness" was indirectly intertwined all through the planning era. The present stage of economic governance in India, at the completion of 60 years of political freedom (1947-2007), represents an ambiguous philosophy which weeps for the woes of the poor, but sides with the shinny life style of the rich segment. The 60th year of economic independence is best celebrated by a firm social foundation to build an "inclusive growth" society benefiting all sections.

Having posed the problem: Will the aim of inclusive growth be achieved?, *M.Y. Khan* pinpointed that the United Progressive Alliance (UPA) government has made a success effort to offer several benefits to the rural areas through the Budget allocations and schemes. But their successful implementation will depend on how effectively corruption could be kept at bay and how accountable the authorities are. Indeed, neither the GDP growth nor of employment reflects any inclusiveness. With the growth having become more technology-oriented and capital-intensive, its fruits are getting evenly distributed. There is clearly a need to focus on common people.

T.S. Papola brought out very clearly that reducing imbalances in regional development will be an essential ingredient of strategy for inclusive growth. A first step in making economic growth more inclusive is to identify the groups that have been excluded from the past growth and examine why they could not participate in the growth process in the first instance, we need to look at the composition of growth in terms of sectors and activities. What is the relationship and sequence in change in disparities in economic indicators and development indicators? The question assumes particular significance in view of the observation that while inter-state disparity in most economic indicators has increased whereas indicators of human development declined!

Taking stock of the banking sector growth between December 2001 and December 2006 financial inclusion, *V. Jagan Mohan* found out that there are uneven levels of penetration in each population segment more so at semi-urban and rural segments. The majority of India's population in the urban, semi-urban and rural areas appears to be still underserved by the banking industry, leading to financial exclusion. The Bottom of Pyramid (BOP) of the financial system is not structurally enabled to contribute to the macro-objectives of financial inclusion and credit penetration. The situation certainly calls for some bold out-of-box initiatives. *C.J. Punnathara* in his analysis based on latest progress and trends in banking industry insisted that for nurturing greater equity and accelerate economic development, the early gains in inclusion should be transformed into financial deepening as well. For the newly empowered bank customers should be enabled to extend their financial activity into an array of products, leading to all-around economic development.

Bhanoji Rao discussed the importance of human resource development as integrated in the Eleventh Plan. It is gratifying that the plan hopes to evolve strategies for secondary schooling that will emphasise the public responsibility. Further, the Planning Commission should come up with innovative ideas to ensure an enabling environment with zero corruption for private institutions to thrive in higher education. Above all, top priority to corruption is vital to ensuring private and public sector efficiency so as to promote human development by getting the best from health and educational expenditure by the government and the people.

Part III raises the issues involved in inclusive growth. Out of the trends analysis of the Indian economic development for the past sixty years, *S. Iyyampillai* found out that the increased growth rate of GDP, which was expected to solve the problems of poverty illiteracy, ill-health, unemployment, social unrest and terrorism, has miserably failed by market-led growth. Exclusion is the built-in strategy in the market economy. Unless the government takes care of the marginalized and left-out people, inclusive growth will not be become a reality. In his well-argued paper, *V. Mohanasundaram* pointed out that many suggestions and policy measures are indicated to achieve a higher rate of economic growth, but concrete policy guidelines are not available for an equitable distribution of income and wealth. Inclusive growth and good governance should go together. At the same time, caution must be exercised, as populism and symbolism can distort India's recent development agenda.

While analysing the three years performance of the UPA Government, *Ranabir Ray Choudhury* convinced that growth is bound to be imperfectly distributed in an economy like India's even if development policy is made as inclusive as possible. It would appear that there is no fundamental conflict between "inclusiveness" of growth policies and the phenomenon of "rowing inequality" because the two relate broadly to two different sectors of the economy. However, this would have been unacceptable if the poor had remained where they were at the beginning of the growth exercise. In his analytical paper, *C.J. Punnathara* diagnosed that despite several programmes in place to bridge the rural-urban gap and correct regional imbalances, Bharat—spatially, socially and economically—remains India's poor cousin and inter-state economic disparity remain as divisive as ever. He advocated that it might be more prudent for the government to focus on social inclusiveness and equitable growth rather than pursuing the dreams of bridging regional inequalities.

P.V. Indiresan pointed out although the Approach Paper has the three objectives of expansion, inclusion and excellence, the Eleventh Plan itself concentrates on expansion and inclusion with little attention to excellence in education. In the matter of education, inclusion should be for the poor. To reach education to the poor, not restrict it to the politically privileged, the government must think of bussing rural children to well-equipped schools, give gifted children the choice of going to private schools and invoke the public-private partnership framework for vocational education. *Sherly Kurien* emphasized that human development which holds the key for all types of development has to form the core of all "inclusive growth" policies. This can be done only through more investment in health sector and better health delivery services. Prioritizing for children offers India a unique opportunity to a celebration of human development missing this opportunity could prove costly.

In his argumentative paper, *G. Narasimha Raghavan* raised the question: Is inclusive growth exclusive of environment? The Approach Paper's vision that the 11th Plan must integrate development planning and environmental concerns. India needs growth coupled with social justice and due care of environment. One without the other is an insecure gesture to national development agenda. To Raghavan including environment in a national level policy has be accompanied by pointers that would help in integrating environment into mainstream growth process. To *R. Christopher Rajkumar,* the rationale behind the interlinking of rivers should make use of the surplus water for better regional development. It should be spelt through actions towards 'just' and "equitous water management". The access to water is to be ensured i.e., physical access, equal distribution and local monitoring and evaluation.

In their joint paper, *G.M. Bhat* and *Shabir Ahmad Padder* made a thorough study of the challenges and options of inclusive growth in the globalised India. When certain groups of people are not even "included" in the growth process there is no question of the benefits of growth: trickling-down" to them. Thus the notion of "trickle-down" is not merely non-operational, it is irrelevant. By ensuring inclusive growth, the Eleventh Plan would set out economy on a growth path, which would finally liberate millions from the perennial scourges of poverty, ignorance and disease. In general, our development strategy has be to sensitive to all social groups' interest.

It is true that "inclusiveness" and "inequality" are intertwined, but also incompatible in the Indian socio-economic system. After 60 years of political independence, economic security of all sections should be ensured through effective distribution of inclusive growth's benefits enriching the standard of living of common people.

P. JEGADISH GANDHI

Part I

DYNAMICS OF ECONOMIC GLOBALISATION

1

India : A Developed Nation before 2020?

A.P.J. Abdul Kalam

Friends, I am delighted to address you all, in the country and those living abroad, after working with you and completing five beautiful and eventful years in Rashtrapati Bhavan. Today, it is indeed a thanksgiving occasion. I would like to narrate, how I enjoyed every minute of my tenure enriched by the wonderful association from each one of you, hailing from different walks of life, be it politics, science and technology, academics, arts, literature, business, judiciary, administration, local bodies, farming, home makers, special children, media and above all from the youth and student community who are the future wealth of our country. During my interaction at Rashtrapati Bhavan in Delhi and at every state and union territory as well as through my online interactions, I have many unique experiences to share with you, which signify the following important messages:

1. Accelerate development : Aspiration of the youth,
2. Empower Villages,
3. Mobilize rural core competence for competitiveness,
4. Seed to Food: Backbone for agricultural growth,
5. Defeat problems and succeed,
6. Overcome problems through partnership,
7. Courage in combating calamities,
8. Connectivity for societal transformation,
9. Defending the nation : Our pride, and
10. Youth movement for Developed India 2020.

Now let me share with you each of the messages.

ACCELERATE DEVELOPMENT : ASPIRATION OF THE YOUTH

While there were many significant events during my tenure, a question from a little girl Anukriti of Sri Sathya Sai Jagriti Vidya Mandir School, of Darwa village from Haryana, during children's visit to Rashtrapati Bhavan on May 22, 2006, rings in my mind ever after. Anukriti asked me, "why India cannot become a developed nation before the year 2020". I appreciated the question and said it was indeed a thoughtful question and assured her that her dream would be taken to the highest institution of the nation and we would work for it to achieve before 2020. This question reflects how the desire to live in developed India has entered into the minds of the youth. The same feelings are echoed by over fifteen lakh youth, whom I have met so far and who represent the dream of the 540 million youth of the nation. The aspirations of the young to live in a prosperous, safe and proud India should be the guiding factor in whatever profession we contribute.

EMPOWER VILLAGES

Friends, I recall my visit to Nagaland on 26th October 2002, soon after my assuming office as President. It was a unique experience for me at Khuzama village to meet tribal village council members and discuss with them the village progress and the dream of village citizens. I was very happy to see the empowered village council functioning with financial powers and taking decisions. I saw a prosperous village with fruits and vegetables production. However, there is a need for providing physical connectivity in Nagaland through quality roads for enabling faster movement of products from villages to the market. That meeting gave me a powerful message about the transformation which can take place to the 600,000 villages of India, if all the villages are empowered to deal with their development and are well connected among themselves and with the urban societies.

MOBILIZING RURAL CORE COMPETENCE FOR COMPETITIVENESS

Now I would like to talk about the initiative of Periyar Maniammai College of Technology for Women, Vallam, Tanjore of Providing Urban Amenities in Rural Areas (PURA) complex involving 65 villages with a population of 3 lakhs. This includes provision of three connectivities—physical, electronic and knowledge—leading to economic connectivity. Periyar PURA has health care centers, primary to post-graduate level education and vocational training centers. This has resulted in large-scale employment generation and creation of number of entrepreneurs with the active support of 1000 self-help groups. Two hundred acres of waste land has been developed into a cultivable land. The villagers are busy in cultivation, planting Jatropha, herbal and medicinal plants, power generation using bio-mass, food processing and above all running marketing centers. It provides a sustainable economic development model for the whole region. During the last eight months, people of Periyar PURA villages technologically supported by Periyar Maniammai College of Engineering for Women have worked with experts from Japan External Trade Organisation (JETRO) on various products, for which core competence and raw material are available in Thanjavur district. They developed internationally competitive prototypes for 55 life style products with support of JETRO specialists and feedback from exhibitions at Delhi and Tokyo. This co-operative venture has enhanced the innovative ability of the people of all the 65 villages enabling them to develop and produce internationally acceptable products. I have seen similar type of PURA being established in many states. The whole country needs 7000 PURA to bridging the rural-urban divide.

SEED TO FOOD : BACKBONE FOR AGRICULTURAL GROWTH

Let me now share with you, the enriching experience I had, while meeting more than 6000 farmers from different States and Union Territories visiting Rashtrapati Bhavan. They evinced keen interest in the Mughal Gardens, the Herbal Gardens, the Spiritual Garden, the Musical Garden, the Bio-diesel garden and the Nutrition Garden and interact with the Horticultural specialists. Recently, during my address to the agricultural scientists while participating in a National Symposium on "Agriculture cannot Wait", I summarized the many practical suggestions given by farmers. We have to double the agricultural production with reduced land, reduced water resources and reduced manpower and improve the economic conditions of the nation through the principle of "Seed to Food" since agriculture is the backbone of the nation. We should empower the farmers to protect and nurture the fertile land for second green revolution. Meeting the Scientists and the Farmers has given me the confidence that the nation is poised to increase the agricultural GDP growth by atleast 4% per annum through the partnership of farmers and agricultural scientists and industries particularly for value addition.

DEFEAT THE PROBLEMS AND SUCCEED

On the evening of February 24, 2007, at Coimbatore, I had a very beautiful experience. As I got ready for meeting the first person out of twenty appointments, a wheel chair was in sight with a smiling person probably in his late fifties; unfortunately he has no hands and legs. His radiant face was revealing his happy state of mind. He introduced himself as Vidwan Coimbatore SR Krishna Murthy. I greeted him and asked him how this had happened. He smilingly said that it was from by birth. He thanked God, his parents, teachers and many others for giving him confidence, training and help. I asked him, what I could do for him? He said, "I don't need anything from you. I would like to sing in front of you". I readily agreed. He sang melodiously the Saint Thyagraja's pancha ratna kriti entharo mahanubavulu in Sriragam giving me a glimpse of his talent. I was quite touched. What is the message? Despite being physically challenged, the latent talent of music could blossom in this person with his positive attitude and perseverance, encouraged by the parents, teachers, academics and rasikas. Now he wants to give, give and give his art to inspire others. Of course, by his merit of music, in July 2007, he performed in the Rashtrapati Bhavan art theatre.

OVERCOME THE IMPACT OF DISASTER THROUGH PARTNERSHIP

I had the opportunity to experience the Indomitable Spirit of the people and children of Jammu & Kashmir even as they were just recovering from the devastating earthquake in 2005. I visited Urusa village on 26th November 2005 which has been adopted by the Western Air Command, Air Force for providing relief and medical aid to the residents of that area. When I went there, I found that the school building had been severely damaged. I met all the school children and the village citizen of Urusa. The villagers apprised me of their losses and had all praise for Army and Air Force role in rescue and relief operations along with state government. I appreciate the courage of the people of Urusa in defeating their problems. They have actually become the master of the problem rather than allowing problems to become their master. Despite the severe loss due to the earthquake, the children and the members of the village participated in the relief operation with the Armed Forces bravely and were smiling when I went to meet them. They interacted with me and said that the school was functional in the temporary tents. Here, I also witnessed the participation of acting Chief Justice of Jammu & Kashmir along with State Government authorities in on-the-spot settlement of relief grants to be provided to the victims whose houses had been damaged in the earth quake. I have experienced many such acts of courage from our citizens when faced with severe challenges.

COURAGE IN COMBATING CALAMITIES

In 2005, I met the Tribal Council Leaders, Students, Children of Chuckchucha village during my visit to Car-Nicobar

Islands. While various reconstruction and rehabilitation activities were in progress, during the discussions with the members of tribal council, I realized the unique trait among the Car-Nicobar islanders. Even though there were many human losses due to the Tsunami of 26 Dec. 2004, the tribal islanders had taken possession of affected victims as their children and there is nothing like orphanage in Car-Nicobar Islands. Touched by their courage, I composed few verses called "Sea Waves" which reads as follows:

Sea Waves

We are the children of Sea waves,
Sea waves are my friends.
When they become angry,
Sea waves give the challenges.
God has given the courage,
To challenge the sea waves.
And we will succeed,
We will succeed
With Almighty's grace.

All the members who were gathered in the village sang the poem with me and exhibited lots of courage and enthusiasm even though they had gone through severe suffering during the Tsunami.

CONNECTIVITY FOR SOCIETAL TRANSFORMATION

I addressed the Pan African Parliament on 16 September 2004, at Johannesburg, South Africa. This was attended by 53 member-countries of the African Union, where I proposed the concept of Pan African e-Network for providing seamless and integrated satellite, fiber optics and wireless network connecting 53 African countries at an estimated cost of US $ 100 million.

As part of the project 12 universities (7 from India and 5 from Africa), 17 Super Specialty Hospitals (12 from India and 5 from Africa), 53 tele-medicine centers and 53 tele-education centres in Africa will be connected. The pilot project on tele-education and tele-medicine in Ethiopia has already been commissioned. Indira Gandhi National Open University has taken up the MBA Course for 34 Ethiopian students of Addis Ababa and Harmaya Universities. As regards, tele-medicine, the specialists from CARE Hospital, Hyderabad are providing one-hour live tele-consultation to doctors in Black Lion Hospital, Addis Ababa in Cardiology and Radiology since November 2006. Using the Pan African network the Heads of the State in all the 53 countries will be connected for instant communication. I am extremely happy that Indian experience in bringing the benefits of technology to the people has enabled us to work with Africa to bring societal transformation in the African continent.

DEFENDING THE NATION: OUR PRIDE

I visited KUMAR in Siachen Glacier located at 17,000 feet altitude held by the Indian Army, had a memorable underwater journey in INS Sindhurakshak and flew in a Sukhoi-30 fighter experiencing 2.5 g. In these three experiences, I personally felt proud of our ever vigilant Soldiers, Sailors and Air Warriors performing their tasks beyond the call of their duty even in the most adverse circumstances natural and man made. During the last five years, I had an opportunity to present colours to many regiments, participate in number of passing out parades, meet the troops who were going to undertake peace missions and interact with the family members of our Defence Forces. Our Defence Forces are in a beautiful mission. When the nation sleeps during night, Members of our Defence teams are awake to guard us and remain vigilant to counter any threat. The Nation cherishes the valour, commitment and devotion to duty of our Defence Forces. Similarly, I had opportunities to interact with members of our para-military forces, central and state police personnel including internal security forces who are making immense contribution in augmenting the safety and security of our citizens under difficult conditions.

YOUTH MOVEMENT FOR DEVELOPED INDIA 2020

Recently, in Hyderabad, I met a group of citizens who are putting into practice the motto of transforming of our youth into enlightened citizen. The Lead India 2020 Foundation created by Dr. N.B. Sudershan at Hyderabad is training thousands of students in many districts of Andhra Pradesh in partnership with the District Administration. Particularly, I happened to know the transformation which has taken place among the students of Medak district. As per the district authorities the impact of the training on the students is visible in terms of self-discipline, love for their parents and teachers shedding of stage fear and recognition of their duties towards the nation. I talked to Ms. Padma, a student leader from Andhra Pradesh Tribal Welfare School, Nalgonda who related how she weaned her father away from smoking after imbibing the spirit of the 10 point oath from the Lead India Training Camp. This gives me an assurance that the youth of our country are on the right path through this mission-oriented programme. With the ignited minds of the 540 million youth below the age of 25, which I consider is the most powerful resource on the earth, under the earth and above the earth, we have to empower the youth through value-based education and leadership.

CONCLUSION

I was touched by the variety of Indian panorama, emotional content of the tune, cultural diversity and unity of minds in the vast land of ours. I have cited these examples just to give a glimpse of the richness of our tradition and effort being taken by different agencies to preserve it. There are also many new adventures by institutions and individuals. I have experienced many of them and learnt a lot about my country and our people. Even while pursuing our economic growth, we need to do a lot to preserve the rich and diverse treasures of our culture and civilization. It is our duty for our future generations. This has to be done in a much larger scale through countrywide participation of multiple institutions. Our country is blessed with natural resources, has shown considerable progress in the last sixty years, and above all we have hard working people particularly the power of the 540 million youth of the country. Every sector of our country has given me the confidence that India can become a developed nation well before 2020. Whomsoever, I met they constantly ask what they can give to the nation. We should constantly strive to empower such members of the society. With this spirit, I am extremely happy that we are on the right path. Here I am reminded of a famous poem:

> "When you wish upon a star,
> Makes no difference who you are,
> Anything your heart desires,
> Will come to you"

This poem is true to all of us, and particularly for our youth and if they aim great, I am sure they will reach close to the target or the target. My dear citizens, let us resolve to continue to work for realizing the missions of developed India 2020 with the following distinctive profile:

1. A Nation where the rural and urban divide has reduced to a thin line.
2. A Nation where there is an equitable distribution and adequate access to energy and quality water.
3. A Nation where agriculture, industry and service sector work together in symphony.
4. A Nation where education with value system is not denied to any meritorious candidates because of societal or economic discrimination.
5. A Nation which is the best destination for the most talented scholars, scientists, and investors.
6. A Nation where the best of health care is available to all.
7. A Nation where the governance is responsive, transparent and corruption free.
8. A Nation where poverty has been totally eradicated, illiteracy removed and crimes against women and children are absent and none in the society feels alienated.
9. A Nation that is prosperous, healthy, secure, peaceful and happy and continues with a sustainable growth path.
10. A Nation that is one of the best places to live in and is proud of its leadership.

Finally let me thank each one of you for showering your love and affection on me throughout the last five years by your cooperation and support.

Dear citizens, I conclude my address by sharing with you my mission in life which is to bring connectivity between billion hearts and minds of the people of India in our multicultural society and to embed the self confidence that "we can do it". I will be always with you, dear citizens, in the great mission of making India a developed nation before 2020.

May God bless you, Jai hind.

— Text of the Farewell Thanksgiving speech to the Nation, July 24, 2007

Institute Urges Kalam to Lead in Cleansing India

The Vellore Institute of Development Studies (VIDS) has urged former President of India Dr. A.P.J. Abdul Kalam to spreadhead a movement to cleanse the Indian society as part of his vision 'Developed India by 2020'.

In a memorandum sent to him, founder director of the VIDS Dr. P. Jegadish Gandhi has pointed out that Kalam himself should take the lead to realise the dream of a cleaner and richer Indian society.

He referred to the speech made by Kalam at the Platinum Jubilee celebration of the Annamalai University, Chidambaram, in 2004 wherein the former President suggested the formation of youth core groups to fight corruption.

Gandhi said that Kalam has already brought out significant changes in the thoughts of children, youth, politicians, religious leaders, industrialists and philanthropists through direct social dialogue dynamics, though he considered the total eradication of corruption to be a 'Herculean task'.

Gandhi also urged Kalam to initiate steps to convert PURA (Providing Urban Amenities in Rural Areas) into a people's movement by involving all sections of the society in all states.

Kalam has kindled many State Governments, private organisations and NGOs to divert their efforts towards creating more economically viable and technologically sustainable Providing Urban-amenities in Rural Areas (PURA).

—*The New Indian Express, July 25, 2007*

2

Promise of Globalisation

JOSEPH E. STIGLITZ

Globalisation has been a double-edged sword. To those able and willing to seize the opportunities and manage globalisation on their own terms, it has provided the basis of unprecedented growth. China and India, two countries with 2.4 billion people together, have for more than a quarter century been growing at historically unprecedented rates. They have taken advantage of globalisation of knowledge and of markets.

But elsewhere, matters have not worked out so well. There is growing disparity between the richest countries and the poorest countries, and growing inequalities within most countries around the world. The number of people in poverty in Africa has doubled in the past two decades. And globalisation, as it has been managed, has contributed to both of these problems. For instance, the last trade agreement, the Uruguay Round, signed in Marrakesh in the spring of 1994, was so unfair that the poorest countries of the world were actually made poorer, In the North, global competition has helped drive down wages of unskilled workers, exacerbating similar trends coming from changes in technologies and the weakening of labour unions.

Economic theory never said that everyone would gain as a result of globalisation. It said that the winners could compensate the losers, not that they would. And they haven't. Some say that globalisation is inevitable, but that is simply wrong: the extent of globalisation, as conventionally measured, for instance, by the ratio of trade or capital flows to GDP, was actually stronger before the First World War than in the interwar period. And unless we ensure that globalisation has more winners—and few losers—there can be a backlash against globalisation. Indeed, in many quarters, one can already see such a backlash taking shape.

This would be unfortunate—both for those in the developed and the developing countries. Standard economic theory emphasizes that opening up markets provides opportunities for each country to take advantage of its comparative advantage, and provides enhanced scope for efficiency gains from economies of scale. But there is an even more compelling argument for globalisation: the encounters between different cultures, the new opportunities which globalisation brings, as well as the enhanced competition that accompanies, all these mean that globalisation can, in fact, be a tremendous spur for innovation and creativity.

MAKING GLOBALISATION WORK

An alternative world is possible globalisation can be managed differently. In *Making Globalization Work,* I explain how this can be done. The problems that have been encountered are not inevitable. They are a consequence of the particular way that globalisaton has been managed—or mismanaged—especially in the post-Cold war world. I lay out a set of reforms—some small, some large, some that will take years to be brought about, some that are already in the process of being made—that will at least make globalisation work better.

From a global perspective, making globalisation work will require a fairer trade regime, a true development round, not what the advance industrial countries have tried to sell as the development round. It requires redressing the imbalance between capital and labour market liberalization. It requires an intellectual property regime markedly different from that embodied in TRIPs, the intellectual property provisions of the Uruguay Round, which was both bad for global science and for developing countries. What is needed is an intellectual property regime that helps narrow the knowledge gap that separate developed from less developed countries—not one which reduces access to knowledge and denies access to life-saving medicines, but which, at the same time, provides little incentive for research in the diseases that plague the developing countries.

Making globalisation work will also require a legal regime which provides cross-border protection for firms, but also imposes on them responsibilities, e.g., concerning the environment and worker rights. It will require doing something about the most pressing global environmental problems, especially global warming: it will do us little good to make economic globalisation work, if our planet suffers as a consequence. And as is so often the case, the poorest are the most likely to suffer the most—a third of Bangladesh will be submerged, and incomes, already low, will likely fail even more.

There are challenges too within India in making globalisation work. The countries that have been most successful have managed globalisation on their own terms, taken a pragmatic course, eschewing ideologies and the kind of market fundamentalism on which the Washington consensus neo-liberal policies were premised. For instance, capital market liberalization has, around the world, been associated with greater instability, but not greater growth.

Intellectual property is important, but a poorly designed intellectual property regime can actually retard innovation and growth, it is a mistake for India (of any other developing country) to imitate America's intellectual property regime: as in so many other areas, one-size-fits-all policies do not work, and an intellectual property regime which was designed for America would not necessarily be appropriate for India. Worse still, America's intellectual property regime is not working well for America: it may be enhancing profits for the pharmaceutical industry, but it is impeding the advancement of science. It is especially important that generic medicines are available. It is a matter of life and death: the poor simply cannot afford brand name medicines.

In coping with globalisation, it is important too that one makes sure that credit is available to all sectors of the economy; in too many cases, financial services liberalization has been followed by the dominance of foreign banks, which make credit available to foreign enterprises and large domestic enterprises; but the flow of credit to small and medium size enterprises and the rural sector dries up. There are ways of dealing with these problems; but, first, one has to recognize that there is a problem.

So too, around the world, globalisation has been associated with growing inequalities, and unless policies are put into place to counter these, there can be increasing political and social instability, of the kind so manifest in Latin America.

The problem, as I have said, is not with globalisation, but with the way globalisation has been managed. The reforms I have suggested will at least make globalisation work better. With the reforms, globalisation has a chance of living up to its promise and its potential, of improving the living standards, not just of the rich in the richest country of the world, but of the rich and the poor, in both the developing and the developed world.

3

Why Globalisation is in Trouble?

BRANCO MILANOVIC

INTRODUCTION

Historically, the dominant power tends to support globalisation as a way to increase the ambit of its influence, expand trade and gain economic advantage, co-opt. new citizens and possibly show the advantages of its own pax. This was the case with the Roman, British and now American-led globalizations. But recently, the rich West—which saw globalisatoin as a prelude to "the end of history"—is having second thoughts. Two fears drive this unease with globalisaton: The first is a fear of job loss due to competition from low-wage countries. The second is the fear of ethnic and cultural dilution due to increased immigration.

CHINA-INDIA FACTOR

The cause of the first fear is a fast re-emergence on the world stage of China and India. For students of history, the rise of China and India is not a surprise. The two countries are just recapturing the ground lost during the 19th and most of the 20th century. Before the Industrial Revolution, China's and India's combined output accounted for one half of the world's total. Now, after a quarter-century of China's spectacular growth, and more than a decade of India's growth acceleration, the two countries contribute less than a fifth of total world output.

Although their share is, in the long-term historical sense, still below what it used to be, it has nevertheless increased dramatically compared to where it was 30 years ago. The rise of the two Asian giants, reflected in their dynamic trade, large Chinese export surpluses and India's role as an outsourcing centre and a potential leader in information technology, has made the West wonder whether it can compete with such hardworking, cheap, plentiful and yet relatively skilled labour.

IMMIGRATION PRESSURE

While the fear of job loss is driven by fast economic growth of the two giants, the fear of immigration is, ironically, caused by the slow economic growth of the rest of the developing world. The people who try to reach the shores of Europe or cross from Mexico into US come from the countries that have disastrously fallen behind Western Europe and the US during the last quarter century.

In 1980, Mexico's real per-capita income, adjusted for the differential price level between Mexico and the US, was a third of that in the US. Today, the ratio is almost 4.5 to 1. The poor Africans who land daily on beaches of the Spanish Canary Islands come from the countries that have seen no economic growth in 50 years. Take Ghana, a country often touted as an African success case: Around its independence, in 1957, its income was one half of Spain's today, it is one-tenth. Immigration puts a similar pressure on low or medium-skilled jobs in the West as do cheap imports from China and outsourcing to India. And indeed, wages of low and medium-skilled workers in the rich countries have failed to keep pace with incomes of educated workers at the top of the pyramid. While the median US real wage has not risen in real terms over the last 25 years, real wages of the top 1 per cent have more than doubled. The richest 1 per cent of Americans today controls almost 20 per cent of total US income, a proportion higher than at any time since the Roaring Twenties. The U-turn of inequality—a sharp increase that started during the Thatcher-Reagan era, after a long decline—has affected, to a varying extent, all Western countries.

BEYOND JOBS AND WAGES

But at stake is something more profound than a threat to jobs and stagnant wages in a few : "exposed" sectors. After all, the West is no stranger to structural change, Ricardo in his *Principles* written in 1815 discusses labour dislocation "occasioned" by the introduction of machinery. The Western countries handled the decline of powerful industries like coal, textile and steel. Economists have never been sympathetic to the protection arguments of sunset industries: In an expanding economy, structural change is necessary and inevitable; jobs lost in one industry will reappear as new jobs in another industry.

The difference now is that the twin challenge undermines the consensus upon which the West's welfare state was built since World War II. To understand why, recall that the Western welfare states rest on two building blocks: Those of ethnic and social solidarity. The first building bloc implies that one is willing to be taxed if certain that aid will flow to somebody who is ethnically or culturally similar. But once large stocks of immigrants with different and not easily adaptable, social norms, arrive, that certainly is no longer. More immigrants will strain the already-tattered solidarity among citizens of rich European countries.

The second building block of the welfare state is class solidarity. For its to exist, there must be relatively similar economic conditions between classes so that one can reasonably expect that for social transfers paid out of his pocket today, he may be compensated—if the need arose—by a similar benefit in the future. If, for example, unemployment rates are relatively equal across skill levels, then the highly skilled will pay for unemployment benefits but if unemployment rates are different, the highly skilled may opt out.

As the income divide widens in the West between the rich and the highly educated who have done well, and the middle-classes and the unskilled who are merely scraping by, the second building block on which welfare capitalism was built crumbles. Economic inequality also translates into a cultural divide. "Ethnic" migrants who fill the rungs of low-paid workers are not the only ones economically and culturally different from today's Western elites; the elites are also growing more different from their own poorer ethnic brethren.

NEW SOCIAL CONTRACT

So far reaching, these developments require an entirely new social contract—a redefinition of capitalism no less. Such fundamental changes are not easy to come by when the threat is subtle, continuous, incremental and far from dramatic in a daily sense. Difficult decisions can be postponed, and neither politicians nor the electorate have an appetite for change. A battle of attrition regarding who would bear the costs of adjustment ensues, and this is at the heart of Europe's present immobilism.

Why is the development of "new capitalism" and rethinking of the old social contract so much more difficult for Europe than the US? First, for an obvious reason, because Europe's welfare state is much more extensive, more embedded in ordinary life, and its dismantlement is more socially disruptive. Second, because a low population growth—or in many countries, a decline—necessitates continuing large immigration. But, and this is the crux of the matter, Europe struggles more in absorbing immigrants that the US.

Historically, of course, Europe was not a society of immigrants. Europeans were happy to receive foreign workers as long as they would do low-paying jobs and stay out of the way. This quasi-apartheid solution preserved immigrants' culture, which then, most famously in the Netherlands, was found to clash with some European values. Immigrants, more so their daughters and sons, were not happy to remain in subaltern jobs. And while Europe was good about welcoming them to its soccer and basketball teams, it was more stingy when it came allowing them to direct operating rooms or boardrooms.

A SOCIAL REVOLUTION

The bottom line is that Europe needs no less than a social revolution: Replacement of its welfare state, and acceptance that Germans, French or Italians of tomorrow will be much darker in their skin colour, composed of individuals of various religions, and in many respects indeed a different people. As fusion of Frankish ethnicity and Latin culture created France, a similar Christiano-Islamic and Afro-European fusion may create new European nations, perhaps with a different outlook on life and social norms. No society can accomplish such epochal transformation quickly and painlessly.

II

In the rich world globalisation had driven the wedge between social classes, while in the poor world, the main divide is between countries: Those that adjusted to globalisation and, in many areas, prospered and those that adjusted badly and, in many cases, collapsed. Indeed the Third World was never a bloc the way that the first and second worlds were. But it was united by its opposition to colonialism and dislike for being used as a battlefield of the two then-dominant ideologies. As the second World collapsed and globalisation took-off, the latter rationale evaporated, and a few countries, most notably India and China, accelerated their growth rates significantly, enjoying the fruits of freer trade and larger capital flows.

FISSURE LINES

And although these two countries adapted well to globalisation, there is little doubt that their newfound relative prosperity opened many new fissure lines. Inequality between coastal and inland provinces, as well as between urban and rural areas, skyrocketed in China. So did, and perhaps by even more, inequality between Southern States, where the hub cities of Chennai and Bangalore are located, and the slow-growing North-East. For China, which still may face political transition to democracy, widening inequality between different parts of the country, could have disastrous consequences.

But another large group of Third World countries, from Latin America to Africa to former Communist countries, experienced a quarter century of decline or stagnation punctuated by civil wars, international conflicts and the plight of AIDS. While between 1980 and 2002, the rich countries grew, on average, by almost 2 per cent per capita annually, the poorest 40 countries in the world had a combined growth rate of zero. For large swaths of Africa, where about 200 million people lie, the income level today is less than it was during the US Presidency of John F. Kennedy.

For these countries the promised benefits of globalisation never arrived. The vaunted Washington Consensus policies brought no improvement for the masses, but rather a deterioration in the living conditions as key social services became privatized and more costly as was the case, for example, with water privatizations in Cochabamba, Bolivia, and Trinidad, electricity privatization in Argentina and Chad. They were often taken over by foreigners, and to add insult to injury, Western pundits arrived by jets, stayed in luxury hotels and hailed obvious worsening of economic and social conditions as a step toward better lives and international integration.

A NEW IMPERIALISM

For many people in Latin America and Africa, globalisation appeared as new, more attractive label put on the old imperialism, or worse as a form of re-colonisation. The Left-wing reaction sweeping Latin America, from Mexico to Argentina, is a direct consequence of the fault lines opened by policies that were often designed to benefit Wall Street, not the people in the streets of Lima or Caracas. Other Third World states—particularly those at the frontline of the battle between communism and capitalism, with ethnic animosities encouraged during the Cold War, efforts by Washington and Moscow to get the upper hand in the conflict—exploded in civil wars and social anomies. That part of the world associates globalisation with disappointment (Because Washington Consensus never delivered), resentment (because others got ahead) and poverty, disease and war.

In several sub-Saharan African countries, life expectancy at the turn of the 21st century is not only where it was in Europe almost two centuries ago but is getting worse. In Zimbabwe, between 1995 and 2003, life expectancy declined by 11 years to reach only 39 years. Ideologies which proposed some economic betterment and offered self-respect to many people in Africa (from Kwame Nkrumah's African socialism to Julius Nyerere's "cooperative economy") and parts of the former Communist bloc (Tito's "labour management") all collapsed and have given way to self-serving oligarchies that justified their policies, not by calling on their own citizens, but by publishing excerpts from reports written by the World Bank and the International Monetary Fund.

'GOVERNMENTS SANS GREATNESS'

In the Third World as a whole, globalisation, at best, produced what Tocqueville, with a touch of aristocratic disdain, called a government of the commercially-minded middle classes, "a government without virtue and without greatness"; at worst, it produced governments of plutocrats or elites unconcerned about their own populations. Globalization thus appeared in the poorest and weakest countries at its roughest. Perhaps the greatest casualty of the money-grabbing global capitalism was loss of self-respect among those who have failed economically—and they are preponderantly located in the poorest countries.

The desperate African masses who want to flee their own countries leave not only because incomes are low and prospects bleak, but also because of a lack of confidence that either they or their governments, no matter who is in power, can change life for the better. This despondency and loss of self-respect is indeed a product of globalisation.

In the past one could feel slighted by fortune for having been born in a poor country, yet have as compensation a belief that other qualities mattered, that one's country offered the world something valuable, a different ideology, a different way of life. But none of that survives today.

MORAL SUPERIORITY

The problem was, strangely, noticed by Friedrich Hayek. Market outcomes, Hayek argued, must not be presented as ethically just or unjust because the market is ethically neutral. But to buttress the case for global capitalism, its proponents insist in an almost Calvinist fashion that economic success is not only good in a purely material sense, but reveals some moral superiority. Thus winners are made to feel not only richer but morally superior, and the converse: The losers feel poor and are supposed to be ashamed of their failure. Many people do, but understandably not all take gladly to such judgment. An interesting coincidence of interests emerges between the desperate masses and the rich in advanced countries. The latter, educated and with considerable property "interests," are, economically, often in favour of greater Third World competitiveness and migration since, either as investors abroad or consumers of cheap labour services at home, they benefit from low-wage labour.

This unlikely coincidence of interest lends some superficial justification to the claims of George Bush and Tony Blair that the opponents of free-trade pacts work against the interests of the poor. The problem that the (US) President and the (British) Prime Minister fail to acknowledge, or perhaps even to realize, is that many of the policies urged by their governments on poor countries in the last two decades have indeed brought people to their current point of desperation.

Sandwiched between this unlikely "coalition" of the global top and the global bottom, are globalisation's losers: The lower and middle-classes in the West, and those in the "failed" states, not yet sufficiently desperate to board the boats to Europe or cross the US border at night. They too lost in terms of their national sovereignty and personal income. They may not gladly accept, though, that they are morally inferior. At first sight, they do not seem likely to derail globalisation because their power is limited. Yet in a more interdependent world with an easy access to deadly weapons, politics of global resentment may find many followers.

4

Towards an Inclusive Globalisation

MANMOHAN SINGH

PRELUDE

When I came up to Cambridge in the mid 1950s, the Cold War had frozen the world into two blocs. India had won independence a few years before and under the leadership of Jawaharlal Nehru was trying to establish its own place in a divided world. For Indians it was an era of hope, and there was great optimism about the prospect of development.

Today the world appears radically altered. The cold War is history. A new age of freedom has harnessed to it new technologies that have transformed production and communication. The dismantling of state control has unshackled economic forces. More countries are now integrated into a global economic system in which trade and capital flow across borders with unprecedented energy. The age of freedom is also the age of economic growth. Prometheus has truly been unbound.

A very significant feature of the global economy is the integration of the emerging economies in world markets. In fact, the weight of global economic activity is gradually shifting to these emerging economies. They now account for more than two-fifths of world exports compared to a fifth 25 years ago.

In many parts of the developing world, especially India and China, per capita incomes are doubling or are expected to double over every decade. This will lift millions of people out of poverty. This pace of change is unprecedented, far exceeding what was witnessed during the Industrial Revolution in Europe. Freer trade and financial flows in the world as a whole are helping to contain inflation, keep interest rates low, and sustain higher levels of investment.

In my own country, the economic reforms we initiated in the early 1990s have made our economy more competitive. Indian business is responding to new market opportunities. India's growth is underpinned by a vibrant and growing entrepreneurial class. Indian youth is keen to get into technical and scientific institutions—helping India gain salience as a knowledge-based economy. Our country, I believe, is now on growth path of 7 to 9 percent per year, while maintaining price stability. The proportion of people living below the poverty line is declining.

SOME CONCERNS

These achievements of the era of globalisation should not blind us to the new anxieties that globalisation has brought in its wake. The reach of globalisation has brought in its wake. The reach of globalisation is yet to touch many parts of the world. Moreover, the evidence suggests that the process has not removed personal and regional income disparities. In many developing countries, growth is bypassing the rural areas. Also, in the face of stagnation in their real pay, the working classes in industrialized countries are becoming fearful of the opening of markets. The gap between the rich and the poor is widening. This, coupled with the inability of the public sector to provide adequate and quality services in health and education, and cater to the needs of the poor, is causing resentment and alienation. This is nurturing divisive forces and putting pressure on the practice of democracy.

INCLUSIVE GLOBALISATION

These are real and palpable concerns and they cannot be ignored. I suggest to you that we address these vital concerns by making globalisation an inclusive process. We need to work for inclusive globalisation. This calls for a new global vision. That vision must ensure that the gains from globalisation are more widely shared. It is a matter of deep concern that the Doha Development Round of trade negotiations has reached an impasse. If trade is to be an instrument of combating poverty and spreading manufacturing capacities more evenly in the world, it is vital that barriers to the export of agricultural goods from developing countries be eliminated.

Nearly two-thirds of the population of developing countries live in rural areas. In the developed world this falls to less than ten per cent. My appeal is that developed countries should not allow short-term national interests to prevail at the cost of promoting freer trade and combating poverty. The prosperity of so many cannot be sacrificed for protecting the interests of so few. The price of myopia is heavy on the exchequers of the developed world. The issue also has profound moral dimensions.

To convince people in poor countries abut the benefits of globalisation we must take a more enlightened view in liberalizing trade in services and labour intensive manufactures, in which developing countries are competitive. I see trade not only as a means to prosperity, but also as peace building. Collectively we need to devise an enlightened approach in approaching negotiations over the reduction of harmful gas emissions, intellectual property rights in the production of life saving drugs, transfer of technologies that help to combat poverty and such issues.

Prosperity is not divisible, Neither is global peace possible without the eradication of poverty. As Jawaharlal Nehru said in his address to the Canadian Parliament in 1949. "There can be no security or real peace if vast numbers of people in various parts of the world live in poverty and misery. Nor, can there be a balanced economy for the world as a whole if the underdeveloped parts continue to upset that balance and drag down even the more prosperous nations."

CONFLUENCE OF CIVILIZATIONS

The best efforts to eradicate poverty will be in vain if our societies and nations are threatened by the spectre of terrorism and extremism. Open societies like India and Britain are more vulnerable to this threat. The very openness of our societies makes us more vulnerable. Yet we must fight terrorism without losing the openness or the rule of law that guarantees the freedom of the individual.

I believe that terrorism can be defeated only by combating fundamentalism and promoting respect for diversity. Britain, the land of John Stuart Mill and Bertrand Russell, the cradle of common law, liberty and democracy, has a unique role to play in fighting fundamentalism. India too has its own pluralistic traditions and openness to other cultures. The legacy of Mahatma Gandhi and Nehru ordains that we remain committed to combating fundamentalism. We do not believe in a "clash of civilizations." What we believe in is enrichment of the human condition through cultural inclusiveness and a "confluence of civilizations."

As democracies we must also stand together in making governance across the world more democratic. As a democracy we aspire to a world in which global institutions are more democratic and more representative of all the peoples of the world. The governance processes of global institutions of today—be they Bretton Woods institutions or the UN Security Council—reflect the realities of the world as it was more than half a century ago.

A more inclusive global process that carries the population of the world with it calls for a reform of these institutions, in which the developing world will have a greater voice. Not to do otherwise is to risk alienation and to render ineffectual the global system. I look to Britain, the Commonwealth and other great nations of the world to join forces in bringing about such a reordered global system.

— Excerpted from the Prime Minister's speech at the University of Cambridge on October 11, 2006 on the occasion of his being awarded the honorary degree of Doctor of Law

In his address on the 61st Independence Day here today, Dr. Singh promised that the Government would pursue policies that would help in rapid industrialisation, while reassuring farmers that their welfare was at the core of all concerns.

The Prime Minister said that the final shape being given to a national policy for rehabilitation and resettlement for all those displaced by major projects would ensure that displacement did not lead to impoverishment; that those who lose land do not lose livelihoods and those who have lost employment get better opportunities.

"India cannot become a nation with islands of high growth and vast areas untouched by development. It is, therefore, essential that we create new employment opportunities outside of agriculture."

"If employment generation is the best weapon against poverty, then industrialisation is the most effective means to create new job opportunities".

Initiatives

The Prime Minister announced a slew of initiatives including extension of the National Rural Employment Guarantee Act across the country, a programme to invest Rs. 25,000 crore in agriculture and old age pension to citizens over 65 years and living below the poverty line.

The Government also plans to open 1,600 new industrial training institutes (ITIs) and polytechnics, 10,000 vocational schools, 50,000 skill development centres and provide vocational training to 100 lakh students annually with the active help of private sector.

—15.08.2007

5

India in a Globalising World

MONTEK S. AHLUWALIA

INTRODUCTION

The problems posed by globalisation have been much discussed in recent years and it is interesting to recall briefly how perceptions about globalisation have changed in this period. The early 1990s were characterised by a highly positive assessment of globalisation especially in the West. The collapse of Communism in Russia and Eastern Europe, and the enthusiastic conversion of these countries to market economics, created an environment of triumphalist optimism which was reflected in Francis Fukoyama's premature pronouncement of "the end of history". Many in the industrialised world advocated a drastic reduction in the role of the state and freeing of markets—domestic and external, including liberalisation of capital markets—as a simple and tested formula for accelerated development. It was felt that countries only had themselves to blame if they failed to follow this recipe.

Experience did not validate this simplistic view. In some of the emerging market countries, especially in Africa and Latin America, it became evident that adoption of the conventional package of reforms did not always lead to rapid growth. The liberalisation of capital markets also proved to be a source of problems in certain circumstances, as several emerging market countries experienced severe financial crises from which recovery proved to be a prolonged process, and where the poor were often the worst hit. The industrialised economies also saw growing opposition to globalisation arising from high unemployment rates and fears of lost job opportunities. Careful research repeatedly established that these losses had more to do with technological changes than competition from cheap imports, but public perception remained otherwise, and protectionist fears fanned anti-globalisation sentiments.

This is the background in which India, the world's largest democracy, has been charting her course in a globalising world. Democracies encourage debate and there is a great deal of it in India on issues connected with globalisation.

Politicians of all political parties in India know that globalisation is a reality. Many of them also know that all countries that have grown rapidly have done so by exploiting opportunities in world markets and this can only be done if the economy is globally competitive. But there are also the fears about the impact of globalisation which need to be addressed. These fears relate to two types of negative fallouts. First, there is apprehension that globalisation, and the policies of openness associated with exploiting the opportunities it offers, may lead to negative effects on GDP growth. Second, there are concerns that even if aggregate growth is not adversely affected, indeed even if it increases, globalisation may have severely disruptive distributional effects hurting the economic interests of particular groups, sectors or regions causing a loss of income and an increase in poverty.

INDIA'S GROWTH PROSPECTS

Let me first focus on India's growth prospects in a globalising world. India's experience certainly suggests that there is no reason to fear that globalisation will hurt India's growth prospects. On the contrary, India has experienced a distinct improvement in growth in the period when its policies reflected the compulsions of globalisation, compared with the 1960s and 1970s, when the Indian economy grew relatively slowly at an average of around 3.5 per cent per year. Growth accelerated to an average of around 5.8 per cent per year in the 1980s and 1990s and the economy is currently growing at about 6.5 per cent. The present government has targeted a growth rate of between 7 and 8 per cent for the near future. Since population growth has slowed down from 2.2 per cent prior to 1990 to around 1.8 per cent at present, these figures imply that the projected acceleration in the growth of per capita income is greater than in the growth of GDP.

International agencies and independent scholars agree that the economy can achieve growth rates of 8 per cent or so provided supportive steps are taken. A much quoted recent study by Goldman Sachs identified Brazil, Russia, India and China as the set of large emerging market countries projected to grow rapidly over the next thirty years. Within the group, India's potential growth rate was projected to be the fastest—around 8 per cent per year—faster even than China which is currently, and has been for many years, the fastest growing economy but is expected to slow down in future. According to this study, by 2040 India will become the third largest economy after the USA and China. This projection has been adopted by the US National Intelligence Council's 2020 report "Mapping the Global Future".

Are these projections credible? There are good reasons to believe that they are.

KEY DETERMINANTS OF GROWTH

Economics tells us that, per capita income in an economy depends upon several key determinants and growth of per capita income depends upon changes in these determinants over time. The first is resource availability, i.e. capital per unit of labour and the quality of human capital. The level of technology available to a country is obviously, an important determinant, and so is the set of policies and economic institutions which together determine the efficiency with which resources are used, given available technology. In an open economy, it is particularly important for the policies to be such that the country can take full advantage of the opportunities provided by interaction with the rest of the world and this aspect has become especially important in a globalising world, where technology has created new opportunities for trade and other interaction which simply did not exist earlier.

Based on these considerations, I have no doubt that India is well positioned to accelerate ftom its present 6.5 per cent growth rate of GDP to around 8 per cent in the near future. As far as the availability of capital is concerned, this depends upon the rate of investment, which, in turn, is constrained by the rate of domestic savings and the sustainable level of foreign inflow. India's domestic savings rates have risen to a very respectable level of 27 per cent of GDP, and could rise further reflecting the age composition of the population, which is at the stage where the dependency ratio is expected to keep falling. The weak spot in the savings picture is public savings, which is negative, though the latest figures show welcome improvement in this dimension.

In a globalising world, domestic savings can be supplemented by investment flows from abroad and India has reoriented policies towards foreign investment to welcome such flows. India at present attracts only about $ 5 billion of FDI compared with $ 60 billion for China. The government has set the target of raising foreign investment to three times its present level and is taking steps to remove policy impediments to such flows in several areas. With continuing improvement in domestic savings, and an increase in FDI from under 1 per cent of GDP to say 2.5 per cent, India can achieve rates of investment of close to 30 per cent which should suffice to sustain 8 per cent growth, Investment rates in China are much higher—around 40 per cent of GDP—but there is reason to believe that China's very high investment rates reflect some degree of inefficiency in the use of capital.

Human capital is another resource that determines growth and there are two somewhat different dimensions that are relevant. One is the availability of skilled manpower and the other relates to entrepreneurial ability. India has a large pool of technical and higher skilled manpower, reflecting long established socio-cultural biases in favour of education and also the emphasis placed on higher education almost immediately after independence. The country produces about 170,000 graduates in engineering and technology annually; not a large number in relation to the population but very substantial as an absolute flow. While quality varies, the best institutions such as the Indian Institutes of Technology and the Indian Institutes of Management, all part of the Nehruvian legacy, are truly world class. Familiarity with English has proved to be an important advantage, especially in some of the new growth areas created by globalisation such as IT enabled services. These endowments make India a potentially attractive production base, offering high level skills at a fraction of the cost in the industrialised world. The picture is less encouraging when it comes to basic education of the labour force.

The other dimension of human capital relates to private entrepreneurship and this is one of India's major strength. India has a long tradition of private enterprise which flourished even in the period when economic policy strongly favoured the public sector. In those years, businessmen operated in a domestic market, where government control limited domestic competition and high protective barriers limited foreign competition, clearly not an environment that encouraged genuine entrepreneurship. Industry profited more from its. ability to 'manage' the bureaucracy and obtain benefits, of one kind or the other, from a system of control that was highly discretionary and non-transparent. There has been a major change in the business environment in the past two decades thanks to economic reforms and this has had a powerful impact on the private sector. Indian firms have re-oriented themselves to deal with both domestic and foreign competition and many have begun to establish or acquire subsidiaries abroad to compete more effectively in a globalised world. Earlier fears that lowering of tariff barriers would lead to a flood of imports that would swamp Indian industry, have been dissipated and Indian industry today is confident about its ability to compete in a globalising world. Some of the best Indian firms have even listed on foreign stock exchanges and now have substantial foreign institutional stakeholders, who are an important force, pushing for greater transparency and better corporate governance. These changes are not easily quantified, but they are real nonetheless and they are an important reason for being optimistic about faster growth in the years ahead.

ECONOMIC POLICES AND INSTITUTIONS

Economic policies and institutions also play a central role in determining growth prospects. Economists, probably focus too much on the role of policies, and tend to underplay the importance of institutions, because policies can be changed over relatively shorter periods while institutions take much longer to create and to mature. I will touch on institutions also, but for the moment let me emphasise that India has seen major changes in economic policies over the past two decades which will help it to perform more effectively in a globalising world.

The process of economic reforms began in the mid 1980s, following a recognition that India's performance in the 1960s and 1970s was below its potential. Mr. Rajiv Gandhi was the Prime Minister at the time, and he was keenly aware that East Asian countries were outpacing India and a restructuring of economic policies was necessary if India was to realise her growth potential. This was the period when the extensive government controls, which existed earlier, on private investment and technology decisions began to be liberalised. Indian private companies were encouraged to expand in scale and induct contemporary technology. Access to foreign technology was made easier and foreign investment began to be viewed as a mechanism for injecting new technology into the economy. Prime Minister, Rajiv Gandhi was also personally convinced of the importance of telecommunications and paid special attention to the modernisation of this sector. He also encouraged the application of computers and the development of the software industry. These policy initiatives paid rich dividends 10 years later, when India emerged as the most globally competitive emerging market country in software and IT services.

Economic reforms, were intensified in the 1990s following a serious balance of payments crisis in 1991. The present Prime Minister, Dr. Manmohan Singh, was the Finance Minister at the time, and was the architect of those reforms. The internal liberalisation begun in the 1980s was carried further, and was combined with a gradual process of external liberalisation, including lowering of import duties, removal of quantitative restrictions on imports and a major liberalisation of foreign direct investment. The 1990s also saw the start of a process of financial reforms aimed at introducing greater competition and tightening prudential norms in the banking sector, stock exchanges and capital market institutions and the insurance sector.

These reforms were accompanied by efforts to strengthen institutions appropriate for the functioning of a market economy. India is fortunate in this area because it already had commercial and legal institutions necessary for functioning as a market economy in a globalising world. The institutions, I have in mind, are an independent judiciary and the rule of law, the prevalence of acceptable accounting standards, functioning stock exchanges and corporate practices. In a globalising world, these institutional characteristics, sometimes called 'soft infrastructure' to distinguish them from the traditional 'hard infrastructure' of roads, ports, railways, etc. are an important positive factor, especially for attracting foreign investment. India's institutions were broadly patterned on those in the industrialised countries though their functioning certainly needed to be improved. Several steps were taken in this direction, including especially in the area of modernising stock exchange practices and introduction of corporate governance rules. Gaps remain in certain areas such as bankruptcy laws, where procedures take far too long, but the basic structures are in place and they are increasingly being pushed to conform with best practices internationally.

The response of the economy to the reforms that have already taken place gives some grounds for optimism about the future. The reforms of the 1980s produced a distinct improvement in economic performance as the growth rate of GDP, which had earlier averaged only around 3.5 per cent accelerated to an average of 5.8 per cent per year in the 1980s. This was not only much better than in earlier years, it was also better than growth rates in Latin America and Africa in the 1980s which decelerated in the period, later described as 'the lost development decade'. However, India's growth remained well below growth rates achieved in China, which grew at about 8.5 per cent in the 1980s, or even Malaysia and Thailand, which grew at 6 per cent and 7.4 per cent respectively.

The intensification of reforms after 1991, including especially the external liberalisation, was expected to push the economy to a distinctly higher growth path. It appeared to do so initially, as GDP growth averaged 7.5 per cent per year between 1994-95 and 1996-97. India appeared ready to transit to a faster rate of growth and the government even targeted growth at 8 per cent for the Ninth Plan period (1997-2001), but this was not achieved. Growth slowed down in the second half of the 1990s and the average growth rate for the 1990s was not very different from that in the 1980s. More recently, the growth rate has accelerated to around 6.5 per cent but this is well below the growth rate targeted.

The fact that the reforms of the 1990s did not produce significantly faster growth than observed in the 1980s, has led some critics to question whether the reforms of the 1990s, including especially the liberalisation of trade policy and foreign investment, were appropriate or even necessary. The reforms initiated in the 1990s were indeed essential and the reason why growth did not accelerate as much as expected was because the reforms were incomplete in some important respects.

The reforms of the 1990s, were essential because the earlier reforms initiated the process of internal liberalisation, but they did not address the issue of international competitiveness, which required extensive liberalisation of trade policy and liberalisation of foreign investment. In the absence of action in this area, there was not enough improvement in export competitiveness. India's share of world exports had been declining steadily from 2 per cent in 1950 to 0.4 per cent in 1980. This decline began to be reversed in the 1980s but the share increased only marginally to 0.5 per cent in 1990. The balance of payments remained under pressure and the economy resorted to external borrowing, leading inevitably to a deterioration in external debt ratios. Not surprisingly, a loss of confidence in 1990 precipitated a reversal of debt flows and produced a crisis.

The reforms of the 1990s, including the shift to a flexible, largely market determined exchange rate succeeded admirably in correcting this weakness. India's export share in world trade increased from 0.5 per cent in 1990 to 0.8 per cent in 2002. This is still a modest figure, but I should add that it does not include earnings from software exports and from business process outsourcing, which have become very important in recent years and are themselves, indisputably, the outcome of the liberalisation of the 1990s. Higher export earnings in the 1990s have been supplemented by larger flows of foreign direct investment and investments by foreign institutional investors (FIIs) in the stock market. The total inflow from both these sources was around $ 6 billion until 2002-03 and then shot up to $ 16 billion in 2003-04, mainly because of a surge in FII inflows.

The disappearance of the 'foreign exchange constraint' is a major benefit of the economic reforms of the 1990s. It has enabled successive governments to take a number of steps essential for enabling India to compete in a globalising world. Most important of these has been the reduction in import duties, implemented by successive governments albeit at a very gradual pace. There was a brief reversal in this process in the late 1990s, but it was soon resumed, indicating a reasonable consensus on this issue. Indian import duties are still too high-nearly three times higher than in China—but the present government is committed to bringing them down to levels comparable to East Asia and significant reductions were implemented in each of the two budgets presented by the government thus far. Interestingly, Indian industry is no longer alarmed at the prospect and representative industry organisations have publicly recommended a gradual process of duty reduction.

ECONOMIC REFORMS AND SLOW GROWTH RATE

Let me now turn to the question why the reforms of the 1990s did not lead to significantly higher rates of growth of GDP than achieved in the 1980s. I believe there are two reasons for this. First, the reforms in India have been deliberately implemented in a gradualist fashion, a gradualism that reflects the compulsions of India's highly pluralist and participative democracy. It has the obvious disadvantage that the benefits of reforms take time to surface and this may account, to some extent, for the less than expected acceleration in growth. It also tries the patience of investors around the world who worry about the endless debates and controversies and their impact on the process of economic change. However, it has the distinct advantage that it builds a broad consensus in favour of the reforms being attempted, thereby giving them greater political sustainability. This is evident from the fact that the Congress government, in the first half of the 1990s, which initiated the reforms was succeeded by a short lived left of centre coalition which was followed by a right of centre coalition, and despite these changes the broad direction of economic reforms was continued.

A second reason for the lack of a significant acceleration is that the reforms were incomplete, in some important respects. The most important shortcoming is the inability of the reforms to ensure adequate expansion in infrastructure. Rapid growth in a globalising world requires good infrastructure to attract investment and ensure competitiveness. India's infrastructure is distinctly poorer than in most of the competing countries of East Asia and this has discouraged investment in manufacturing, which in turn has led to inadequate growth in this sector. The Ninth Plan (1997-98 to 2001-02) had targeted a growth rate of 8.2 per cent in the industrial sector against which the actual achievement was only 4.6 per cent. The Tenth Plan (2001-02 to 2006-07) targeted industrial growth at 10 per cent but the achievement in the first 3 years is only 7 per cent per year.

The slow growth of industrial production in the second half of the 1990s is a major cause of concern about the growth process because of its implications for employment. Employment in the organised sector—which is basically the modern sector which generates high quality jobs—has actually fallen in recent years. Indian firms, facing the pressure of domestic and external competition, are downsizing the labour force in their effort to improve productivity and cut costs. This process of improving productivity is unavoidable but it underscores the need to achieve higher growth. Had industrial sector grown not at 6.7 per cent, as it did in the first three years of the Tenth Plan, but at 10 per cent which was the target, the economy would have seen expansion in organised sector jobs notwithstanding the improved productivity. The failure of the economy to generate rapid growth in the industrial sector stands in sharp contrast to the performance in IT enabled services which have grown very rapidly albeit from a low base and where India has been able to penetrate world markets. It is interesting to note that global competitiveness in these services depends not on hard infrastructure as much as upon telecommunications connectivity, where India has done well.

Inevitably, the growth witnessed over the past 15 years is continuously evaluated in terms of its impact on poverty. Critics often argue that the growth produced in the period of reforms has not reduced poverty, but this is not true. Poverty has declined from 40 per cent in 1987 to around 23 per cent in 2003. While the decline is welcome, the performance falls below expectations and targets. India still has a very large number of around 250 million below the poverty line, and the poverty line is very minimal, only $ 1 per day.

Another dimension in which the growth witnessed in the 1990s is less than satisfactory relates to regional balance. Available evidence suggests that even in the first half of the 1990s, when growth accelerated compared with the 1980s, there was an increase in regional disparity in growth, with some of the poorer states actually growing more slowly than in the 1980s. It is not true that the rich got richer and the poor poorer. Two of the richest states, Punjab and Haryana, actually slowed down while some of the poorer states, especially Rajasthan and West Bengal did better than in the 1980s. None of the poorer states experienced an actual decline in per capita GDP. However, some of the largest low income states, especially Uttar Pradesh, Bihar and Orissa grew more slowly than they did in the 1980s. None of this is surprising. In the pre-liberalised world of industrial licensing, investments were deliberately directed to the more backward states and the resulting inefficiencies in production were sustainable because of protection. With liberalisation of industrial licensing, investment could be expected to flow where productivity was higher and some states would have lost out in this process.

Regional imbalances in growth combined with lower than expected growth and insufficient growth in employment were bound to cause tensions, especially in a functioning democracy where globalisation has raised awareness and expectations.

Failure to meet expectations leads to electoral defeat and that is what happened in India in May last year. I do not mean to suggest that election outcomes depend on any single factor and there were other important social issues also involved. But in so far as economics was an issue, the previous government went into the election under the slogan 'India Shining', suggesting that its economic policies had produced results which justified reelection. The electorate clearly thought otherwise.

The election results were described in some quarters as a vote against reforms. This is, in my view, a misreading. The truth is that while me previous government had not reversed the process of reforms initiated by the Congress in 1991, and had even carried it forward in several areas, they had not delivered the high growth rates that were expected and were necessary to create high quality jobs for the new entrants to the labour force. Such growth that occurred was also seen as benefiting only a few. The software and business process outsourcing sectors were clearly 'shining', but performance in critical areas such as agriculture was unforgivably poor. Between 1980 and 1996, agricultural GDP in India grew at about 3.2 percent per year, hut after 1996, it decelerated massively to 1.5 per cent per year. With 60 percent of the population depending upon agriculture as their primary source of income, the deceleration of agricultural growth to 1.5 per cent clearly showed that the economic reforms had by-passed the rural population.

The critical message of the last election is that the process of economic reforms must generate a wider spread of benefits to be politically sustainable. This calls for a faster pace of growth including in the industrial sector and a better sectoral balance in growth, with much greater attention to the agricultural sector. The present government has read this message dearly. It has indicated that the reforms will be pushed ahead to accelerate growth to 7-8 per cent in the short-term. It will also work to make this growth more 'inclusive' and distributionally fairer.

The general strategy of pushing forward with economic reforms involves action on many fronts. It includes continuing with the process of opening up the economy by reducing customs duties, reducing bureaucratic hurdles which make the investment climate less attractive, continuing with the process of reducing the list of items reserved for production by the small scale sector, and continuing with financial sector reforms. A sensitive area which is important for promoting expansion in labour intensive sectors, but where it is necessary to build a consensus, is the need for greater flexibility in labour laws.

TOWARDS MORE INCLUSIVE GROWTH

Three areas which are crucial for achieving a more inclusive growth and are receiving priority attention are health and education levels especially in rural areas, revival of momentum in agriculture, and improving the quality of infrastructure. Let me comment briefly on each of these.

PRIMARY EDUCATION

India's primary education and health indicators lag behind other East Asian countries, not only in comparison with the levels prevailing in these countries today, but even compared to the levels 30 years ago when they began to grow more rapidly. China, in particular, invested heavily in these areas in the early stages of development, with the result that when economic reforms were introduced in the early 1980s, adult literacy was already 85 per cent. In contrast, adult literacy in India in 1991 was only 49 per cent. It can be argued that a base level of literacy of 49 per cent is not enough to generate 8 per cent growth. In a globalising world which places a high premium on skills and knowledge, improving these indicators should be a matter of the highest priority. As Amartya Sen has pointed out, "This will not only improve human welfare directly, it will also contribute to economic growth over a longer period and furthermore, it will improve the ability of the poor to participate more fully in the growth process."

The government has embarked on a major programme to strengthen primary education, especially in rural areas. The aim is to ensure that 100 per cent of children complete five years of primary schooling by 2007. The programme also includes training teachers to improve the quality of instruction, and the provision of mid-day meals to all primary school children. This will improve the nutrition status of children from poorer families and also encourage school attendance thereby helping to reduce drop out rates, which are too high. The cost of these programmes is being met by imposing a cess of two per cent on all taxes earmarked for this purpose.

RURAL HEALTH SERVICE

A parallel effort is being made in the area of health, concentrating initially on rural areas, where public health facilities are grossly inadequate. A new National Rural Health Mission, has been launched which aims at expanding the availability of public health centres at the village level combined with strengthening of referral health facilities for groups of villages. Improving facilities for assisted childbirth is a critical area where more needs to be done. India's total health expenditure as a percentage of GDP is around five per cent, which is comparable with that in other countries, but public expenditure on health is less than one per cent of GDP much lower than in other countries. The government proposes to raise this to two per cent of GDP over the next seven years.

I must emphasise that while it is necessary to increase public spending in both health and education, this is only one part of what is needed. Equally important, and probably more difficult, is the need to ensure that the money made available is spent well. This is best done by involving the local communities in supervising and monitoring public agencies which provide these services. This function should be performed by the elected bodies at village, district and intermediate levels which provide the third level of democracy, supplementing elected legislatures at the state and national level.

Constitutional Amendments were introduced in 1994 making it mandatory for states to constitute these elected councils and this was a major step in bringing democracy to the grass-roots. What has been achieved is impressive; at any given time there are 3 million elected representatives of whom 30 per cent are women. A great deal remains to be done to strengthen the capacity of these bodies and empower them to supervise local functionaries, but I have no doubt that, in due course, these bodies will take on larger responsibilities and contribute greatly to good governance and increased accountability.

FOCUS ON AGRICULTURE

The second area where corrective steps are needed relates to agriculture. We need to more than double the growth rate in agriculture from 1.5 per cent observed in recent years to around 4 per cent, and this requires much more than a business as usual approach. The present government is undertaking a comprehensive review of policies in agriculture and related areas such as irrigation, water management and conservation, agricultural research and extension, rural roads, etc. Large investments are needed in these areas, as also policy changes, including policies on sensitive issues such as the pricing of irrigation water and pricing of electric power to agriculture. The government has already announced a major Food for Work Programme (soon to be converted into, an Employment Guarantee Act) aimed at providing at least 100 days of employment at the minimum wage to one member of each poor household in designated rural areas. This is designed as a measure of income support for the rural poor but the programme can also be dovetailed with plans for creation of rural infrastructure by the wage costs of infrastructure development being met though the programme.

Indian agriculture will also have to expand its focus beyond producing foodgrains, towards agricultural diversification, including especially dairying, poultry and horticulture. The scope for development of food processing industries is very large. At present, only about 2 per cent of horticulture production in India is processed compared with 20 per cent or more in many countries. Wastage due to poor handling and spoilage from the farm to the consumer is as high as 25 to 30 per cent and this is reflected in low prices paid to farmers. The development of modern agro-processing would help increase farm incomes but it is currently hampered by outdated laws governing the marketing of agricultural produce which make it difficult for corporations to enter into contract purchase arrangements with groups of farmers. Contract farming would enable farmers to grow the specific varieties needed for agro-processing, with the buyer providing the planting material, extension services, advice on appropriate pesticides and a cold chain from the farm to the processing plant. The laws governing the food processing industry also need to be modernised.

Agricultural modernisation will present new challenges to Indian farmers. India is climatically well suited to the production of high value horticulture, including organically grown crops, which can be marketed in Europe, but this will require compliance with phyto-sanitary standards and European food laws. Biotechnology has the potential of greatly increasing yields of crops tailored to the soil and moisture conditions prevailing in India. However, there are apprehensions and environmental concerns as the development of genetically modified crops faces challenges from NGOs internationally and domestically. India is actively engaged in the WTO negotiations, looking for larger market access for its products and it will have to do its part in the process of opening up. However, opening agriculture creates legitimate fears because of the persistence of heavy subsidisation of agriculture in industrialised countries. Opening up the agricultural sector also exposes farmers to risks when international prices fall. Farmers need to have access to instruments of risk management to deal with such situations such as liquid forward markets and these require institutional development which takes time.

INFRASTRUCTURE

The third area where a complete overhaul of policies is needed relates to infrastructure development. Any visitor to India also familiar with East Asia is immediately struck by the fact that India's infrastructure services, by which I mean the availability and quality of electric power from the utilities, the road network, ports, airports, rail transport, etc., are far behind East Asia. I have already mentioned that inadequate progress in this area is probably the most important reason why the reforms introduced in the 1990s did not accelerate growth as much as was expected. The government is paying special attention to this area. The Prime Minister has established a committee on infrastructure, under his chairmanship, to systematically review policy issues in each of the infrastructure sectors, and to determine an agenda for policy change and monitor implementation.

The investment required to upgrade India's infrastructure is massive and cannot possibly come entirely from the public sector. The strategy being adopted is to increase public resources directed towards infrastructure development and to use them in a manner which most effectively leverages private investment in these areas. In some areas, such as telecommunications, private investment in infrastructure has already taken-off. There are a handful of strong private sector service providers, investing aggressively and competing for market share with the erstwhile public sector telecom companies. The government has recently increased the limit on foreign investment in this sector from 49 per cent to 74 per cent. At the other end of the spectrum are rural roads, where also large investment is necessary, but will have to come entirely from the public sector.

ROLE OF PRIVATE SECTOR

Between these two extremes are a number of sectors where private investment is possible, but there are sector specific problems and policy constraints that need to be overcome. Private investment in ports is relatively easy. Several minor ports are being developed entirely in the private sector, and in the major ports, expansion of new capacity has been successfully privatised. The private sector can also play a major role in airport development. A private sector airport in Kochi has been in operation for some years, and two more have been approved recently for Bangalore and Hyderabad. Bids have also been invited from private investors interested in the development of Mumbai and Delhi airports as joint ventures, with management control in private hands, and the concession is expected to be awarded later in the year.

Roads have been traditionally built only in the public sector but it is proposed to entrust significant portions of future National Highway development to private investors on a BOT basis. The revenue model envisages the investor receiving earnings from tolls, with a capital subsidy to make the project financially remunerative. One such project has recently been completed. Thirty more private sector BOT projects are expected to be awarded in the course of the year.

The most difficult area, of course is electric power. The power utilities in most states are financially unviable, thanks to a combination of large electricity losses in distribution, arising from stealing of power, usually in connivance with the distribution staff, and unrealistically low electricity tariffs for certain categories of consumers. The solution clearly lies in setting rational power tariffs and improving the operational efficiency of the distribution segments. The initiative in this area lies largely with the state governments and some progress is being made. Regulators have been set-up in almost all states and have started prescribing electricity tariffs. Two states have privatised electricity distribution, but it is too early to tell whether this shift to private ownership will succeed in reducing losses. Most states have adopted a more limited strategy of separating generation, transmission and distribution into separate companies, and then trying to improve the performance of the distribution company through better management systems. The net result is that despite false starts in the past, some private investment in electric power generation is taking place but not as much as is needed. This can be expected to increase as the distribution companies become financially more viable.

I have listed only some of the major initiatives in the area of infrastructure to give an idea of what is being done. This is a complex area where the reforms needed often require deeper institutional change. Progress will be uneven across states, but I have no doubt that there will be success stories and these will be rapidly replicated, if not in all states, certainly in many. Better infrastructure is central to achieving larger inflows in foreign investment in manufacturing and generating faster growth in this sector which is critical for expanding employment.

MACROECONOMIC STABILITY

Finally, I must emphasise that reforms need to be pursued in a framework of macroeconomic stability. India's macroeconomic parameters are stable, but some of them are riot at comfortable levels. There is concern that India's fiscal deficit is too high, and this has been so for quite some time. The government recognises this as a problem and hopes to correct it over time, working within the framework of the Fiscal Responsibility and Budget Management Act, which prescribes a time path for reducing the fiscal deficit of the central government. The states are also being encouraged to adopt similar legislation. As an incentive, they have been offered restructuring of their outstanding debt liabilities to the centre on favourable terms, if they agree to enact fiscal responsibility legislation.

Fiscal balance requires action on both expenditure and revenues. On the expenditure side, the government must contain the growth of public expenditure as much as possible by withdrawing from areas where public spending is not essential or effective, while actually expanding it in other areas where it is necessary and presently inadequate. On the revenue side, there is need for steady pursuit of tax reform, especially reform of tax administration, which should permit larger resources to be raised even at the existing tax rates. An important development in this area is the recent adoption by 19 out of 27 states of a VAT system for sales taxes (which are levied by the states) under which credit will be allowed for sales taxes paid at earlier stages. Experience suggests that this will have a very favourable effect on revenue collection.

I hope the picture that emerges from my lecture is one of an India grappling earnestly with the challenges posed by globalisation, and finding solutions to these challenges within the framework of her democratic polity. As in the past, policy reform in India will continue to be a gradualist process. The present government is a Congress led coalition, with outside support from the Left parties. The partners of the coalition have all subscribed to a consensus document, the National Common Minimum Programme (NCMP).

This document outlines a credible framework to push the reform forward, in a manner which takes care of the deficiencies in past policies and prescribes important corrective steps. The document indicates transparently some important constraints on policy. For example, the government will not privatise profit making public sector companies though it can sell minority equity in such companies. Similarly, the government is against 'automatic hire and fire' policies, but it will work together with labour to determine desirable changes in the labour laws to give greater flexibility. I recognise that many investors want stronger action in precisely these areas, but democracy is about working within constraints defined by political acceptability. I have no doubt that it is possible to define a reform programme within these constraints, which makes sufficient progress in many important areas to enable India to achieve eight per cent growth per year, and a much more 'inclusive' and socially just growth than in the past.

If we succeed, India could emerge, within 10 years, as an economy well on the way to achieving middle income status, with a much broader middle class whose economic well-being is more directly linked to the growth process than is the case today. In Nehru's memorable phrase, "We will have brought about India's second tryst with destiny."

—Text of the Twenty-seventh Jawaharlal Nehru
Memorial Lecture, London, April 20, 2005

6

Globalised Indian Economy : Structural Changes and Challenges

M.R. Aggarwal

INTRODUCTION

The word "globalization" which appeared for the first time in 1961 became widely known and used by economists, politicians during the last 20 years of the last century. Globalization may be defined as a process of increasing economic integration and growing economic inter-dependence between countries in the world economy. It is associated not only with an increasing cross-border movement of goods, services, capital, technology, information and people, but also with an organization of economic activities which straddles national boundaries. In general, this process is mainly driven by the forces of "competition" and "efficiency" of the market mechanism.

This paper aims to examine the need and rationale of economic reforms introduced in 1991, the economic performance during the era of reform years and to suggest a pragmatic approach for the coming decade under the current waves of globalization for India for achieving the goal of overall faster growth with equity.

The globalization of the world economic and social structure in terms of increased volumes of capital, trade and immigration is certainly one of the key characteristics of the present times, describing how the relationships among countries have changed since Second World War II. This may be labeled as the second globalization era. GATT (1947) and now WTO (Jan.,1995) which is wider in scope as compared to GATT and other Bretton Woods Institutions, i.e. IMF and the World Bank and its Associates are now promoting the process of globalization through the liberalization of trade, capital and advancement of technology around the world and infact are its main pillars. The quick availability of the information and its drastic decline in costs, falling transactions cost have further speeded up this process. In fact at present the world is growing smaller and smaller due to the interdependence of the markets. This process, it may be that noted here, is not new as the first era of globalization remained on the international scene with gold as the medium of exchange during the period 1870-1914. During the Inter-war period, thereafter the notion of "free trade in principle" lost much of its charm, mainly because of the excessive trade and payments restrictions used by one country against another. But it again got momentum immediately after the Second World War. This was based on the wisdom of the conventional pure theory of international trade which establishes the superiority of free trade over trade with restrictions, i.e. of competition, the invisible hand, over interference indeed; the theory fundamentally is an extension of the theory of optimization. Free trade in principle is the main prescription of the pure theory for achieving optimality in resource allocation and acceleration in economic welfare more so at the global level. But during the Post-War 2nd years the movement towards the formation of regional groupings, primarily in the form of customs unions or free trade areas, both in the developed and developing, countries, got momentum, with the belief (which is debatable) that a customs union or a free trade area is a step towards free trade in a number of contiguous countries.

The working of the GATT, founded by 23 countries in 1947 was amazingly successful during the Post-War II period despite its inherent weaknesses as far as the reductions in the rates of tariffs were concerned among the countries of the world, thus advanced the basic objectives of free market and competition through the process of trade and capital liberalization. This is the sole reason that the different regions of the world are integrating with the global economy (Table 6.1)

India after attaining independence adhered strictly to 'inward looking import substitution' policies behind huge tariff walls and highly restrictive quantitative restrictions and regulations with attendant disincentives for exports due to: (i) gradual realization that the market forces wont operate efficiently and could not be relied in the long-run, and (ii) acceptance of Keynesian framework, which accorded a leading role to state as an economic actor, for sustaining rapid rates of economic growth with equity. The various instruments, used by India to achieve the aim of "shared growth" could be listed as follows: (i) Though it was realized in the various plans that the private sector should and can contribute significantly in the acceleration of the process of growth, but massive investments in the public sector was made to generate surpluses for capital formation; (ii) The private sector was regulated extensively through discretionary direct controls and carefully monitored in a way as to play a supporting role to state enterprises; (iii) Increasing use of industrial licensing and controls to promote growth in some of the basic industries and hence to balance aggregate supply to demand was resorted; (iv) The government, besides entry barriers, introduced strict exit barriers to protect the workers from being unemployed, e.g. under the Industrial Disputes Act a firm with one hundred or more workers could not retrench workers and cannot resort to closures without a prior permission of the Government. (v) A highly restricted and bureaucratic import licensing system through high rate of tariffs and non-tariff barriers, was backed by an equally complex system of "export incentives", providing a huge subsidy to exporters, was used to support import substitution inward looking policies for industrialization; (vi) In

TABLE 6.1

Integration with the Global Economy—India and Other Countries (1990-2001)

	Merchandize Exports		*Trade in Services*		*Growth of real trade less GDP growth*	*Gross Private Capital Inflows*		*Foreign Direct Investment (Inflows)*		*Foreign Direct Investment (Outflows)*	
	1990	*2004*	*1990*	*2004*	*1990-2004*	*1990*	*2004*	*1990*	*2004*	*1990*	*2004*
(1)	*(2)*	*(3)*	*(4)*	*(5)*	*(6)*	*(7)*	*(8)*	*(9)*	*(10)*	*(11)*	*(12)*
India	13.1	25.0	3.4	8.2	6.8	0.8	5.9	0.1	0.8	0.0	0.2
World	32.4	44.9	7.89	10.5		10.3	28.4	1.0	1.6	1.2	2.2
High Income—Europe	44.4	59.4	11.1	14.8		13.4	41.3	1.1	1.3	1.7	2.6
High Income	32.3	41.5	8.0	10.5		11.0	32.0	1.0	1.3	1.4	2.4
Low and Middle Income	32.5	58.1	7.0	10.3		5.9	11.9	0.7	2.6	0.1	0.5
Low Income	24.1	37.8	0.3	9.4		2.7	6.9	0.4	1.4	0.0	0.2

Source : World Bank Indicators, 2006.

the agricultural sector, public policies in the form of price support procurement, input subsidies and provision of commercial credit, were adopted for providing necessary incentives to farmers for adopting modern agricultural techniques. Lastly, strict control, under FERA-1974, on the operation of direct foreign investment in general and in banking, insurance and the extra active industries was placed. The export sector which was more or less neglected during the 1950s however received serious attention of the planners in the mid-1960s due to mounting balance of payments imbalances but the balance of payments crisis, revised doubts regarding the efficacy of the state-led-industrialization strategy. The Government in the 1970s, due to growing levels of unemployment, and under employment inflation which hurt the most the poorer and weaker sections of the society and for increasing agricultural surplus, adopted various anti-poverty alleviation programmes, thus shifting the emphasis from "quantitative dimension" to "qualitative dimension" of growth strategy. In the early 1980s, besides persistent macro-economic crisis, the economy was confronted with a high rate of inflation due to over expansionary fiscal policies. It was explicitly realized that "too much" use of the interventionist policies by the state, administrative controls in the various sectors are highly detrimental to economic growth. Hence selective and small doses of trade liberalization coupled with the policies of decontrol deregulation in some of the core sectors of the economy though half-heartedly, were being tried to restructure the economy to manage both the aggregate demand and aggregate supply; but could not be pursued far, maybe due to political compulsions. It was also felt that an adequate agricultural and export policy which are causing serious impediments to the future growth of India. The macro-economic crisis reached its peak in 1990 with current account balance as percentage of GDP backed by a rate of inflation of 9.9 percent despite India's record economic performance (6.0 percent) due to the high rate of industrial growth of 5.9 percent and domestic savings ration of 21.9 percent as percentage of GDP. The overall rate of growth of GDP was 6.0 percent which even surpassed the "rate" achieved by industrialized countries, Eastern European countries and other developing areas during 1983-1989 and was far higher as compared to the rate of growth of 4.9% achieved during the period 1975-82. These "imbalances" at macro-level represent an "excess demand" or "shortage of savings" and given the limited scope of internal borrowing due to underdeveloped capital market were financed primarily through external commercial loans which resulted in a rise in foreign interest payments and external debt service ratio which reached to 2.2 percent of GDP in 1990. Limited foreign exchange reserves were reduced to levels which were not even sufficient to finance to two weeks of imports. Serious attempts backed by strong economic reasoning through the introduction of various reforms under SAP and stabilization programmes were initiated in the various sectors by the Government, to reduce these "imbalances" while maintaining high rates of growth. The reforms under SAP help in increasing the rate of growth by enhancing the productivity in the various sectors through the opening of economy in trade, industrial, financial and services sectors and overall reduction in the role of the state. The main aims of these reforms are to achieve macro-economic stability, curb the speed of inflationary pressures, and revitalize the economy by removing the powerful breaks on production productivity and efficiency in the different sectors of the economy.

POST-REFORM PERIOD : (1991-2005)

The performance of the Indian economy during the "reform years" is commendable as measured, in terms of rates of growth of GDP, exports, ratios of savings to national income, gross fixed capital formation, level and rate of inflation and current account deficit and in fact confirms that economy is on a high growth trajectory. The rate of growth of real GDP remained above 6% since 1993 while the ratio of savings to national income increased from 21.9% to 29.0%, the fixed capital formation rose from 23.0% to 26.0% during the period. The average rate of inflation fell from 9.9 to 5.9% and the current account deficit as a percentage of GDP declined from 3.3 to 1.6%. Foreign currency reserves net of gold holding and SDRs rose signifies India has come a long way on the road of reforms but there is still a long way to go (Table 6.2).

TABLE 6.2
Macro-Economic Performance of Indian Economy (1995-2005)

(*Percentage*)

	1995	1996	1997	1998	1999	2000	2001	2002	2003	2004	2005
(1)	(2)	(3)	(4)	(5)	(6)	(7)	(8)	(9)	(10)	(11)	(12)
GDP growth rate	7.3	7.8	4.8	6.5	6.1	4.4	5.38	3.8	8.5	7.5	8.1
Agricultural sector growth rate	-0.9	9.6	-2.4	6.2	0.3	-0.1	6.2	-6.9	10.0	0.7	2.3
Industrial sector growth rate	11.6	7.1	4.3	3.7	4.8	6.5	2.7	7.0	7.6	8.6	9.0
Services Sector Growth Rates	10.5	7.2	9.8	8.4	10.1	5.5	7.1	7.3	8.2	9.9	9.8
Gross domestic savings rates	25.1	23.2	23.1	21.5	24.9	23.5	23.6	26.5	28.9	29.1	29.0
Growth domestic investment rate	26.9	24.5	24.6	22.6	26.0	24.2	23.0	25.3	27.2	30.1	30.3
Inflation rate	10.2	9.4	6.8	13.1	3.4	3.8	4.3	4.0	3.9	3.8	4.5
Current account balances	-1.7	-1.2	-1.4	-1.0	-1.0	-0.6	0.7	1.3	1.8	-0.9	-1.3
Change in money supply	11.0	18.7	17.7	18.2	17.1	15.2	14.3	16.8	13.0	16.7	17.1
Merchandise export growth rate	20.3	5.6	4.5	-3.9	9.5	21.1	-1.6	20.3	20.4	24.9	26.0
Annual average exchange rates	32.43	35.43	36.31	41.26	43.05	44.94	47.19	48.61	46.58	45.32	44.10

Source : World Bank Economic Indicators (Various issues).

TABLE 6.2A

Annual Average Compound Growth Rates of Per capita GDP Growth

(*Percentage*)

	1820-2001	*1820-1913*	*1913-1950*	*1950-1973*	*1973-1980*	*1980-2001*
Developed World	19.0	1.3	1.2	3.3	1.9	1.9
Eastern Europe	8.8	1.0	0.6	3.8	2.1	0.2
Former USSR	6.7	0.8	1.8	3.3	0.8	-1.6
Latin America	8.4	0.8	1.4	2.6	2.7	0.3
Asia	6.9	0.4	0.1	3.6	2.8	2.3
China	6.0	-0.1	-0.6	2.9	3.5	5.9
India	3.7	0.3	-0.2	1.4	1.4	3.6
Japan	30.9	0.8	0.9	8.1	2.3	2.1
Africa	3.5	0.4	0.9	2.0	1.2	-0.1

Note : Unemployment rate on current daily status basis.

Sources: 1. Planning Commission—1 (2001). Report of the Task Force on Employment Opportunities.

2. NSSO (2005), Report No. 506, pp. 87, 90.

3. Maddision (2001) and UN/DESA.

In some quarters it is forcefully argued that the state under the present economic scenario will have little role to play as an economic actor which is totally a mistaken view. The role of state under perfect competition markets, information and absence of externalities ignoring the problem of income distribution, no doubt is minimum but it had and continued to play a significant role when there exists "imperfections" in any sector of the economy. In India what actually has happened during the pre-reform era is that the state has attempted to do of what it cannot or should not do and it has done practically little where it should have actually done. The need of the hour is to redefine the role of the state. It must off-load many of its responsibilities on to the private sector which could be performed efficiently by it, and should intervene systematically and through multiple channels in the different sectors to foster the agents of development. For example, it must create a healthy social sector by providing basic services, education infrastructural facilities, partly through the socialization of PSUs profits specify the rules of the game ... players both in the private and public sector, and create a sound and stable macro economic and; physical environment as these can't be left to the market forces. The growth experience of East Asian economies is quite instructive in this regard. The export led growth strategy based on transnational private foreign investment without doubt paid rich dividends in these countries. The high degree of openness and rates of growth in exports, on the basis of multiple regression, are found to be statistically significant and positively correlated with the changes in real income. However, an in-depth examination of the various policies pursued by them in the past clearly reveal, that the state, besides guiding the "market" at various levels played an active but selected interventionist role through budget discipline, managing exchange rates, devising institutional framework which exerted strong discipline on the private sector, and use of scarce resources. In other words, favourable external environment, "getting the prices right" and "getting the policies right" worked in a mutually reinforcing manner for their remarkable performance, both in economic and social sector.

ECONOMIC GROWTH AND STRUCTURAL CHANGES IN INDIA DURING THE REFORM YEARS

Generation of productive employment has become one of the major issues of worldwide concern since unemployment and underemployment have been significantly higher in many parts of the developing world including India. Although the world economy is becoming highly integrated through the flow of trade, investment and the other short-term and long term financial flows and offers growing opportunities for economic expansion has also created social dislocation and unrest in the society. It is creating wage and income disparities carrying the degree of social disintegration. Therefore, in spite of globalization national policies are quite important in determining the level of employment. We need a society which is very competitive and also compassionate in today's world. It is not only necessary to have wider role of the state but also to have an efficient government.

The classical development model of economics is closely linked to the changes in the structure of production. According to this rule, industrialization from the agriculture became driver of change and overall productivity increase as a result of the reallocation of labour from low to high productivity. According to this view, capital accumulation through a high rate of savings and investment still holds ground in any economy as these are needed to support the industrial development. It is presumed here that external shocks and erratic domestic policies are conducive to negative growth. In other words, it means that the importance of industrial development was central to development thinking.

In other words, it means that the significance of industrial development was central to classical development model. It follows from the following that capital investment is essential to economic development and growth, as it is a major carrier of technological change and productivity increase. It also plays a central role in the development of infrastructure and the construction of urban centers, where manufacturing and services cluster. Further, capital accumulation also sets off structural changes. Economic transformation thus will require changes in patterns of accumulation as new resources are invested in new sectors of the economy, thus increasing their contribution to overall output. Higher economic growth and convergence are associated with increase in investment per capita. Following Tables 6.3 to 6.8 show that India's economic growth has been exceedingly good as measured by rate of economic growth (6.2%) as compared to the 1991 period. The saving and investment rates have been very good, by any measure but the rate of economic growth has been made possible by a high rate of growth in services sector, which has been consistently more than 7% but the contribution of agricultural sector which is around 2% is very low. The little contribution of this sector over the variant years brings the structural transformation of the Indian economy but side by side what has happened to be productive employment generation. Rate of inflation along with unemployment has gone up. The 11th Plan approached proper seeks to achieve more than 8% with a further acceleration to 9% during the coming years. Agricultural sector remained a passive sector. (Tables 6.3 to 6.8).

TABLE 6.3
Growth of Output of India and Selected Countries

	Gross Domestic Product		Agriculture		Industry		Manufacturing		Services	
	Average annual % growth		Average annual % growth		Average annual % growth		Average annual % growth		Average annual % growth	
	1990-2000	2000-04	1990-2000	2000-04	1990-2000	2000-04	1990-2000	2000-04	1990-2000	2000-04
(1)	(2)	(3)	(4)	(5)	(6)	(7)	(8)	(9)	(10)	(11)
India	6.0	6.2	3.0	2.0	6.3	6.2	7.0	6.5	8.0	8.2
Malaysia	7.0	4.4	0.3	3.4	8.6	4.2	9.5	4.4	7.3	4.7
Philippines	3.4	3.9	1.7	2.4	3.5	2.4	3.0	3.9	4.0	5.8
Singapore	7.7	2.9	-2.6	-1.1	8.8	1.2	7.9	3.2	7.5	3.7
Sri Lanka	5.3	3.7	1.87	0.4	7.0	2.5	8.1	2.0	5.7	5.6
United Kingdom	2.7	2.3	-0.2	1.2	1.5	-0.1	—	—	3.5	2.9
United States	3.5	2.5	3.7	-0.7	3.7	0.0	—	0.6	3.4	2.5
World	2.9w	2.5w	1.8w	2.1w	2.4w	1.4w	-w	1.0w	3.1w	2.3w
Low Income	4.7	5.5	3.1	2.7	4.9	6.0	5.8	6.5	5.9	6.7
Middle Income	3.8	4.7	2.0	3.4	4.3	5.6	—	—	3.9	4.1
Low and Middle Income	3.9	4.8	2.3	3.2	4.3	5.6	—	—	4.2	4.4
High Income	2.7	2.0	1.0	-1.3	1.9	0.3	—	0.7	3.0	2.0

Source: World Development Indicators, 2006.

TABLE 6.4

Structure of Output of India and Selected Countries

	Gross Domestic Product		Agriculture		Industry		Manufacturing		Services	
	$ millions		% of GDP		% of GDP		% of GDP		% of GDP	
	1990-2000	2000-04	1990-2000	2000-04	1990-2000	2000-04	1990-2000	2000-04	1990-2000	2000-04
(1)	(2)	(3)	(4)	(5)	(6)	(7)	(8)	(9)	(10)	(11)
India	316937	691163	31	21	28	27	17	16	41	52
Malaysia	44024	118318	15	10	42	50	24	31	43	40
Philippines	44312	84567	22	14	35	32	25	24	44	54
Singapore	36901	106818	—	0	—	35	—	29	—	65
Sri Lanka	8032	20055	26	18	26	27	15	15	48	55
United Kingdom	989524	2124385	2	1	35	26	23	—	63	73
United States	5757200	11711834	2	1	28	22	19	15	70	77
World	21735592	41290409t	6w	4w	33w	28w	22w	18w	61w	68w
Low Income	609821	1239169	32	23	26	28	15	15	42	49
Middle Income	3238587	7156777	16	10	39	37	25	18	46	53
Low & Middle Income	3849026	8395211	18	12	37	36	23	18	45	52
High Income	17887372	32900093	3	2	33	26	22	18	65	72

Source : World Development Indicators, 2006.

TABLE 6.5

Unemployment Rates* for 50th Round (1993-94) and 60th Round (January-June 2004) of the NSSO (All India)

	Rural						
	Males				Females		
Round	*Usual*	*CWS*	*CDS*		*Usual*	*CWS*	*CDS*
(1)	*(2)*	*(3)*	*(4)*	*(5)*	*(6)*	*(7)*	*(8)*
60th (2004)	24	47	90		22	45	93
50th (1993-94)	20	30	56		14	30	56
	Urban						
	Males				Females		
Round	*Usual*	*CWS*	*CDS*		*Usual*	*CWS*	*CDS*
60th (2004)	46	57	81		89	90	117
50th (1993-94)	45	52	67		83	84	105

*Unemployment rates (number of persons (or person days) unemployed per 1000 persons (or person days)).

CWS: Current Weekly Status, CDS: Current Daily Status.

Source : NSSO's 60th Round Survey on Employment and Unemployment conducted in January-June, 2004.

TABLE 6.6

Unemployment Rates Among Rural and Urban Males and Females in India

(*Percentage of Labour Force*)

	Rural Areas			*Urban Areas*		
Year (Round)	*Males*	*Females*	*Persons*	*Males*	*Females*	*Persons*
1977-78 (32nd)	7.1	9.2	7.7	9.4	14.5	10.3
1983 (38th)	7.5	9.0	7.9	9.2	11.0	9.5
1987-88 (43rd)	4.6	6.7	5.3	8.8	12.0	9.4
1993-94 (50th)	5.6	5.6	5.6	6.7	10.5	7.4
1999-2000 (55th)	7.2	7.3	7.2	7.2	9.8	.7
2004 (60th)	9.0	9.3	9.1	8.1	11.7	8.8

Note : Unemployment rates are on CDS basis.
Source : Same as Table 6.1.

Table 6.4 clearly reveals that the contribution to GDP by the service sector during 2000-04 was 52% while that of agriculture decreased from 31% to 21% during same period.

Table 6.5 which gives the unemployment rates for the 50th round and 60th round clearly shows that unemployment rates between rural and urban males and females, on CWS, CDS basis have increased during these rounds.

Table 6.7 which gives unemployment rates on all India basis and in the major states of India shows that even in advanced states like Gujarat, Haryana, Punjab and Himachal Pradesh and Maharashtra have registered an increase in unemployment rates after the introduction of reforms. The poor states remained poor, i.e. Bihar Madhya Pradesh, Orissa, Rajasthan.

Table 6.8 which gives the growth rate of employment in the organized sector during 1991-98 shows that the employment in the public sector and overall has declined. It is true that it has increased marginally in the organized price sector. This means that the labour force has become dependent on private sector.

Structural transformation in must of the countries of the world during the period 1995-05 show that first of all

TABLE 6.7
Unemployment Rates in Major States of India (Percent of Labour Force)

Sl. No.	States	Unemployment Rate					
		1987-88	1993-97	1999-200	2004		
					Rural	Urban	Persons
(1)		(2)	(3)	(4)	(5)	(6)	(7)
1.	Andhra Pradesh	7.35	6.67	7.94	10.63	9.54	10.17
2.	Assam	5.09	7.96	8.00	7.65	7.87	7.76
3.	Bihar	4.04	6.25	7.35	6.97	9.63	8.26
4.	Gujarat	5.79	5.73	4.63	7.87	5.54	5.74
5.	Haryana	7.59	6.59	4.67	7.31	9.67	8.47
6.	Himachal Pradesh	3.12	1.82	2.93	6.54	10.07	8.28
7.	Karnataka	5.06	4.89	4.61	10.95	6.69	8.99
8.	Kerala	21.19	15.50	20.77	23.88	16.62	20.28
9.	Madhya Pradesh	2.86	3.42	4.60	4.91	7.29	6.01
10.	Maharashtra	4.67	4.97	7.09	10.19	9.50	9.86
11.	Orissa	6.44	7.28	7.38	12.20	9.69	10.99
12.	Punjab	5.07	3.08	4.15	9.50	7.43	8.42
13.	Rajasthan	5.74	1.33	3.06	3.87	4.17	4.01
14.	Tamil Nadu	10.36	11.44	12.05	18.49	11.03	15.09
15.	Uttar Pradesh	3.44	3.45	4.27	3.57	6.80	5.19
16.	West Bengal	8.13	9.87	14.95	12.58	12.17	12.36
	All-India	6.09	6.03	7.32	9.00	8.83	8.91

TABLE 6.8

Growth Rates of Employment in Organized Sector

(Percent)

Year	*Public Sector*	*Private Sector*	*Total organized*
1991	1.52	1.24	1.44
1992	0.80	2.21	1.21
1993	0.60	0.06	0.44
1994	0.62	1.01	0.73
1995	0.11	1.63	0.55
1996	(-)0.19	5.62	1.51
1997	0.67	2.04	1.09
1998	(-)0.09	1.72	0.46

Source : Planning Commission.

employment shift from agricultural to industrial and then to services sectors (Table 6.9).

The impact of stabilization has to be judged in the medium term by its effect on growth and employment but the NSSO has undertaken a study on incidence of poverty status in this context. It is encouraging to see that for the first time in 50 years, the number people below the poverty line has touched a figure below the 300 million mark, despite an increase in population. But from the foregoing the sharp decline in poverty figure has shown that the inequalities in income and employments have increased (Table 6.10).

The seminal study by Kuznet in 1955, and in 1963 advanced the hypothesis of the 'inverted U-shaped". According to him inequality in income first increases and then decreases. This pattern of growth was also indicated by Adelman and Monis, Ohima and many others. The conclusion in this study is that it takes a long time before the poor 20% experience any increase in the income share. But the level of per capita income explains only small part of the variation in inequality.

India has faced a problem of jobless growth, the people below the poverty line and the youth unemployment and employment of children (5-14 years of age).

TABLE 6.9

Employment in Developing Countries has Shifted out of Agriculture into Manufacturers and Services Trends in Sectoral Shares in Employment, 1995-2005

(Percent)

World region	Agriculture			Industry			Services		
	1995	2005[a]	Changes (%)	1995	2005[a]	Changes (%)	1995	2005[a]	Changes (%)
(1)	(2)	(3)	(4)	(5)	(6)	(7)	(8)	(9)	(10)
World	44.4	40.1	-9.7	21.1	21	-0.5	34.5	38.9	12.8
East Asia	54.4	49.5	-9.0	25.9	26.1	0.8	19.7	24.4	23.9
South East Asia and the Pacific	55.3	43.3	-21.7	15.4	20.74	34.4	29.1	36	22.9
South Asia	64.1	61.2	-4.5	13.4	14.1	5.2	22.5	24.6	9.3
Latin America and the Caribbean	23.4	17.1	-26.9	20.2	20.3	0.5	56.4	62.5	10.8
Middle-East and North Africa	30.8	26.3	-14.6	20.3	25	23.2	48.9	48.7	-0.4
Sub-Saharan Africa	70.1	63.6	-9.3	8.2	8.9	8.5	21.7	27.5	26.7
Developed economics and the European Union	5.1	3.7	-27.5	28.7	24.8	-13.6	66.1	71.4	8.0
Central and Eastern Europe and CIS	27.9	22.7	-18.6	27.5	27.4	-0.4	44.6	49.9	11.9

Source : ILO 2006; Bank staff calculations.
CIS : Commonwealth of Independent States.
(a) Indicative.

TABLE 6.10
Incidence of Poverty in India

Year	No. of People below poverty line (million)	% to total Population	Rural number (million)	%	Urban number (million)	%
1993-1994	320	36.0	244	37.3	76	32.4
1999-2000	260	26.1	193	27.1	67	23.6

Source : Economic Survey, 2006.

TABLE 6.11
Employment Elasticities and Labour Productivity (1980s and 1990s)

	Elasticity		Productivity growth (Labour) 1980-2001 (Percentage)
	1980s	1990s	
Bangladesh	0.550	0.495	1.5
China	0.330	0.129	5.2
India	0.324	0.312	3.2
Indonesia	0.435	0.370	1.8
Malaysia	0.682	0.406	2.8
Thailand	0.335	0.193	3.0

While India is having more than 6% rate of average consistent growth during this period employment has not keep pace with the rate of growth and labour force. As a result, increasing unemployment has given rise to the fears of job less growth in India has also to confront with the youth unemployment reflecting mismatch between demand for labour and supply of labour. It is reflection of the imperfect labour market. The high rate of growth of labour force, the substitution of labour with capital from abroad and the labour becoming a fixed factor from variable factor gives rise to unemployment and under employment and jobless growth.

TABLE 6.12

India's Global Position in Terms of Socio-demographic Parameters

Country	at Life expectancy birth (years)	Under-five mortality rate (per 1,000 live births)		Infant mortality rate (per 1,000 live births)		mortality ratio (per 100,000 live births)
	2000-05	1990	2003	1990	2003	2005
(1)	(2)	(3)	(4)	(5)	(6)	(7)
China	71	49	37	38	30	56
India	63	123	87	80	63	540
Nepal	61	145	82	100	61	740
Pakistan	63	128	103	96	81	500
Sri Lanka	74	23	15	19	13	92
Bangladesh	63	144	69	96	46	380
South Asia	63	126	91	84	66	NA

NA : Not available.

Source : UNDP, Human Development Report, 2005.

Though economically India has achieved after the reform a high rate of growth in terms of per capita income but India's global position in terms of socio-demographic parameters is not very much encouraging as compared to 1980s and other countries of the world, i.e. Life expectancy at birth (years), Under-five mortality rate (per 1,000 live birth) Infant mortality rate (per 1,000 live births) mortality ratio (per 100,000 live births).

Meaning the total number of years in which income per head was less than in the previous year, which do not therefore represent a period of uninterrupted decline.

There has been failure of growth process in the last 50 years in most of the developing countries. There has been negative growth in many countries at different levels of development. Some of these are oil producers with relatively high levels of per capita income. There are some countries which are poor in terms of per capita income. The collapse of growth in countries which are the producers of the commodities. They have come to believe that there is the natural resource a curse which may not be so.

New European Union 25 encompasses the old European Union 15, plus Cyprus, the Czech Republic, Estonia, Hungary, Latvia, Lithuania, Malta, Poland, the Slovak Republic and Slovenia.

Looking at the long view of the whole table the so called convergence hypothesis since 1820 and more particularly after 1944 between the Western Europe and USA and south on the basis of GDP per capita, rates of GDP growth and the ratios of GDP never took place. The gap instead of becoming smaller and smaller did infact widened. Africa and USSR and some of the developing countries continued to diverge even during the period of golden age.

Lastly, the state must provide "good governance" as far as possible to achieve higher rates of economic growth. Though it is very difficult to define and operationalise this concept but according to the World Bank, "good governance" in the conduct of public and private social business is based upon three major pillars, viz. "accountability", i.e. creation of institutional network for assessing the financial performance, transparency (making available accurate and timely information to the

TABLE 6.13

Unskilled Workers in Developing and Developed Countries (2030) Growth in the Global Labour Force 2001-30

World Region	All workers (millions)			Unskilled workers (millions)			Skilled workers (millions)		
	2001	2030	Growth (% per year)	2001	2030	Growth (% per year)	2001	2030	Growth (% per year)
(1)	(2)	(3)	(4)	(5)	(6)	(7)	(8)	(9)	(10)
World total	3077	4144	1.03	2674	3545	0.98	403	598	1.37
High income countries	481	459	-0.16	327	276	-0.58	154	183	0.60
Developing countries	2596	3684	1.21	2347	3269	1.15	249	415	1.78
East Asia and the Pacific	1060	1279	0.65	988	1163	0.56	71	117	1.70
China	773	870	0.41	740	816	0.34	33	54	1.72
South Asia	632	1005	1.62	589	925	1.56	42	81	2.27
India	473	712	1.42	441	653	1.36	32	59	2.10
Europe and Central Asia	236	233	-0.04	195	192	-0.06	41	41	0.02
Middle-East and North Africa	119	205	1.88	87	144	1.74	32	61	2.25
Sub-Saharan Africa	313	617	2.36	293	573	2.33	20	44	2.74
Latin America and the Caribbean	236	345	1.32	194	273	1.19	42	72	1.85

Source : World Bank Staff Calculations.

TABLE 6.14

Countries with at Least Seven Consecutive Years of Decline in Real Per capita Income, 1950-2001*

	Period of decline	*Real GDP per capita in the first year of decline*	*Real GDP per capita in the last year of decline*	*Percentage decline in period*	*Total number of years of negative growth between 1950 and 2001*
(1)	*(2)*	*(3)*	*(4)*	*(5)*	*(6)*
Region and country		(1990 International Geary-khamis dollars)			
Africa					
Cameroon	1986-1994	1695	978	42.3	11
Cote d Ivoire	1985-1994	1798	1214	32.5	23
Democratic Republic of the Congo	1974-1983	842	587	30.2	32
	1986-2001	598	202	66.2	
Djibouti	1984-1998	1802	1092	39.4	29
Liberia	1979-1989	1230	889	27.7	26
Libyan Arab Jamahiriya	1979-1995	7565	2321	69.3	25
Madagascar	1971-1978	1246	1007	19.2	26
	1979-1988	1076	784	27.2	
Namibia	1981-1988	4159	3478	16.4	14

(*Contd.*)

TABLE 6.14 (*Contd.*)

(1)	(2)	(3)	(4)	(5)	(6)
Sao Tome and Principle	1985-2000	1486	1226	17.5	25
United Republic of Tanzania	1976-1985	620	519	16.3	24
Uganda	1971-1980	871	577	33.7	21
Latin America and Caribbean					
Bolivia	1978-1986	2715	2074	23.6	17
Cuba	1957-1965	2406	1988	17.4	20
Haiti	1980-1994	1304	753	42.3	29
Jamaica	1973-1980	4130	3121	24.4	17
Nicaragua	1983-1993	2169	1308	39.7	22
Venezuela	1977-1985	11251	8521	24.3	23
Western Asia					
Iraq	1979-1986	6756	3759	44.4	22
Qatar	1980-1991	29552	6467	78.1	30

Source : UN/DESA, based on Maddison (2001).

TABLE 6.15

Intraregional Trade Share in Selected Regional Groups, 1980-2004

Region	*1980*	*1985*	*1990*	*1995*	*2000*	*2001*	*2002*	*2003*	*2004*
(1)	*(2)*	*(3)*	*(4)*	*(5)*	*(6)*	*(7)*	*(8)*	*(9)*	*(10)*
East Asia 15	35	37	43	52	52	52	54	55	55
Emerging East Asia 14	22	28	33	39	41	41	43	44	44
ASEAN + 3	30	30	29	38	37	37	38	38	39
NIE 4	6	7	12	16	16	15	15	15	14
ASEAN 10	18	20	19	24	25	24	24	24	24
SAARC	4	3	3	4	4	4	5	6	5
Central Asia	—	—	—	—	7	7	6	6	5
NAFTA	34	39	38	43	49	49	48	47	46
Mercosur	11	7	11	19	20	18	14	15	15
Old European Union 15'	61	60	66	64	62	62	63	63	62
New European Union 25'	61	60	67	67	67	67	68	69	68

Source : East Asian Visions, Perspectives on Economic Development, Indermit Gill, Yukon Huang and Homi Kharas (2006).

TABLE 6.16
The Big Divergence : Developing *versus* Developed Countries, 1820-2001

	GDP per capita (1990 International Geary-Khamis Dollars)					
	1820	*1913*	*1950*	*1973*	*1980*	*2001*
Developed World	1204	3989	6298	13376	15257	22825
Eastern Europe	683	1695	2111	4988	5786	6027
Former USSR	688	1488	2841	6059	6426	4626
Latin America	692	1481	2506	4504	5412	5811
Asia	584	883	918	2049	2486	3998
China	600	552	439	839	1067	3583
India	533	673	619	853	938	1957
Japan	669	1387	1921	11434	13428	20683
Africa	420	637	894	1410	1536	1489

Ratio of GDP per capita to that of the developed world

	1820	*1913*	*1950*	*1973*	*1980*	*2001*
Eastern Europe	0.57	0.42	0.34	0.37	0.38	0.26
Former USSR	0.57	0.37	0.45	0.45	0.42	0.20
Latin America	0.58	0.37	0.40	0.34	0.35	0.25
Asia	0.48	0.22	0.15	0.15	0.16	0.18
China	0.50	0.14	0.07	0.06	0.07	0.16
India	0.44	0.17	0.10	0.06	0.06	0.09
Japan	0.56	0.35	0.30	0.85	0.88	0.91
Africa	0.35	0.16	0.14	0.11	0.10	0.07

general public and clarity about the rules/regulations and decisions of the government) and predictability (informing public about the existence of laws, regulations and policies to regulate society both well defined rights and duties). Though all of these are mutually supportive but "accountability" particularly in the Government expenditure under several heads takes the lead. In reality "bad governance" makes even "good economics" as "bad economics". The experience of "East Asian economics" growth is quite instructive in this regard. The great and immediate threat to India's economic stability is not "political instability" but "bad governance", particularly measured in terms of "corruption and inefficiencies at all levels.

THE EMERGING GLOBAL TRADING ENVIRONMENT

Inter-nationalization of trade and finance are the two major elements of the SAP. Various empirical studies have concluded from the growth experience of the East Asian Economies, ASEAN region during the last three decades and the historical experience of the gold standard during 1870-1913, a golden period of globalization, that the "degree of openness" or the policy of "getting the prices right" was one of the major factors in accelerating the process of economic development, because, besides increasing healthy competition, through the allocation of available resources of the trading partners optimally, it enabled the partners to obtain need expansion and operation imports, raw materials, technical know-how, skills and even entrepreneurship, and helped encourage the movement of capital, weakened inefficient monopolies and of course increased the size of the narrow home market more than otherwise would be possible. However, during the last two decades, in particular, international economic environment has become quite unfavourable and even shaky as far the South is concerned due to the advent of "regionalism" and "bilateralism", increased use of neo-protectionism (grey area measures) intra-industry trade among Northern countries, and slow down in the rates of growth of USA, greater EC and Japan due to past disinflationary policies. This group of G-3 is India's principal trade markets, it must be noted here.

The first wave towards regionalism was launched with the creation of "Unions of Six" and "Union of Seven", i.e. EEC and EFTA in the late 1950s with the decision to form NAFTA comprising of USA, Canada and Mexico and the creation of Asia Pacific Economic Co-operation Forum—a loose grouping of 18 Pacific Rim countries including USA, Japan and China. In 1994 the Forum committed themselves to form FTA between members by 2010 for the higher income countries and 2020 for lower income countries. USA also aimed to form a FTA embracing 34 democracies in the Western Hemisphere except Cuba by 2005. The EC was enlarged from 9 members to 12 in 1986 and 15 in 1994, and now 27 in 2007. A common market consisting of Brazil, Argentina, Uruguay and Paraguay in Latin America came into force in 1995 (Mercosur). Within Asia, Malaysia announced in 1990 the formation of East Asian Economic Grouping. A member of smaller arrangement including the ASEAN free trade are (AFTA) and SAPTA also came into existence. The world is witnessing a "paradoxical situation". As the pace of globalization is gaining momentum, the urge among the countries all over the world to club together at regional level is becoming stronger. The share of world trade in 1994 of these main groupings stood at around 61% of the total world trade. According to WTO, it has been notified of almost 180 regional trade arrangements. India is not a member of any of these groups except SAPTA where the intra-regional trade is virtually negligible. It would be very difficult for India under these circumstances, to increase her rate of growth of exports in the markets of G-3 despite all its efforts to integrate with the world trading system. However, India cannot and should not be an "innocent bystander" and must meet the challenge of growing regionalism by joining ASEAN and taking a lead in strengthening the intra-regional trade, keeping in view of the long run interests of less developed areas of SAPTA and opening the markets particularly for those who have absorbed a major share of intra-imports. It is quite true that the world economy of today is dominated by G-3 and their policies *vis-a-vis* the rest of the world will define the future path of the trading system, but it is equally true that for the future of global world trading system, each regional group must make a commitment and ensure to foster "freer" and "fairer" and nondiscriminatory open "multilateral trading system" by reducing tariffs simultaneously for the non-members and strictly adhering to the various provisions of WTO.

Non-tariff barriers include quantitative restrictions OMA export restraints, non-automatic licensing, quotas and prohibitions and price controls, i.e. anti-dumping, countervailing actions and voluntary export restraints, and are more binding in nature as compared to tariffs. These non-tariff barriers though under the "Uruguay Round" have been reduced to large extent but still are highest in USA, and Canada in the case of semi and finished manufactured goods as compared to the raw materials, agriculture, forestry and fishing (World Development). There is practically little or no change in the case of Japan even after the signing of "Uruguay Round". Even the ratio of tariffs except in the case of EU, are still the highest on the finished and semi finished products as compared to other categories. In other words, these barriers which increase with the degree of processing would reduce significantly the export opportunities for South and India by raising prices to the consumer and thereby restricting demand. The "low wage argument" advanced by the rich countries in favor of, such barriers, seems to be unconvincing because wages are only one element in total costs and the competitive advantage in different industries depend as much on such other determinants of costs as the state of their technological advance, capital stock, benefits of economics of scale and the price of raw inputs. From the low wages paid may be much more than offset by the low productivity of labour so that labour cost per unit of output may in fact be higher as compared to industrialized countries. One of the major factors which made the "process of globalization"(1870-1913) a grand success was the virtual absence of non-tariff barriers, intra industry and intra firm trade. Practically the whole world may enter, if this trend continues what "Friedman" calls into an "era of managed trade". In fact, a more or less similar situation may emerge at the global scene, if appropriate economic measures are not taken by G-3, which was witnessed after the First World War when trade dependency ratios increased despite rising wave of protectionism and the South including India may become to a large extent the victim of the world deteriorating economy.

It is argued that with the internationalization of capital, these dominant constraints will be overcome which in turn will increase income, output and employment. The classical gold standard survived as the financial flows were mainly long-run in nature, stabilizing and was mostly related to trade and investment. The Bretton Woods system era was based on a consensus among the founding fathers, that capital flows unrelated to trade and investment be discouraged and was based on a number of positive adjustment mechanisms such as capital controls, exchange rate adjustment and wide spread use of fiscal tools. However during 1990s, there have been rapid swings in these flows due to the upcoming of the Euro-dollar market, shifting of the project loans by the World Bank/IMF to balance of payments adjustment, besides being short-term and speculative in nature. The major repercussions of these flows are to raise rates of interest and lower exchange rates but less stable which in turn further cause violent changes in "macro-economic problems" due to the "destabilizing nature" of these flows. This unpredictable nature of international flows has not been incorporated in the standard theory of foreign borrowing. Growth costs would be severe in those countries which are caught up in the debt trap. The rigid exchange rate system of Bretton Woods system which collapsed under its own weight and the fluctuating exchange rate system which in fact has been turned into a complete managed floating exchange rate system do not seem to be workable, keeping in view of the interests of the Southern World. India is yet to go for full convertibility of rupee on capital account. And after the introduction of full convertibility, the movement of these flows would have a serious "repercussion". The possible solution lies under the present circumstance is the urgent need of devising an "intermediate position" which should regulate the fluctuations of exchange rates under "target zones" and heavy taxes on "purely speculative" activities. This could be best achieved if there is a serious governance in terms of a co-operative agreement among G-3 which should effectively check these unpredictable flows, so that the occurrence of recent East Asian crisis and Mexico crisis in 1995 be minimized.

From the foregoing it is clear that no doubt India has achieved a higher rate of economic growth but the inequalities in income and unemployment between India and other countries and within the states of India have increased after the introduction of reforms.

The broad generalizations which emerge from the foregoing analysis are that the final success of the policies of globalization and market friendly reforms from the point of view of the South and India's overall economic and social growth will to a great extent depend on the complete agreement between G-3, regarding adjusting their macro-domestic policies consistent with global framework of co-operation and not confrontation, maintaining stable macro-economic environment by stabilizing as far as possible the exchange rates and the rates of interest limiting the speed and strength of the speculative short-term financial transactions across borders progressively reducing the non-tariff barriers on the finished and semi-finished products of the South, coupled with the concerted efforts made by India in the neon future to expand and deepen the ongoing domestic liberalization apart from strengthening intra-regional trade at SAPTA and creating a favorable climate for good "governance".

References

Aizenman, Joshua and Yothin Jinjarak (2006), Globalization and Developing Countries: A Shrinking Tax Base?

Akyuz, Yilmaz (2004), Trade Growth and Industrialization: Issues, Experience and Policy Challenges, Geneva.

Baro, Robert J. and Xavier Sala-i-Martin (1992), Convergence, *Journal of Political Economy,* (Chicago).

Bourguignon, Francois and Christian Morrison (2002), Inequality among World Citizens, 1820-1992, AER.

Carcovic, Maria and Rose Levine (2002), "Does Foreign Direct Investment Accelerate Economic Growth?", Minnesota.

Dollar, David (1992), Outward-Oriented Developing Economies Success, Princeton, New Jersey : Evidence from 95 LDCs, 1976-1985, *Economic Development and Cultural Change,* Vol. 10, No. 3.

Driffield, Nigel and K. Taylor (2002), Spillovers from FDI and Skill Structures of Host-Country Firms, *Discussion Papers in Economics,* No. 24.

Feld, Serge (2005), Labour Force Trends and Immigration in Europe, *International Migration Review,* Vol. 39, Issue 3.

Gabriele, Alberto (2004), Exports of Services and Economic Growth in Developing Countries, Geneva : UNCTAD, UNCTAD/DITC/TNCD/MISC/2003/6.3.

Ghose, Ajit K. (2004), Capital Inflows Aid Investment in Developing Countries, *ILO Employment Strategy Paper,* No. 2004/11.m

Grilli, Enzo R. and Maw Cheng Yang (1988), Primary Commodity Prices, Manufactured Goods Prices and the Terms of Trade of Developing Countries : What the Long-run Shows, *World Bank Economic Review.*

Haggard, Stephan (2004), Institutions and Growth in East Asia, *Studies in Comparative International Development,* Vol. 38, No. 4.

Hummels, David, Jun Ishii and Kei-Mu Yi (1998), Vertical Specialization and the Changing Nature of World Trade, *Economic Policy Review,* Federal Reserve Bank of New York.

J. Michall Finger, ERD Working Paper Series No. 21, Economic and Research Department (ADB), The Doha Agenda and Development: A View from the Uruguay Round—Sept. 2002.

Kaldor, Nicholas (1957), A Model of Economic Growth, *Economic Journal,* Vol. 67.

Kaufmann, Daniel, Aart Kraay and Massimo Mastruzzi (2004), Governance Matter III: Governance Matters III: Governance Indicators for 1996-2002, World Bank, 5 April revised.

RIS: World Trade and Development Report, 2007.

Taylor, Timothy, The Truth about Globalization, The Public Interest, Spring 2002.

UNCTAD, Trade and Development Report (1999), Report by the Secretariat of the UNCTAD, also WTO, Trading into the Future Introduction to WTO (1999).

United Nations, Global Economic Prospects, Managing the Next Wave of Globalization, 2007.

United Nations, *World Economic and Social Survey,* 2006.

7

Impact of Globalisation on Indian Agriculture

A. Ranga Reddy and M. Sampath Kumar Raju

INTRODUCTION

Globalisation is the process of integration of economics across the world through Cross-border flow of factors, products and information. The Universal economics liberalization which gathered momentum in the last two decades of the twentieth century, reinforced and enforced by the World Trade Organisation, seems to have made globalisatoin irreversible and un-stoppable. "All institutions have to make global competitiveness a strategic goal. No institution, whether a business, a university or a hospital, can hope to survive, let alone to succeed, unless it measured up to the standards set by the leaders in its filed, any place in the world". Globalisation, of course, is not a new phenomenon. The period 1870 to 1914 experienced a growing trend towards globalisaton.

The new phase of globalisation which started around the mid-20th Century became widespread, more pronounced and over changing. Since, the late 1980's by gathering momentum from the political and economic changes that swept across the Communist Countries and the economic reforms in other countries. The latest multi-lateral trade agreement seeks to substantially liberalise international trade investment, and the technological and communication revolutions. Globalisation may be considered at two levels, viz., at the macro-level and at the micro-level. The paper highlights the macro-changes of globalisaton on Indian Agriculture. The first part deals with globalization and second, on Indian Agriculture.

Drivers of Globalisation

The world economy has been emerging as a global or transnational economy. Globalisaiton is a process of development of the world into a single integrated economic unit. The transnational economy is a borderless world economy characterised by free flow of trade and factors of production across national borders. "In the mid-1970s, with the OPEC and floating of the US dollar—the world economy changed from being international to transnational. The transnational economy is characterized by money flows rather than trade, money and capital markets increases, market maximization rather than trade, money and capital markets increase, market maximization rather profit maximization, trade become function of investment, decision-making shifts from national State to regional blocs, genuine organized information and entire world turns into a single market for production". Globalisation represents the increasing integration of the world economy based on five inter-related drivers of change. They are international trade, financial flows Communications, technological advances and population mobility.

Stages of Globalisation

Normally, a firm passes through different stages of development before it becomes a truly global corporation. Typically, a domestic firm starts its international business by exporting. Later it may establish joint ventures or subsidiaries abroad. From an international firm it may then develop into a multinational firm and finally into a global or transnational one. Ohmae identifies five different stages in the development of a firm into a global corporation. A domestic company moves into new markets overseas, company takes over activities on its own. Domestic-based company begins to carry out its own manufacturing, at overseas. The company moves towards a genuinely a global mode of operation. This is what Akio Morita of Sony has termed as global localization.

Benefits of Globalisation

Foreign Capital, if properly utilized, can make substantial contribution to the economic development of a nation. A classical example is the communist China. Productivity grows more quickly when countries produce goods and services in which they have comparative advantage. Living standards can go up faster. Increase in competition would make companies more cost and quality conscious, and innovative. Global Competition and imports keep a lid on prices, so inflation is less likely to derail economic growth. Liberalisation and global competition enhance consumer choice and consumer surplus. An open economy spurs innovation with fresh ideas from abroad. Export jobs often pay more than other jobs. Unfettered capital flows give the country access to foreign investment and keep interest rate low. Globalisation opens up enormous domestic and global opportunities for firms in developing countries. Despite discriminations of the global economic order against them, there are chances of developing countries benefiting from trade.

Survival of the Fittest in Globalisation

Globalisation brought number of challenges for the individuals, firms and countries. Certainly, globalisation will doom the future of those who fail to meet these challenges effectively. (a) In a competitive environment, a firm can survive only if it is efficient. Cost efficiency is to be promoted either by cutting size of labourers or other inputs. (b) Attracting foreign investment is a real challenge, as is evident from the fact that the FDI inflow of India is far below the target. (c) Liberalisation increases the economic inequality. Even in China, the liberalization has created many islands of affluence. The fast growth of Chinese economy has reduced poverty. Naisbitt points out that there were as estimated 200 to 270 million Chinese living in absolute poverty in 1978 and their number came down to 100 million by 1985. (d) small and medium firms often have some edge over the large ones in respect of standardized products or technologies. The new patent regime should be expected to help the Indian industry by promoting it to give added thrust to R & D and enabling Indian firms also to develop patented products. (e) The domestic and Cross-border M & As pose a serious Challenge to governments in ensuring fair competition. (f) Liberalisation will be successful only if the policy is proper and clear and there is the required political mandate, will and boldness. Lack of clarity regarding privatization; lack of boldness to implement labour law reforms, downsizing, bureaucratic hurdles and so on are retarding India's reform process. Lack of clarity in policies and delays can make the situation worse instead of realising the objectives of liberalization. E.g. Tata Steel had bagged corus for 12.1 billion.

Impact of Globalisation on India

With the new economic policy ushered in 1991, there has been a change. Globalisation has in fact become a buzzword in the Indian firms now and many are expanding their overseas business by different strategies.

Negative Factors

The Indian business suffers from a number of disadvantages of globalisation like bureaucratic culture not encouraging, high costs of many inputs, poor infrastructure facilities, obsolescence technology, resistance to change, poor quality image, supply problems, small size, lack of experience, limited R & D, growing competition and trade barriers. There is a view that globalisation is another form of imperialism, to exploit the resources of developing countries.

Positive Factors

There are number of favourable factors for globalisation. India had enough human resources, wide-based industrial business, growing entreprenuership, growing domestic market, niche markets, expanding markets, transnationalisation, large number of Non-resident Indians, encouragement of economic liberation, cut throat competition among global strategies.

II

MOVING TOWARDS CORPORATE AGRICULTURE

India has to support one sixth 1.2 billion of world population in the 2 per cent of land area (247 M. ha) and one per cent of global precipitation (400 M. ha.m). India is endowed with a natural wealth of diversified soil types heterogeneous climate conditions and biodiversity. The variabilities are with (1) Abundant sunshine and equitable temperature regimes provides conditions for round the year cropping, (2) To adopt diversified farming system to include livestock, tree crops, horticultural crops and aquaculture to ensure food security and prosperity to country men. (3) The other side inherited scarcity and poverty from the colonial rule. Through systematic planning to harness natural resources and technological development, Indian Republic surged ahead from scarcity to self-sufficiency, marginal surplus on food front in new millennium. The apprehensions of Thomas Malthus about the human ability to produce food to match the needs of human numbers, fortunately, did not come true.

Globalisation and economic liberalization have direct impact on production process, commercialization of agricultural products and social structure, it is capital intensive and offers opportunities for educated youth to participate. To compete with global market, cost reduction and quality improvement in production system will be indispensable; consequently shrinkage in labour and greater expectation on labour productivity. In future, corporate will play a lead role in Indian agriculture, effective partnership building will be warranted to bridge/reduce the severe disparity between rural and urban population. Agri-business should strike a partnership with farmer for covering his produce to satisfy market needs. This type of inter dependence between the farmer—Customer—Corporate would Constitute a socio-economic matrix (ITC, Pepsi, Mother Dairy, etc. are examples).

Agri-business

It is a profit-motivated enterprise that involves providing agricultural supplies and or the processing marketing and distribution of agricultural materials and consumer products.

Agri-business Companies provide input supplies to the production of agriculturists. The production agriculturist produce food, fibre etc, and the output is taken by agri-business companies that process, market and distribute the agricultural products. Many services are needed in agriculture, transportation, storage, refrigeration, credit, finance and insurance. Agri-business manufactures furnish farmers with supplies and equipment needed to produce and protect their crops. Hundreds of agri-business trade organizations, committees and conferences, were to be executed to educate, promote, advertise, coordinate for their agricultural products. Millions of people are employed in agri-business throughout the world. To uplift *kisan,* give him fishing rod and teach him how to fish. Otherwise he is bound to turn into a Naxalite. Blood revolutions in Russia and China were started by just such disgruntled farmers.

Precision Farming

At present, the average farm worker supplies over 150 persons with food and fibre. Annual consumption of food is 600 kgs per person, production is 50 tonnes of food. This productivity frees others from food production and pursues careers in science, medicine, computers and many other fields.

Precision farminag combines crop planning, including tillage, sowing chemical application, harvesting and post harvest processing of the crop. The five major objectives of comprehensive precision farming are—increased production efficiency, improved product quality—more efficient chemical use, energy conservation, soil and ground water protection. Precision farming requires the use of digitally, geographically referenced date in cropping operations.

Most of agri-business is small business. When it comes to jobs small business is not small in the number of people they employ. Entrepreneurs are people who have vision, diligence and persistence to flow through. An entrepreneur is a person who accepts all the risks pertaining to forming and operating a small business. A business succeeds only when it fills an economic need. Determine what type of business is needed. Many new business succeed they provide a product of service that others need for which they are willing to pay.

Agro-Industries

Agro-industries are considered an extended arm of agriculture, but in India it has not received as much attention as agriculture, while agriculture contributes about 18 per cent of India's GDP the value added by the processing industry is only 8 per cent of total food production. The size of the domestic market is Rs. 3,50,000 crores (Rs. 350 billion). An average Indian spends 53 per cent of his/her income on food. The domestic demand of processed food is not only huge but is growing fast it tandem with the economy. If more incomes are to be generated in the rural areas to improve the lot of farmers, it is imperative to accelerate the growth of the agriculture sector and agro-industry segment.

The focus on value addition in agri-sector is vital for comprehensive development of the rural economy. Since food processing industry creates job, demand for agri-raw materials, leads to diversification and commercialization of agriculture, enhancing the income of the farmers and creating surplus for export of agro-foods. The broad-based development of food processing industry will improve both the social and physical infrastructure of rural India. Some of the critical areas that require immediate attention are strengthening the infrastructure like cold storage, improving the production process in the agriculture sector, relaxing or removing stringent laws and regulations, and ensure reliable power supply.

Bio-Village Development and Future of Food Insecurity

Rural environment is to be changed. Globalisation is a capital intensive and has vast scope for better-educated personal. An inefficient and outdated technology farmer may not sustain in agriculture. The new technology and better distribution networks allow farmers to succeed in agriculture. Agriculture is to be adopting industrial approaches. New technologies such as no-till or minimum till, precision farming, drip irrigation and genetically altered crops are attempts to increase profitability, stability and sustainability. It is estimated that assuming India's share in world exports improves from 0.5 per cent to 1.0 per cent, trade gains may conservatively be placed at 2.7 billion US dollars per year. Although agricultural exports are increasing in value terms, their share in India's total exports declining. It declined from 33 per cent in 1980 to 13.5 per cent in 2000-01.

India is also losing competitiveness because the very step increase given to administer prices and rising administrated prices have not only resulted in weakening India's competitiveness. They have also resulted in creating the dilemma of mounting stocks of food grains along with persistence of large scale poverty. High prices have tended to price out the poor from the market.

Further, Lester Brown has predicted that India may have to import 50 million tones of food grains and China over 20 million tones by 2030. These estimates are based on the basis of three major criteria, increasing population, increasing purchasing power and increasing degradation of life supporting systems. The first two will increase the demand for food. The last one will reduce potential to produce the food we require. This is why partnership between all sectors assume great importance. Care of nature counters care of civilizations.

Bio-village programme is pro-nature, pro-poor, pro-women development paradigm. It seeks sustainable agriculture and rural development by concurrently attempting to mitigate the twin concerns of the present times, namely, creeping degradation of the resources base and persistence or rural poverty. Technologies and interventions are needed, which are ecologically compatible, economically viable and socially acceptable. Technology empowerment, Agri-export zones contract farming through corporate culture, organized rural force intellectual property Rights, Biotechnology, Information technology were new agencies entered into agriculture sector for farmers' growth.

A Threat to Sustainable Ecology

Ecology is the science of the distribution, abundance and activity of life. It is the science of environmental awareness, ethics, stewardship and remediation. The distribution of organisms and agricultural system is dictated by global and attitudinal climatic belts of temperature and by availability of water soil types and other organisms. The community, its physical environment and the interaction between organisms and the physical environment comprise the ecosystem, which some scientists regard as the basic of ecology. Community can be measured by their bio-diversity. Gentleman farmers are likely to increase conservation of rare endangered species. It is estimated that 60,000 species will be eliminated in the fore-seeable future and 50,000 will be at risk cf extinction in the next half a century. Sustainable development was defined by Weed (1983) to mean development, which meets the needs of the present generation without jeopardizing the needs of future generations.

In fact, of the 304 Million ha. of cultivated land in India as much as 175 million ha. suffer from environmental degradation—wind and water erosion—water logging, salinity, alkalinity caused by reservoirs and water rise and mismanagement of soil and water resources. Further, green house gases remain in the atmosphere for decades for centuries. The CO_2, concentration has increased from 290 ppm hundred years ago to 350 ppm, and likely to increase to 440-500 ppm by 2100. CO_2 emission has to be cut. The global increase in CO_2 and other green house gases may enhance the lower atmospheric temperature by 11.5 C to 4.5 C by the year 2030. This will result in the melting of Pole ice Caps and rise in sea level. Such an increase in sea level will cause flooding in many coastal wetlands. 10-15 per cent arable and productive coastal land will be lost. Ecology protection and promotion are must for global community to avoid nature's havocs and disasters. Modern agriculture, technology, training to farmer community, soil moisture water management, credit supply leading, marketing, price mechanism, global markets are to be pushed into agriculture sector and forced to shift, marginal, small medium farmer to non-agriculture areas.

Rural Women Disempowered in Globalisation

Before British Rule India's villages were self-sufficient which, were destroyed by British rule. Gradually, Independent India turned towards World Bank, IMF, USA, which intervened and made too few and too much urbanization like Highways, flyovers, Hi-tech cities, Computerization, English Education, Foreign Direct Investments, etc. than rural development. Urban markets were became villains in exploiting rural people, rural styles and rural markets. Presently, Special Economic Zones (SEZs) are also helpless to rural. E.g. Nandigram, Singure, Chittoor, Rural goods and services were become cheaper, but urban goods and services were found dearer. During 1998 to March 2006, around 4,500 farmers went for suicides. Due to male and virtue of Head of the households' suicide, the next Head, women were helpless to run that family especially children's health, education and employment. Many rural women went to prostitute homes in a distant places like Pune, Mumbai, and Goa. Many studies revealed that 60 per cent of women were behind for every successful farmer and farming. Unfortunately, even 2 per cent of women had no property rights. Many women and children of middle income households were in malnutrition situation and prone to diseases. Many households were in outdated cultures like Mathangi, Jogini, Basivini are still prevailed. Globalisation had generated, high degree of consumerism, which is supported by cable televisions. This phenomenon made the people not to go for physical labour. Two-third of rural women were under helpless position. The basic ideology is that State is withdrawing from active role in developmental strategy, market forces were entered into development. So women were again pushed back. Entry of Multi-national corporations, Seed insecurity, un cooperative agricultural markets and corporate cultures penetration into rural economy made women position pushed to on knife edge. In fact, women education, 50 per cent women empowerment through legislation, girl child promotion in career development, women reservation in Parliament, would bring some positive effects on rural India, in general and women in particular. However, globalization entry into rural India would destroy the good old professions like Jajimani system and traditional agriculture itself. At the end farm households would be rehabilitated into service sector by making corporate farming.

CONCLUSION

The objective of globalisation is to bring cheap and quality goods and services to all people of global in one market, so that welfare for all is ultimate achievement, Provided, people are efficient with modern technology then only the fruits would go to that area. In fact, Indian agriculture is not so advanced. It has to improve its nature and extent through corporate farms, Agri-business, Agri-industry, Ecological protection, Bio-village development, so that it can remove rural poverty and promote employment opportunities. Globalisation is to be taken as an opportunity to flourish with prosperity of agriculture and agro-based industries. Certainly, Indian farmer would become a global trekker and enjoy the flavour of different markets, prices and goods for sustainable agriculture.

References

Peter Drucker, (1999), Management Challenges for the 21st Century, Harper Business, Newyork.

Peter R. Drucker (1990), The New Realities, Mandrin, London.

John. D. Sullivan (2000), Preparing in the Global Economy, *Economic Reforms Today,* November 1.

Kenchi Ohmae (1991), The Borderless World, Fontana, London.

John Naisbitt (1994), The Global Paradox, Nicholas, Barely Publishing, London.

P.M. Thomas, S. Sen, R.R. Sriram (2007), Iron Willed. It is a Steel Plated Victory, *The Economic Times.*

G.S. Bhalla (2004), Globalisation and Indian Agriculture (19), Academic Foundation, New Delhi.

Sitaram Yechury, Globalisation: Impact of Indian Economy for Desh Bhagat Yadgar Committee Seminar.

S. Subramanian (2004), Globalisation and Sustainable Agriculture.

R. Maria Saleth (2004), Agricultural Strategy for a Globalisation Economy; Continuing and Changing, edited by C.G. Krishna Swamy, S.R. Keshava, Ravi M. Tirlapur, Better Expression, Dept. of P.G. Studies and Research in Economics, Bangalore University, Bangalore.

Jagadish Bhagawathi (2007), Outsourcing is as Good or Bad or any Kind of Trade, *The Economic Times,* January 29.

Joseph Stiglitz (2002), Globalisation and its Discontents, Penguin Books, New Delhi.

Agriculture's SOB Story

- Total investment in the sector has fallen from 7.07% of agricultural GDP in 1976-80 to 6.69% during 2001-03.
- From 3.51% of agricultural GDP during 1981-85 period, public investment fell to 1.89% 2001-03, i.e. half the earlier levels.
- The fall in investment is sad as it is crucial for stepping up farm sector growth from the current 1.8% to 4% targeted in the 11th Plan.

8

'Inclusive' Globalization and Food 'Security'!

I. John Mohan Razu

INTRODUCTION

Our Government, policy-makers and bureaucrats, who are prone to treating liberalization, privatization and globalization, as ends in themselves, are even now promising to usher-in capital account convertibility and have kept the doors wide open to global investors and retailers of the world. They believe and hope that the flight of foreign capital across the borders would certainly bolster economic growth and progress. Those who believe in this type of theory should read Joseph Stiglitz's latest book, *Making Globalization Work,* which de-mystifies and de-mythologizes their basic assumptions. The neo-liberal dogma that has dominated international economic policy for three decades and our country for about a decade and half has widened income gaps, sharpened conflicts and deepened misery. In an era of globalization, humanity is increasingly caught up on all sides and do not know which way to turn. The essence of his argument is to evolve ways and means for globalization to work. Globalization is at work, but the benefits of globalization have not reached all. The proponents of globalization claim that globalization would bring about a win-win situation, but the opponents categorically foresee that in a globalizing world there would be few winners and many losers.

As against this backdrop, an attempt is made to bring to the fore some of the dominant understandings of economic globalization (for and against) thereby positing its historical antecedents and manifestations. More importantly, I intend to grapple with the interplay between economic globalization and the Eleventh Five Year Plan and show how economic globalization has influenced politics and programmes especially the agricultural sector. Further, the terminologies and accent are turned by the Government at the Centre such as "inclusive growth" and "food security" which is interrogated, analyzed and evaluated with facts and figures.

I

THEORISING GLOBALIZATION

Broadly speaking, the term globalization[1] means, integration of economies and societies through e-mail, e-banking, e-governance, e-finance, e-commerce and e-net. Globalization has also furthered the flow of goods and services, movement of people, labour and capital across the globe at a rapid pace than ever before. One cannot ask for proportionality of a particular dimensionality of globalization despite its multi-dimensional character. However, the term globalization is used here in the limited sense of economic integration, which can happen through the three channels i.e., (a) trade in goods and services, (b) movement of capital, and (c) flow of finance. There is also the channel through movement of people within and between countries. Globalization is a historical process, which manifests itself in different forms and flows. The movement toward international integration of national economies is as old as the history of capitalism. For example,

> *Globalization began in the late 15th century with the rise of capitalism and its overseas expansion; the conquest and exploitation of Asia, Africa, Latin America. . . . In other words, globalization was from the outset associated with imperialism (the global linkage was based on European capitalist accumulation through the exploitation of the Third World) and its impetus was always entered around imperial state institutions, specific class configurations, extracting resources from the domestic economy . . . exploitation of the Third World . . . interacting and appropriating resources and exploiting cheap labour and international exchange (on unequal terms) of commodities. Essentially then 'globalization' is hardly a new phenomenon; it is merely a new name, a sub-code for capitalism that subsumes diverse socio-political economic processes.*[2]

In line with the above quotation, if we take into account the components of globalization and the way in which it manifests itself especially the origin, growth and development of TNCs, is undoubtedly a long-term process with a recent acceleration rather than a sudden and qualitative shift. Globalization is a process of rearrangement of the production, labour, capital and the world's resources between peoples and countries. Globalization has also integrated the scattered and dispensed activities. In this process there are beneficiaries as well as victims. Some countries as a whole would benefit and the others lose. In the ultimate analysis some may be integrated and others be marginalized. They include countries, communities, groups and individuals.

II

FENCES AND WINDOWS OF GLOBALIZATION

Despite opening up the economy and having integrated with the global economy, the proponents of globalization assured a win-win situation, but proved to be wrong. Their claims and facts do not match. The gains and losses from globalization can be analyzed and evaluated in the context of the three types of channels of economic globalization identified earlier. According to the standard theory, international trade leads to allocation of resources through integration and opening-up of the economies that is consistent with comparative advantage. This means industrialization, privatization and specialization. All these components in economic globalization enhance productivity. It is assumed that by following this road map international trade in general would augment exports and thus bring in more money to the economy. It is beneficial to the economies of all countries that have embraced market economics. This theory undermines restrictive trade practices and thus states that closed-economies impede growth.

However, even in relation to trade in goods and services, there is one concern. Emerging economies would reap the benefits of international trade only if they reach the full potential of their resource availability. The 'standard theory' clearly advocates that natural and also specialized professional human resources would be made available so that these resources would be optimized to enhance international trade, which in turn will benefit the developing countries. Those who argue for globalization and market-ushered economics say that it requires time. That is why international trade agreements and financial institutions primarily spearheaded by the World Trade Organization (WTO), International Monetary Fund (IMF), World Bank (WB) and the rich industrialized capitalist countries, make exceptions for a longer time frame so that the developing economies would catch-up. Questions that arise now are: what is the time frame? For how long? Special and differentiated treatments under globalization have become accepted principles. How long to wait so that the market-propelled economy would bring in benefits to all? If the basic assumption is market-based economy, would it work only in the long-run, then, in the long-run, people are dead.

Further, the principles of tariffs and quotas in actual practice are used as control mechanisms by the developed economies to protect their work force, goods and services. We live in a protectionist, hegemonic and neo-colonial world. The rich countries are in an advantageous position. They regulate and control the global economic order. By all means, the developed economies push their interests for profit maximization, product and labour protection. Free competition is advocated only when they are benefited. Therefore, protagonists of globalization stress this principle while arguing the case of developing countries, but in reality some of the principles posited need careful scrutiny and analysis.

Having opened up the economies, capital flow across countries has played an important role in enhancing the production-base. This is true since the 1990's. Flight of capital across the globe is one of the major features of globalization. It is assumed that unrestricted flight of capital enables the developing countries to augment saving and surplus which would help the economies of these countries to grow. Does the flight of capital take place in all directions or towards one direction? What is the *modus operandi* employed and how are profits ploughed back, and at what proportions and percentage? Importantly, a major concern with respect to foreign capital is the potential for its sudden withdrawals. There is no regulation to the inflow of foreign capital. Do we have any moderation to the inflow of foreign capital and out-flow of the profits accrued through these investments? The possibility of sharp outflows through the withdrawals of portfolio investment as it happened in Mexico and Argentina is a danger to guard against.

The rapid development of the capital market has been one of the important features of the current process of globalization. Exports, competition, quality promotion, de-regulation, de-control and de-valuation are the prerequisites for international transfer of capital. These prerequisites are connected to foreign exchange reserves and external debt. IMF-WB attach strings for micro-macro credit lending, macro-stabilization and international transfer of capital. However, the volatility in the foreign exchange market and the care with which funds can be withdrawn from countries has often caused panic situations. The most recent examples are the East Asian and Argentinean fiasco.

Hence, "Globalization implies global, social and political change irrespective of whether one identifies globalization as primarily driven by economics or as a cultural phenomenon occurring in the context of technological change and a transformation of life styles."[3] However, "Globalization at a minimum involves the creation of a world economy which is not merely the sum of its national economies, but rather a powerful independent reality, created by the international division of labour and the world market which in the present epoch predominates over national markets. Large-scale, long-term flow of capital, commodities, technology and labour across national boundaries define the process of globalization.[4]

The overall result of these measures, it was assumed and hoped that the fiscal and trade imbalances would be rectified and thus improve the capacity of the government to service its debt obligations. The spending of the Government on the social sector should be drastically cut, and promoting the private sector to push its role in the area of development and progress and social sector initiatives should be suspended until adjustments are carried out. It was hoped that India would import less and export more.

III

GLOBALIZATION DE-MYSTIFIED

The Globalization idea is itself suspect. In its widely expressed usage it argues for a universal incorporation to the world marketplace and the spread of benefits throughout the world. The empirical reality is neither universal incorporation nor the spread of benefits: there are wealthy creditors and bankrupt debtors; super-rich speculators and impoverished unemployed workers; imperial states that direct informational financial institutions and subordinate states that submit to their dictates. A rigorous comparative analysis of contemporary world socio-economic realities would suggest that the 'globalization' conception of 'interdependence' is far less useful in understanding the world . . .[5]

Undoubtedly, globalization has brought several benefits such as infrastructure, knowledge, efficiency, quality, and consumer awareness, dismantling of monopoly in various fields *vis-a-vis* education, consumer goods, transport and a wide range of choices. Further, globalization by revolutionizing technology has narrowed time and space. These gadgets have brought the world so close, beyond our imagination. But the widespread negative impact of globalization on the socially and economically disadvantaged people is such that while integrating the world on one level, the vulnerable category is moving away from the process. Caste divisions are so apparent and deeper than a decade ago. The flagrant manifestations of communalism and economic disparity are getting worse.

The distance between countries has been reduced but those between communities has widened. Global village has become a misnomer. Uniformity between and amongst the rich across the world is becoming attuned to what they consume, the dress they wear, the food they eat and the education they have. Reports by the UNICEF, UNDP, IMF and WB show that the gap between the rich and poor countries is increasing. It is also the same within the developing countries. Let us examine, analyse and evaluate these gaps by taking into consideration the available data, facts and figures at the micro-macro levels.

1997-2006 has been designated as the First United Nations Decade for the eradication of poverty which clearly shows that poverty is no longer a national or continental or third world problem, but global. Since it has assumed a global character at alarming proportions, the nations of the world urged the UN to declare 1997-2006 as the First UN Decade for the eradication of poverty. The articulation and implementation in meeting the challenges, will determine what the distribution of life chances and life choices will be for most people; and what, and where would be the questions before we embark on the very issue of poverty. The challenges are universal in character and therefore the solutions ought to be universal. Yet, the efforts and processes will have to be routed through nation-states and the governments. Nevertheless, in view of socio-economic inequalities and lopsidedness between and within nations, we cannot take for granted the guarantees expressed on the issue of poverty. Instead of narrowing the gap, the forces and process of globalization is widening the gap. For example, a glimpse of two worlds that are juxtaposed portrays the following:

- The fifth of the world's people living in the highest income countries has 86 per cent of world Gross Domestic Product (GDP), 82 per cent of world export markets, 68 per cent of foreign direct investments, and 74 per cent of world telephone lines; the bottom fifth, in the poorest countries, has about one per cent in each sector.

- More than U.S. $ 1.5 trillion a day is exchanged in the world's currency markets.
- The percentage share of the market by the top 10 corporations in each sector in 1998 has: telecommunications, 86 per cent; pesticides, 85 per cent; computers, almost 70 per cent; veterinary medicine, 60 per cent; pharmaceuticals, 35 per cent; commercial seed, 32 per cent.
- Industrialized countries hold 97 per cent of all patents worldwide.
- The 200 richest people in the world more than doubled their net worth in the four years to 1998, to $1 trillion.
- Some 130-145 million legally registered migrants live outside their countries.[6]

The other side of the scenario portrays the following:

- Worldwide, 1.2 billion people are income poor, living on less than $ 1 a day (1993 PPP U.S. $).
- More than a billion people in developing countries lack access to safe water, and more than 2.4 billion people lack adequate sanitation.
- Some 90 million children are out of school at primary level.
- Worldwide, about 1.2 million women and girls under 18 are trafficked for prostitution each year.
- About 100 million children are estimated to be living or working on the street.
- In developing countries there are some 250 million child labourers—140 million boys and 110 million girls.[7]

The above contrasting projections such as affluence and misery cannot be ignored. For example, the deaths of more than 30,000 children every year from mainly preventable causes should raise a serious question? Why? They are visible victims of poverty.[8] Therefore, poverty continues to be the main issue which poses a major challenge to all of us even today. A decent standard of living, adequate nutrition, health care, education, decent work and quality of life, are inter-linked issues when we talk about poverty. We need to keep in mind the dictum—"poverty in the midst of plenty," which I consider a scandal, and an aberration. It is not because of a tiny percentage, but rather a bulk of humanity—for instance, 90 million children are out of primary school, about 790 million people live in hunger and food insecurity, and about 1.2 billion live on less than $ 1 a day (1993 PPP US $). As against this background more clarity may be sought with regard to poverty, its context and other inter-related aspects.

'How free is the market?' It has not even brought the poor within the fundamentals of the market forces. Standard answers are offered for the widening gap between the rich and poor. It is exhorted that the fruits of globalization would automatically be percolated down once the momentum of growth takes place in industry, agriculture and other services. There has been significant growth in all sectors, which is reflected in our country's GDP and GNP. But this overall growth has not helped the poor. Per capita availability and purchasing capacity of the down-trodden has drastically declined. The teeming millions of poor have not experienced any appreciable increase in wages and earnings, despite the economy's progression along the growth path.

IV

GLOBALIZATION CHALLENGED

Globalization is supposed to bring common good for all but instead it is dismantling social and governance institutions and structures that were evolved to reconcile the interests of the rich and poor and enable them to live in peace with each other. It is also widening the differences in income and wealth between nations; creating new beneficiaries and also new victims by the millions. History is repeating itself. Manchester liberalism has been reborn as Chicago school neo-liberalism. As the Manchester liberals did in the early 19th century, the neo-liberals are preaching the virtue of a new "start mantra" in which the Government should withdraw from management of economy altogether and leave everything to the invisible hand of the market. Accordingly, almost all the governments of the world in order to achieve maximum growth turned to market-ushered globalization. But did the market forces regulate in such a way that the fruits of growth were evenly distributed? Instead, the rich have become richer and the poor poorer. Market-ushered economic logic has widened the gap further between and within nations.

This has triggered a powerful wave of protest from intellectuals, civil society organizations, social and political movements, labour unions and environmentalists all over the world. The proponents of globalization dismiss their opponents as Marxists in search of a cause, while the opponents castigate its advocates as propagandists for the transnational corporations and the American Empire. Each side accuses the other and the debate continues. However, given the track-record of economic globalization, one should objectively look into the impact of globalization as against the facts and case studies with all the protests and resistance happening all over the world against globalization, global capitalism and market economics. In such a context the proponents of neo-liberalism keep echoing the "human face" of globalization and "inclusive globalization." Can market economics have a "human face" or ever be "inclusive?"

The logic of economic globalization is to maximize its profit promised on limitless growth and aggressive market expansion. In the process, the impact has been devastating creating havoc and fragmentation. The current scenario posits contrasting realities juxtaposed side by side. Wealth is generated at an alarming level and at the same time the misery that teeming millions face in their day-to-day life is appalling. Poverty and hunger have assumed alarming proportions. Food security has become a key-word. But paradoxically the presence of poverty amidst plenty continues to grip the moral fabric of thinking and concerned people. Growth is visible. What we see is limitless growth driven by the logic of consumerism and movement of capital. At the same time, billions continue to struggle for one meal a day and are unable to make both ends meet.

Despite these contrasting realities, the catch-phrase 'one global economy' is on everyone's mind today. Corporate companies and bio-technology experts keep talking about expanding business aggressively beyond transnational boundaries. Increasingly open economies and decreasing governmental control are contributing to the influx of global players that are breaking geographical barriers more than ever before. The current new world order with a heavy tinge of *laissez-faire* capitalism is propelled by technological revolution. With countries vying for a slice of the economic pie, older fears and knee-jerk protectionism is fast disappearing behind a haze of prosperity. While the lifting of Government control has helped unleash the power of a global economic order, the engine of prosperity has to be shared by all. Is this happening?

V

ELEVENTH PLAN: FOOD 'SECURITY'— A MYTH OR REALITY?

The Eleventh version of the Five Year Plan is nothing but a replica of the old paradigm and plan and non-plan schemes and centre-state fiscal responsibilities. Apparently, new areas have been explored in the planning process to have partnership with private sectors with an aim to making the growth process inclusive in the context of economic globalization and the market economy since these two have started to subsume other facets. This necessitates a better macro-economic management of the economy so that the plan and policy outcomes have an equitable impact on the people. On paper, the write-ups, initiatives and interventions of the Plan proposals look impressive, but whatever is said and claimed is not translated. Implantation of the thrust areas and prioritizing the concerns get diluted and eventually subsumed as per the whims and fancies of those who control and implement the envisioned areas of importance. A number of examples can be cited especially from the Eleventh Plan.

For instance, the impressive 9.4 per cent GDP growth rate registered by the economy during 2006-07 reflects the current phase of high profile growth thereby pulling the economy out from the orbit of low growth to a trajectory of high growth, which is commendable. The new growth figure also enhances the economy's confidence to achieve the targeted 9 per cent growth rate as envisioned by the Planning Commission during the Eleventh Plan (2007-12). The growth rate of 9 to 10 per cent would meet basic challenges facing the country like eradicating poverty and creating jobs for millions. However, the challenge is how to sustain this high growth rate over the years in a country like India where a majority of the population lives in villages engaged in agriculture. Therefore, the overall growth of the economy is predominantly influenced by the performance of the crucial agricultural sector. If growth is not reflected in the agricultural sector, the whole growth momentum would face a reversal. Over and above, it has been assumed that a breakthrough in agricultural production could happen with the introduction of technology which would accelerate the growth process. Further, it is also assumed that if priority is given to the development of the rural infrastructure, which supports the very backbone of agriculture, the growth momentum could be sustained. Have these assumptions helped to achieve the desired growth?

In a context of economic globalization it is essential to ensure that every sector of society, especially the poor, reap the benefits of high economic growth proportionality. If this does not happen, the very sustainability of high growth will be jeopardized leading to social unrest. This is one of the most crucial and serious problems because a sizable proportion of the population is still dependent on this traditional sector. The situation on the ground represents some of the worst problems that affect the country's huge unorganized sector. For example, lack of appropriate technological up-gradation and innovation due partly to backwardness, poor credit flows, lack of institutional linkages between production, marketing and distribution, highly unsatisfactory development of supporting agro-industry, poor credit flow arrangement and inadequate market awareness.

Against this background, the boost of the reform process, the disquiet in our countryside, is becoming difficult to dispel. The advocates of economic globalization claim many things both at the international and national locations across the developed and developing world, more suited to defend the outcome of the Indian reforms. It is not surprising that their claims are a mirage over the harsh reality that the Indian countryside portrays. The situation has become compelling for them to overlook the evidence that raises fundamental questions about the outcome of the market-propelled reform process. It is not only the question of the cotton growers of Andhra Pradesh, or farmers from Wyanad in Kerala, but across the country, we have been witnessing suicides of farmers and others in the thousands involved in the agricultural sector which have been overlooked and undermined. The misery of the peasant producers, landless laborers and small and marginal farmers who face life-threatening problems due to market forces that determine what crops are to be produced and at what quantum. Per capita food grains output has declined since the introduction of economic globalization and reform process in the beginning of the nineties. Even absolute food grains output has become stagnant since the beginning of this decade. Indian agriculture with the GDP growth (from agriculture) has slipped from 3.62 per cent during 1984-85 to 1995-96 to less than 2 per cent between 1995-96 and 2004-05.

The irony however was that while per capita availability of food grains came down by leaps and bounds, the policies of the Government successfully obfuscated this grain reality. In 2002, the Government's stocks went up to 63 million tonnes. This brought the well-known spectacle "empty stomachs, over-filled go-downs" alive in India. There are many factors that could be attributed to the current state of affairs. One of the major factors is opening up of the procuring of food grains to the private sector companies which is leading to a major reduction in the procurement levels of the Government which leaves it with a much lower level of stocks. Over and above, the forward trading of food grains and its future in the commodity exchanges has legitimized speculative trading of food grains. This has led to a sharp rise in the price of food grains. It has been a principle factor for the sharp acceleration of inflation rates. This has affected large sections of the farming community leading to unrest among the poor. In spite of the specific commitment in the National Common Minimum Programme to improve the lives of farmers, the recommendation of the National Farmers' Commission headed by M.S. Swaminathan reported that "agriculture is not only languishing but the situation in our countryside is becoming explosive."

The proponents of reform process find themselves in a tight situation because the growth of GDP faces the threat of getting derailed due to the poor performance of the agricultural sector. The outcome of the Tenth Plan where the growth in agriculture was around 2 per cent is a case in point. Added to these, the paradigm that the National Development Council (NDC) believes is the corporatization of Indian agriculture. According to NDC, corporatization of agriculture is the only way through which the present crisis can be combated. NDC also believes in augmenting public investment within an additional 25,000 crores and providing a national mission on food security with a 20 million tonne additional food grain production. It is hoped that by the end of the Eleventh Plan the agricultural sector and the crises it faces will be set right

The policy makers and others have failed to critically look at the entire gamut of approach of the establishment which still continues to be growth-driven. Investment, infrastructure and technology are all important elements in our search for strengthening the agricultural sector, but not at the human cost. Since agriculture is going to continue as the mainstay of our economy and society, we need to look at the plight of those who are involved in agriculture. Many studies have come out clearly that apart from other subsidiary factors such as unfavourable weather conditions, loan burdens etc., the spread of new water intensive crops and labour-displacing machinery have been major factors for farmers resorting to suicides. Further, many in the rural areas do not have a balanced diet of food, pulses, and vegetables with ghee and milk. For instance,

In Karnataka, where the farmer suicide rate is equally high, the over-emphasis on technology had only alienated a large percentage of farming population from economic growth and development. Karnataka has in fact been in the forefront of adopting any new agriculture technology. No wonder, the more the adoption of new technologies, the more the farm crisis is aggravated.

Not learning any lessons, Karnataka goes about promoting genetic engineering, contract farming and corporate agriculture without even caring to realize its negative impact on the economic viability of the average farm. Nor does it appear keen to ensure the long-term sustainability of farming.

Blindly aping the World Bank model has pumped in huge finances to push in an industry-driven agriculture that has not only exacerbated the crisis leading to an environmental catastrophe but also destroyed millions of rural livelihoods. The biggest tragedy being that Karnataka with the largest number of farm suicides in the country . . .

In reality, Karnataka . . . blindly promotes the commercial interests of the agribusiness companies, food, food retail companies and the IT hardware units. All benefits will accrue to these companies in the name of farmers. In fact, these sectors, along with biotechnology, are being heavily subsidized in the name of efficiency and infrastructure whereas the poor farmers are being divested of their only source of income—their meagre holdings.

In a country where 80 per cent of the farmers, own less than two hectares of land, only five per cent farmers have more than four hectares (Karnataka is no different) the biggest challenge is to ensure how to make agriculture more attractive for these small and marginal farmers. . . . Intensive farming has destroyed the ability of the lands to produce enough food and the mining of groundwater has pushed the water table to a precarious level, the green revolution has in reality collapsed.

This becomes clearly visible from growing farm indebtedness. With nearly half of the farm households at the national level (48.6 per cent) reported in debt, agriculture reforms aim at doubling the flow of credit to the farm sector. Not realizing that doubling the flow of agricultural credit in the next three years is not the answer to the blood bath that is being enacted in the ravaged farm sector, a direct fallout of the green revolution equation going wrong. Majority of the farmers, who continue to take the fatal route to escape the humiliation that comes along with increasing indebtedness, are actually dying because of their inability to repay the loans.

We all know that indebtedness is also widespread where Andhra Pradesh topped the chart, with more than four-fifths of surveyed farmers in debt, followed by Tamil Nadu with nearly three-fourths of farm households reeling under indebtedness. In Punjab, Kerala and Karnataka the proportion is nearly two-thirds. The situation in Maharashtra Haryana, Rajasthan, Gujarat, Madhya Pradesh and West Bengal is no better with more than half of the farmers surveyed under debt. Making available cheap credit to these marginal farming communities will not be helpful. What these poor and marginalized need immediately is income support.

Credit is therefore part of the problem, and how the policy-makers can think of solving the problem (inability to repay the loans) by extending more loans surely defies any sensible logic.

The lure and glamour of industry-driven agriculture is sure to acerbate the existing crisis. The new technology that the multinationals (as well as the Indian Council for Agricultural Research) are planning to provide is so sophisticated that a majority of the farmers will remain outside its ambit. Precision farming is one such misplaced technology that is receiving budgetary support from the Government. Removing the bottlenecks in the commodity supply chain management by amending the APMC Act and also by enlarging the scope of future trading are aimed at helping the new range of middlemen and business . . .

> Government projection notwithstanding, the fact remains that a majority of farmers are keen to abandon agriculture. There is therefore a desperate need to revitalize agriculture, restore the natural resource base and provide for sustainable livelihoods. Any development alternative to ensure long-term food and livelihood security of farmers has to be linked with sustainable agriculture. What is needed is a fresh approach that takes the ground realities into consideration.[9]

The above quotation clearly shows where rural India is headed for. More importantly, we have been witnessing a range of excluded groups increasing every Plan decade. Market-propelled economic globalization has failed to trickle-down to the urban and rural poor. In the earlier Five-Year Plans (Ten Plans) we have created more and more targeted schemes to touch a range of poor categories through a number of programmes with good intentions to promote inclusive growth. The Minimum Support Price (MSP) to farmers is dictated by the choice of planting patterns.

However, with the country marching towards a market economy, the relevance of the MSP is being increasingly questioned. A variety of factors like market complexities that distort supply-demand equation in the domestic and global markets, changes in food habits and crop patterns have serious bearing on this. The Government should focus more on evolving a long-term policy on food security including a strategy for boosting agricultural production along with the offer of short-term incentive to farmers through enhanced MSP. It should go deep into the causes for the current phenomenon of stagnation in food grain production and the large yield gaps in many crops.

Growing food crops is market-driven and corporate-controlled. There is also a trend among farmers to move away from subsistence crops to cash crops, and from cereals to non-food cash crops. With shrinking land resources and corporatization of scarce natural resources the unskilled rural groups are gradually excluded from economic growth. The Eleventh Plan fails to clearly articulate and spell-out the strategic interventions needed to stop the growing food insecurity both in urban and rural pockets, despite India shining slogans.

When we talk of food security, we need to take into account bio-safety. In the name of 'patents' the agri-business conglomerates have resorted to new modes of profit maximization and market expansion which will create more and more problems for food security. For example, the Supreme Court upheld the importance of bio-safety when it comes to Genetically Modified Organisms (GMO), in its recent order. In September 2006, the Court conducted 90 Multi-Location Trials (MLTs), 32 experimental seed productions, 18 strip trials and 5 pollen flow studies for a variety of crops. The Genetic Engineering Approval Committee (GEAC) has announced that no GM rice experimentation will take place in the basmati belt. Meanwhile, there are various developments against GM crops in different states. The Tamil Nadu, Andhra Pradesh, Chhattisgarh and West Bengal Governments have ordered an inquiry into the field trials of GM food and BT cotton.

CONCLUSION

India will continue to remain in the next two decades as an agrarian economy employing a majority workforce in the agricultural and agricultural-related activities. If food production is to be controlled by agri-business Corporations, both vertically and horizontally under the aegis of market economics, the essential subsistence crops would disappear and in its place more and more cash crops would appear. Hence, food security for the present and future generations becomes an important concern across the world. Unless and until we protect our agrarian economy as against the onslaught of market economy the crisis would escalate wherein the farmers resorting to suicides would increase. Millions of landless laborers will be excluded from the market and pushed to vulnerable situations. Therefore, we need to think about public-private partnership for farm and non-farm employment. If both are well developed, inclusion becomes possible because the diverse groups in the rural sector can compete for better incomes.

Echoing a similar concern, Prime Minister Manmohan Singh, had time and again promised to launch a major initiative for the revival of the ailing farm sector. Addressing the 53rd meeting of the National Development Council in New Delhi he highlighted the enormity of the prevailing agrarian crisis. Whenever he visited suicide-affected areas across the country, he was told that the incidence of suicide is on the rise. The suicide rate has risen from one farmer committing suicide every eight hours to one in every four hours. The Rs. 25,000 crore allocation for new farm initiatives to be launched by the states in the next four years, and the 14-point resolution adopted by the NDC that aims at achieving 4% growth in agriculture by the end of the Eleventh Five-Year Plan, with the entire focus on integrating domestic culture with global economy, roping in agri-business, corporate agriculture, and food retail as the savior, the road map worked out is likely to lead to a greater debacle.

Investing an additional amount of Rs. 25,000 crore into agriculture may seem like an huge amount to double the growth rate in agriculture. But if we divide that between 29 states, the average support will not exceed Rs. 1,000 crore, which is like a drop in the ocean. Incidentally, the Government at the Centre while responding to the farm crisis expects growth rate. But in reality the farm crisis revolves around declining sustainability in agriculture and the economic viability of farming. For example, the state of Punjab considered as the food bowl of the country where farm indebtedness both in the formal and informal sectors is around Rs. 26,000 crore, more than the total package allotted for the entire country. However, the 14-point resolution fails to mention the areas of sustainability and the modes that ought to be employed boosting farm incomes. Apparently, the action plan only focuses on improved seed supply, fertilizer availability and revamping state agriculture extension system to reduce yield gaps. In essence, the entire focus of the farm strategy is to allow the private sector to take control of agriculture.

Setting up a time-bound Food Security Mission by enhancing production of wheat, rice, pulses and edible oils by lowering custom tariff thereby allowing cheaper imports, would lead to further disaster. Integrating Indian agriculture with the global economy defeats and contradicts the purpose and rationale of ensuring food security. For instance, India was self-sufficient in edible oils in 1993-94. Ever since the Government began lowering the tariffs, edible oil imports have multiplied which has led the country to be one of the biggest importers. Small farmers growing oil seeds had to abandon their production in the light of cheaper imports.

Autonomous liberalization of the farm sector is witnessing imports of food items at alarming levels. Import of agricultural commodities has gone up by 300% between the years 2000-04. In addition, the Government is planning to further open up farm imports under the Free Trade Agreement with the ASEAN countries. In the years to come, import tariffs on wheat, rice, pulses and edible oils and other crops that are considered crucial for food security would further be lowered. Cheaper imports will negatively impact food security. For a country like India, with 60-crore farmers, policies that are enunciated and imperatives drawn out will spell doom. Indian farmers are not only producers, but also consumers. What is needed is a farming system that allows production by the masses in a sustainable and viable way.[10]

The Prime Minister said, "If a liberalized economy has to succeed, we must allow competitive forces, and private sector should show some self-restraint in this regard." Elaborating on the theme of "Inclusive Growth—Challenges for Corporate India," the Prime Minister reminded the industry of its responsibilities toward the commoners and advocated a "10-point charter for sharing the benefits of economic growth with the less-privileged." He reiterated that "Corporate social responsibility must not be defined by tax planning strategies alone. Rather, it should be defined within the framework of a corporate philosophy which factors the needs of the community and the regions in which the corporate entity function." He emphatically exhorted that "Rising income and wealth inequalities, if not matched by a corresponding rise in income across the nation, can lead to social unrest."

"Inclusive growth" should include and sustain the trend of higher growth rate, providing more employment, reducing poverty and promoting human development. This why the Prime Minister continues to plead with the burgeoning private sector to share the Government's responsibility in building a more inclusive society in which the poor, the farmers and the left-out regions of the country also get a share of the cake. High growth rate makes no sense if the poor remain on the margins and the unemployed remain unemployed, while the rich become richer. Would the private sector operating in a competitive environment driven by profit motive be committed to social responsibilities by sacrificing its logic of greed for the sake of common good and maximum happiness of all and for all?

Notes and References

1. Globalization is defined by proponents in the following ways:

   (a) "The increasing integration of domestic economies with the world economy is generally termed as 'globalization'." The concept recognizes that in the global economy, economic activity is not only integrated, but it is international in scope and global in organization. It is in this sense, globalization does mean, transnationalization of capital, internationalization of labour, globalization of production and homogenization of culture. Thus, globalization implies the functional integration of internationally dispensed activities.

(b) "Globalization involves the creation of a seamless, borderless, global order with increasing denationalization of the nation-state and its sovereignty, whilst steadily and critically altering the nature of the state itself. It also involves the integration of the market and economies through trade investment finance of new labour skills of knowledge or technology and transnationalization of production and internationalization of consumer wants."
(c) Globalization represents the new emergent phase of capitalism which refers to the geographic spread of economic activity across national boundaries thereby absorbing all the countries of the world into one economic unit. The emergent global capitalism or post-capitalism or transnational capitalism is characterized by an increasing concentration of capital. It is in this context, one has to situate transnational corporations (TNCs).
(d) Globalization is a highly differentiated phenomenon that has historically been linked to the concentration and centralization of capital, wealth and power. The driving force has been the cooperation and competition of the imperialist powers.

The critics of globalization look at globalization in the following ways:

Former President, K.R. Narayanan, expressing concern over the import of economic reforms, poverty and injustices in his Address to the nation on the eve of the Republic Day observed that, "our three-way fast lanes of liberalization, privatization and globalization, must provide safe pedestrian crossing for the unempowered." The core message is that, "the three-way fast lanes of liberalization, privatization and globalization" cannot be placed above everything else and cannot be an end in itself.
The Vice-President, Krishna Kant, said, "Forces of globalization and market economy present tempting opportunities. Economic growth could be looked upon as an end in itself. In the process, it is quite easy to forget the rapid economic growth which could be highly exclusionary. It could generate wealth for some while leaving many behind. If unhindered, this may potentially divide civil society. A more wholistic approach could help aid this. Wisdom lies in not losing sight of the big pictures even while painting small ones."
Responding to Shroff, C.T. Kurien argues that, "If globalization is a process, it cannot be understood and evaluated without a clearer notion of what a global economy is or should be and an explication of what are stated to be impersonal forces of market."

2. James Petras and Chronis Polychronism, 'Critical Reflections on Globalization,' in *Economic and Political Weekly,* (September 6, 1997), p. 2249.
3. Martin Weber, 'Engaging Globalization: Critical Theory and Global Political Change,' in *Alternatives, 27* (2003), p. 301.
4. See James Petras, 'Globalization: A Socialist Perspective,' in *EPW*, February 20, 1999, p. 459.
5. *Ibid.*

6. See *UNDP Report 1999*.
7. See *Human Development Report 2000*, pp. 3-6.
8. *Ibid.*, p. 8.
9. See Devinder Sharma, 'Farmers' Suicides and Agriculture Crisis in Karnataka' in *Deccan Herald*, June 14th, 2007, p. 9.
10. Devinder Sharma, "Deepening Crisis," in *Deccan Herald*.

The Prime Minister referred to food security as an important objective of agricultural policy. This is especially so in the wake of stagnation in the production of foodgrains over several years. Fortunately, the yield gaps in foodgrains crops in many areas suggest that we can evolve a strategy for increasing production of wheat by 8 million tones, rice by 10 million tones and pulses by 2 million tones by the end of the 11th Plan period. A food security mission will be launched to achieve these objectives, focusing for each crop on selected districts in States which provide scope for significant yield increases at modest costs. While food security is important, our projections also suggest that production of foodgrains needs to increase by only 2 to 2.5 per cent a year over the 11th Plan period. This means that if agriculture as a whole is to grow at 4%, it will be necessary for other sectors to grow at around 6%. Agricultural diversification into horticulture, dairying poultry and fisheries must therefore form a critical part of our agricultural strategy. We need to pay much more attention to the specific needs of these sectors in the future. Since the produce in all these sub-sectors is perishable, diversification has important implications for modernizing marketing and the development of logistics support, cold chains and downstream linkages with food processing. Amendment of the APMC Act is an important first step in this process. Many states have amended the Act, but they have yet to complete the process by notifying the rules. This must be done. Contract farming is another innovation which is being encouraged by many states. It does not raise the problems associated with corporate farming and it could prove to be a useful method of linking farmers to markets. However, the need for regulation, especially with regard to dispute resolutions needs to be examined.

—*Montek S. Ahluwalia, NDC meeting, May 29, 2007*

9

Financial Globalisation

T.B. Kapali

INTRODUCTION

The Reserve Bank of India envisages an increased role for them—in terms of their taking stakes in Indian entities or even being allowed to acquire Indian banks—from 2009 onwards. The RBI, in its road map released in 2005, laid out a graduated scaling up of foreign bank activity in order to enable Indian banks to better prepare themselves for global competition. The RBI did not formulate any specific road map for the non-banking financial services sector as foreign direct investment in this sector was already permitted under the overall FDI policy. Also, given the pre-dominant role of banks in the overall credit markets (banks accounting for around 95 per cent of all outstanding credit), attention was naturally focused on them.

Systemically, important non-banking financial companies (NBFCs), though, have come under the regulatory scanner more recently with the RBI, formulating updated guidelines on the relationship between banks/such NBFCs.

WATERSHED YEAR

Half way into the 4-year window offered by the RBI, it appears that 2009 could well be a watershed year in the domestic financial sector as regards the market presence and operations of foreign financial intermediaries. The signals for that are coming from recent developments in the non-banking finance sector.

Repco Home Finance Ltd. is the latest in the growing list of non-banking finance companies in which overseas financial entities are eyeing stakes/have already acquired stakes in the recent past. This list includes names such as Chola DBS, Sundaram Home Finance, Dandapani Finance, First India Credit (previously known as Fullerton India which itself was a renamed NBFC taken over by Singapore's Temasek Holdings) and Shriram City Union Finance of the Shriram Group. It is not a coincidence that all the NBFCs mentioned above are South-based. That is only a reflection of the fact that NBFC activity, historically, has been more prominent in the South than in other parts of the country.

The key questions though are: what is driving this phenomenon of foreign financial intermediaries picking up stakes in Indian financial entities? And, what is it that the foreign investors are positioning themselves for? Also, importantly, how will the competitive position of Indian entities be affected by the growing presence of foreign players?

HOUSEHOLD CREDIT

Though all the companies mentioned above are either Tier 2 or 3 size-wise, foreign investors have not been deterred by the current scale of operations of these entities. Foreign direct investment in any sector is driven by long-term growth prospects. And if the statistics relating to household credit in India are any indication, foreign investors in Tier 2 or Tier 3 finance companies are basically positioning themselves for a huge expansion of the overall market itself. There will be enough business opportunities for all levels of market players—be they financial conglomerates in the top category or the Tier 2/3 companies.

As the accompanying table shows, household credit in India is just around 1/10 of the GDP. Leaving alone the mature markets of the West, even in emerging Asian countries such as Korea, Philipplines or Thailand, the ratio is much higher at around a quarter of the countries' GDP.

Cross-country Trends in Household Credit 2005

(*in per cent*)

Item	*Emerging Europe*	*Emerging Asia*	*Latin America*	*Latin Markets*	*India*
Household credit as % of GDP	12	27.5	9.2	58	9.9
Share of household credit in total pvt. sector credit	38.9	31.4	35.7	41.5	24.5
Share of housing loans in total household credit	27.9	54.2.	37.5	77.5	52.7

To look at the figures in perspective, on a GDP of around Rs. 35,00,000 crore currently, household credit—comprising housing loans, credit cards, consumer durable cards. education loans etc.—is around Rs. 3,50,000 crore. Housing loans constitute around 50 per cent of this, i.e. around Rs. 1,75,000 crore. Total credit is around 50 per cent of GDP—about Rs. 18,00,000 crore.

Biz Avenues

One can visualize the business opportunities here with GDP growing at around 8 per cent and more financial deepening resulting in an increase of the share of overall credit (and household credit) in the national output. Foreign investors are basically betting on the pie getting bigger and bigger. They are positioning themselves strategically for the expected explosion in private sector credit in India and that too in segments which are relatively higher margin businesses.

Broader Implications

Significant implications await the domestic financial

markets on the back of the above developments. For one, newer financing techniques such as securitisation of mortgages—not so far tried that much in India but well known in the advanced markets—could gain ground. This is all the more relevant given the RBI's cap on banks' exposures to non-banking finance companies.

The domestic corporate bond markets could get a boost in the process. Risk management in the financial sector may also assume a higher and more rigorous profile enabling lending institutions to offer products which may better match demand.

From the regulator's point of view, the deeper penetration of the Indian financial sector by foreign entities could throw up its own supervisory and monetary policy challenges. Indian banks may have to reckon with newer dimensions of competition as foreign players create niches on both the lending and funding sides.

PART II

DIMENSIONS OF INCLUSIVE GROWTH

10

Approaching the Eleventh Plan

C.P. Chandrasekhar and Jayati Ghosh

INTRODUCTION

The most remarkable thing about the Planning Commission's Approach to the Eleventh Plan, is that there appears to be no planning in it. Planning in the economic sense requires, at the minimum, a constrained maximization exercise—that is, a clear definition of the social goals, which are then sought to be attained as far as possible subject to the prevailing resource, economic, social and technological constraints. This in turn requires a specification of the proposed mechanisms or measures to be employed to attain these goals.

This was certainly present in the earlier Plans of the Government of India. Even in the 1980s, the Plan documents at least had the semblance of such minimum discipline, though it could be argued that by then the governments in power had less inclination to even try and follow them in practice. But the current Approach Paper does not even attempt to provide a clear statement of goals and mechanisms. Instead, it adopts an uncritical "trickle-down" approach to economic growth, by making the basic objective the achievement of a certain target annual GDP growth figure—either 7, 8 or 9 per cent per annum—and effectively assuming that all social goals will be achieved by this.

This reduces any planning exercise to a relatively crude calculation of the projected growth scenarios and the associated requirements of public and private savings and investment as well as sectoral growth rates. These numbers are derived not just through extrapolating from the past but by making (often heroic) assumptions regarding what are perceived to be desired changes, without any consideration of how these different numbers are to be achieved.

THE GROWTH PROCESS

This approach deserves to be explained in more detail. Average annual GDP growth in the Tenth Plan is estimated to be 7 per cent, below the Plan target of 8 per cent but still above the annual rate of any previous Plan period.

TABLE 10.1

Alternative Growth Scenarios for Eleventh Plan

Target annual GDP growth rate	*7 per cent*	*8 per cent*	*9 per cent*
Investment rate	29.1	32	35.1
Current account balance	-2	-2.4	-2.8
Savings rate of which:	27.1	29.6	32.3
Household savings	20.1	20.5	21
Corporate savings	5	5.5	6.1
Public sector enterprises	3.1	3.1	2.8
Government	-1.1	0.5	2.4
Government fiscal balance	-6.4	-6.2	-6
Government revenue balance	2.9	-1.3	0.6
Growth by Sectors:			
Agriculture	3.2	3.7	4.1
Industry	8.2	9.4	10.5
Services	7.7	8.8	9.9

However, certain features of this growth process need to be noted.

First, this respectable average rate of growth resulted from a combination of poor performance in agriculture and improved performance in the other two sectors. More significantly, it was associated with not just higher investment rates but significantly higher savings rates, which in the event have turned out to be higher than investment rates. This is why the current account has actually been in surplus over the Plan period, at an average of 0.7 per cent of GDP.

This needs to be compared with the projections of the Tenth Plan. It is evident from this that the Tenth Plan had approximated the aggregate rates of investment and growth, its projections of the structure of that growth have been completely belied. Thus, agriculture in particular has performed well below target. Most surprisingly, however, the savings rate has been well above target while the investment rate has nevertheless been below target. This is why the GDP growth has been associated with current account surplus rather than deficit.

But it points to a very disturbing feature of the past growth, which is that over the Tenth Plan, the investment rate has fallen well below the potential provided by the domestic savings rate as well as a feasible current account deficit. In other words, investment has seriously under-performed.

In any reasonable planning exercise, surely the first question following upon this should be: Why has this happened? Of course, to take investment and growth alone as the basic macro-economic targets is deeply problematic, as we shall discuss below. But if they are to be taken as targets, then it is incumbent upon the planners to assess the past performance and consider why the outcomes were so different from those that were expected. And the answer to this question should at least inform the strategy for the next Plan.

PUBLIC INVESTMENT

Thus, one major difference between the anticipated and actual in the indicators, which has contributed to the final outcome, is the much lower rate of public investment. This has been only around 7 per cent of GDP compared to the Tenth Plan target of 8.4 per cent. This has critically affected not only the aggregate investment rate, but also private investment, since there are well known synergies between public and private investment. And the relatively inadequate performance of public investment is related to the misplaced perceptions of fiscal constraint that have prevented the government from increasing much needed public investment despite favourable macroeconomic conditions.

This has been marked for both direct public investment (the "capital expenditure" of the government) and investment of public sector enterprises (PSEs), many of which currently hold their profits as reserves or to provide savings for use by government and private sectors rather than engage in active expansion and investment themselves. Indeed, the inadequate investment by PSEs was a major omission of the previous NDA government, which has thus far been continued by the UPA government, and it amounts to a huge waste of public assets as well as enormous unutilized investment potential. It is worth remembering this every time the Centre cries wolf about the shortage of resources available for public investment, and argues that FDI is the only alternative to generate growth.

This past and current practice of inadequate public sector investment (by both government and PSEs) in turn has already had adverse implications for the future. As Table indicates, even the Planning commission's own projections essentially show PSE profits (and therefore savings out of profits) as more or less constant as GDP increases, such that a higher rate of GDP growth is actually associated with a lower contribution of PSE savings. This in turn creates more pressure on government savings, such that the Government is forced into an even more contractionary fiscal stance in these projected growth scenarios, and moving from dissaving to positive saving amounting to 2.4 per cent of GDP in the highest growth scenario.

This is actually a travesty of the idea of public sector involvement in a developing economy, since it takes the government sector and PSEs away from being net investors to being net savers and providers of resources for private investment. Since there are many areas where private investment will continue to be lacking or socially sub-optimal, because of externalities and social returns being higher than private expected returns, that means that all such areas will be underprovided. These include critical areas such as infrastructure, health, sanitation and education, and so on. Yet, amazingly, the Planning Commission actually appears to be envisaging such a scenario in future.

THE FRBM ACT

This self-imposed constraint upon crucial public expenditure is one of the chief macroeconomic drawbacks of the Approach Paper. The Government may argue that the Fiscal Responsibility and Budget Management Act (FRBMA) has left it no choice but to bring fiscal and revenue deficits down to the targets specified in the Act. But the FRBMA has actually become an unnecessary millstone around the Government's neck, preventing it from undertaking necessary expenditures to improve the condition of citizens and to ensure a desirable pattern of growth.

The Approach Paper's section on financing the public sector on financing the public sector plan does indeed recognize some of the difficulties posed by the rigid and indeed unreasonable demands of the FRBMA, and even suggests a postponement of the targets for fiscal and revenue deficits by a period of two years.

But the more plausible argument, of course, is simply that this Act should be scrapped by the same Parliament that chose to bring it in, because it is illogical, puts bizarre constraints on necessary and desirable revenue spending, does not allow anti-cyclical fiscal stances and also—as apparently recognized here by the Planning Commission—militates against higher economic growth.

However, the more pertinent question in this context relates to the growth obsession that is evident in much of the document. In this Approach Paper, the lack of realism or even awareness of recent national and international experience in this regard is evident. The simplistic and discredited "trickle down" argument is assumed to operate in its more benign and dynamic form despite all evidence to the contrary. This completely belies the very title of the document—which suggests that the Government wants to move towards more inclusive growth—

since there is no consideration of changes in the pattern of growth that would be required to make it more inclusive.

PRODUCTIVE EMPLOYMENT

The most critical aspect of growth that determines whether it is more "inclusive" is the extent to which it generates productive employment. This is where growth in India has been so lacking in the past fifteen years. The agrarian crisis has been combined with lack of adequate employment generation in other sectors, and have been the primary causes for the inequalising growth process so far. Yet, in the listing of the major challenges facing the Government at the start of the document, there is no mention of employment generation.

Further, there is no concern with ensuring that the pattern of growth will be such as to generate more employment, or ideas about how to go about this. Instead, several policy initiatives suggested (such as liberalizing the entry of foreign players into retail trade) would actually damage employment among small retailers and petty traders even further, rather than increase it. Similarly, the other great economic challenge facing the country at present—the agrarian crisis reflected in high and unsustainable levels of peasant debt and the lack of viability of cultivation because of the cost-price relationship for many crops—is barely considered on this document.

The Plan projections blithely assume (Table) that GDP in agriculture will grow much faster than it has in the past decade, yet suggests no ways to ensure this. It is simply assumed that diversification into horticulture (which is not feasible for most dryland areas) and contract farming will automatically generate much higher income growth from agriculture. There is no discussion of any planned and systematic state intervention to address the structural and conjunctural forces currently devastating crop production.

In general, therefore, the macro-economic presumptions of the approach are faulty and unlikely to generate anything resembling more inclusive growth. Several other features of the proposed approach are likely to lead to greater economic exclusion and more fragile economic circumstances for millions of people. The Approach Paper is particularly worrying because it suggests that even the Planning Commission, which is the agency within the government that is charges with the task of looking ahead and thinking strategically about the economy, has no intention of doing so.

> The workforce in the unorganised non-agricultural sector at the end of 11th Plan would roughly equal the combined workforce in agriculture and organised sectors having already increased from 44 per cent in 1993 to 66 per cent in 2004.
>
> The approach paper's response to cope with this grim scenario is pathetic. Its main suggestions; one, changes in existing labour laws to spur investments and growth in labour intensive sectors (!)l two, policies to encourage corporate entities to enter more labour intensive areas (!!). The suggestion to induce capital-intensive corporate sector to enter the labour-intensive segment cannot be serious. Capital consciously shuns labour and that explains the phenomenal deepening of capital-intensity. However, at one place the paper faces stark truth: if the corporate sector expands mainly by capturing existing markets from the unorganised sector, the total employment outcome would almost certainly be adverse since each new corporate sector job would displace several people in the unorganised sector.
>
> Three, it offers no explanation why agriculture which engages two thirds of our work force, has been starved of even minimum capital, short-term or long-term. Besides, it sees additional employment prospects only in manufacturing and services and little in agriculture.
>
> It is oblivious to the real challenge there, that is, to combat underemployment and to raise production field by field to absorb more labour.
>
> —*L.C. Jain, Deccan Chronicle, December, 31, 2006.*

11

Inclusive Growth : An Innovative Approach

P.V. INDIRESAN

INTRODUCTION

It is a well-worn cliché that every new Five year Plan is a copy of the first one (more accurately the Second Plan when the basic principles of national planning were formalized). The same is being said about the Approach Paper to the Eleventh Plan. That is not quite true. The latest Approach paper has at least two innovations: One, the idea of "inclusive growth," which is more comprehensive that the idea of poverty alleviation that has held pride of place in the country's economic policy for decades. Two, shift towards Public-Private Partnership with as much as 70 per cent of investment expected from private enterprise and the state playing a supportive role only, not the dominating one it insisted upon all these years. The first is a shift in emphasis; the latter a cultural change. Both will surely transform the nature of our economy and even polity.

What Professor J.K. Galbraith said of the Council of Economic Advisers in the United States applies to the members of our Planning Commission too: "(They) do not function as economists. They function as a priesthood . . . should not be identified with the integrity of the economic profession but with the politics of the president." Likewise, the Planning Commission is not free to produce the best plan that the discipline of economics would suggest; it has not option but make the best of what the compulsions of politics decides.

No Experimenting

Our planners are like ancient *rishis*. They lay down the *sastra,* which everyone must accept. Like the *rishis,* they do think a lot. Instead of sitting under a tree in a Himalayan forest, they do so for months and months in committee rooms of the Delhi jungle. However, like the *rishis,* they only think. They do not experiment; they do not try out new ideas. The West has dominated world economy for centuries because it tries out unconventional ideas. India has suffered because it will not. India will accept only traditional ideas or second-hand ones handed down by foreigners. Original ideas emanated from within India are unacceptable.

As an example, let us take the case of distress among farmers. On the face of it, the problem lies in their inability to repay debts. More credit is the obvious solution. There can be an exactly opposite view. Farmers have had too much-not too little—credit. It may be argued that, even then, high interest rates are ruining them; hence, cheaper credit will relieve their distress. There can be dissent on that score too. When crops fail or when the market collapses, low interest rates may mitigate distress but will not remove it.

Information Asymmetry

In the alternate view, uncovered risk is the true problem, not lack of low-cost credit. At present, farmers face the full burnt of crop failure; merchants who dump unwarranted, excessive or even adulterated stuff on them run no risk themselves. Here is a classical instance of market failure on account of asymmetry of information. Farmers are uninformed or even misinformed about the value of the farm inputs they purchase. It is also a case of management failure. Disjointed farm inputs thrust on the farmers by merchants who maximize sales not optimize them. It this alternate view, the solution is not more credit, nor lower interest but better information that minimizes risk, better management that ensures optimum mix of inputs.

Consider a scheme where the government regulates what merchants sell to farmers by insisting that they sell a complete package, not parts in isolation; share the risk by accepting part of the crop as full payment. In that case, salesmen will not knowingly sell (the way they do now) more than what is not worthwhile nor will they offer an unbalanced package. For the farmer, the collateral is not his entire capital, not the farm itself but only that season's crop. If for any reason the crop fails, the farmer will earn less but is not ruined, will not lose his property. In this system, there is little or no need to have crop insurance, which the Approach Paper has ruefully accepted is too expensive and too complex to work.

Better Governance

This alternative needs no additional investment, but calls for better governance instead. Planners may accept that it is better than giving more credit. Even then, it is unlikely they will be able to implement the idea now that the government has decided to enhance farm credit. Our government has no plan to accept feedback, to make changes once a scheme has been launched.

Rapid growth, inclusive or otherwise, needs better governance even more than clever economics. Hence, the Plan should be deeply involved in the modernization of governance. For instance, it bemoans corruption but has no prescription to offer. It could at least have indicated how it would use the Right to Information Act for the purpose.

Key Information

The Right to Information Act is the best administration

reform since Independence. Unfortunately, confused critics are raising irrelevant questions about disclosure of official notings. In the government system, what officials write is so confusion that no one can be faulted with certainty. Knowing what individual officials say will not improve governance but knowing which hand—usually an extra-constitutional authority-took the final decision will do so. Knowing which official delayed how much will also help. Then, it suffices if the RTI guarantees two pieces of information only. The name of the official responsible for the final decision, and how long each official retained the file.

Government officials operate the way children play the game of "passing-the-parcel". They are paranoid about taking responsibility. Corrupt politicians have taken advantage of that failing. Once it becomes a legal necessity to pinpoint the official responsible for the final decision, as also the extent of delay that each official caused, officials will be forced to act carefully and promptly. Politicians will lose the power they now have to do backseat driving. Corruption will fade away. Decentralisation that the Approach Paper ardently desires will follow automatically.

The Approach Paper has been accused of departing from conventional wisdom. My complaint is that it has not departed enough. Critical issues it lists, such as the Naxal problem, farmers' distress, urban chaos, education muddle, healthcare mess and the like, are all chronic sores. Conventional wisdom cannot solve them; only innovative solutions will. That is where the Approach Paper is a blank; it has few new ideas. In India, new ideas are not sought. Even when they are proposed, they are left to die prematurely for lack of nourishment. So, old problems fester and become permanent sores. The Approach Paper has no answer.

Closed Windows

It is too much to expect that any planner of however superior intellect will come up with the best ideas to solve all national problems. However, planners have the means to glean ideas that appear anywhere in the country; they have a responsibility to identify what is best. In that respect, the Indian bureaucracy rates poorly mainly because it operates in secrecy. Its windows are closed so tight that it permits little light from outside. It believes in committees, not in people; in rules, not in ideas.

A good plan will have, at all times, a window open for untried novel ideas. It will experiment before rejecting new ideas. It will accept feedback and act on that. That is, the Plan should not be a rigid blue print but a process, the way we go about on an adventurous journey.

II

My appeal for including the poor in prosperity is based on wider considerations than economics. Few people are conscious of the fact we are increasing our wealth at the expense of security. Undoubtedly, India is much richer today than it was at the time of Independence. Even the poor are much better off: They are better fed, better educated, enjoy so much better healthcare that they live more than twice as long. On the other hand, family bonds have become weaker to reduce family security. Traditional economic linkages have faded away to reduce job security.

Above all, crime has proliferated. There are parts of the country where more murders are committed in one day than were committed in one year 60 years ago. About a third of the country is virtually under the sway of Naxalites. Few of our capitalists are alive to the danger large-scale rural disaffection posses.

Rural-Urban Disparity

Our poor are disillusioned not because they are getting poorer but because the rich are getting richer faster, because the rich-poor disparity is increasing. There are several reasons behind this but rural-urban disparity is the main one. That is why Naxalites are most powerful, and the government least effective, in the poorest rural areas.

It is true that our shift to capitalism has engineered rapid growth of the economy. However that rapid growth has come at the expense of political stability and personal security. Basking in luxury, many of our rich are blind to growing disaffection among the poor. If they were wise, they would set apart a part of their new wealth for ensuring better security. There is no point in accumulating wealth if we cannot enjoy it in peace. That is why we need Inclusive Growth.

In this connection, rural-urban disparity in bank credit has reached alarming proportions. On an average, urban-dwellers get about Rs. 70,000 worth of bank credit but villagers get less than Rs. 2500—a ratio of more than 25 to one. One can understand disparity of two or even three to one. A disparity of 25 to one is mind-boggling. No doubt, there are attempts to raise agricultural credit but however generous that raise may be, it will never approach the levels of urban credit. Rural development based on agriculture alone will never match urban development.

Wrong Question

We are asking how much more bank credit agriculture can absorb. That is the wrong question to ask; we should be asking instead how villages may be empowered to absorb more credit. We are asking what the minimum rural wage should be. We should be asking instead what minimum facilities poor villagers should have.

In allocating exceptionally large levels of credit to cities, we forget that money fetches much less in such cities as Bangalore (sorry, Bengaluru) than in a village some 30 km away. What wisdom is there to invest 25 times more capital in most expensive cities and invite at the same time more Naxal trouble in the bargain? Is that not unwise use of capital?

No doubt, the government is considering ways and means for increasing investment in the rural areas. Unfortunately, it is beset by marginal thinking. It asks by what percentage it can increase rural investment. It should ask instead how well it should match rural investment with the urban. No marginal increase in the prevailing Rs. 2000-2500 per capita rural investment will take our villages to urban prosperity when cities are getting Rs. 70,000 per capita, and metropolitan areas are commanding even more. Rural investment requires, deserves far, far more than marginal increase; it requires a new vision altogether.

Fortunately, we have in Dr. Raman Singh, Chief Minister of Chhattisgarh, one leader who appreciates the importance of balancing rural-urban investment. Recently, he launched the first state-sponsored PURA project (inaugurated by the President, Mr. A.P.J. Abdul Kalam, on November 7, 2006). The project links a collection of government land by a 40-km ring road and connects 22 villages. Unlike the case with rural roads, Dr. Raman Singh plans to make the ring road a four-lane highway at an estimated cost of Rs. 160 crore. He has already obtained commitments for two hospitals including a 250 bed hospital with attached training center for nurses and paramedical staff, as well as for two modern English medium schools. Two government buses have been introduced to serve the ring road and many more will come when private operators join.

Here is a vision out of the ordinary because whoever thinks of having expensive urban quality roads to link impoverished villages? Here is an investment jump that is 20 times what is normal in rural areas. Yet, the idea is not quixotic tilting at windmills. This large investment on the ring road will pay for itself if no more than 500 acres of adjacent land attract modern business and urban residents. Businesses and residents are bound to come in because they are guaranteed access to quality hospitals and schools with commercial expansion to follow.

Dovetailing Services

This model of rural development dovetails transport, education and health services, with each one of them as good as the best available in cities. This dovetailing of quality services (and not piecemeal, low quality) will attract human capital, spur demand and set-up a virtuous cycle. Thus, PURA will expand on its own steam.

Special Economic Zones (SEZ) are concerned only about commercial issues such as relaxed labour laws, tax concessions and the like. They are classical instances of top-down planning. No wonder, they are mired in controversy. In contrast,

Chhattisgarh's PURA has been planned after months of discussion with village leaders who have all given their consent in writing without coercion and with much enthusiasm.

In the 16th century, the Spanish Armada, composed of the largest fleet of warships ever assembled, invaded England and was routed. History books explain that the much larger Spanish Armada was defeated by the much smaller English ships because the Armada was loaded with soldiers who were of no use at sea where as the English ships were manned by skilled sailors.

Something similar is happening at the SEZsa—overloaded with capital and commercial experts but short of local content. That is why they run the risk of incurring the same fate as the Spanish Armada. On the other hand, PURA is inclusive without being altruistic.

PURA is inclusive in two senses: If includes social development—mass transport, education, health-care and housing; it organize such amenities the same way railways run passenger services: With multiple class of services to cater to both rich and poor alike. The way they have been planned, SEZs are profitable in the short-term but not necessarily in the long-term.

12

'Inclusive' Model of Development

ADITYA PURI

INTRODUCTION

The Hindu rate of growth has moved up to 7 per cent-plus. More important, the economy, with the internal consumption push, has evolved favouably for sustainable growth. Private consumption accounts for 64 per cent in China, 55 per cent in Japan, and 58 per cent in Eurpoe. *The 'inclusive'* model of development is a political, social and economic imperative. The focus of the model is the poor and is, therefore, inherently biased to consumption-led growth. *Corporate India* is strategically focused on market expansion based on geography (rural) and lowering price. *Our problems*—infrastructure, saving, FDI and vested politics—have reached the inflection point of crisis-induced decisions.

India has, through a combination of the above, transitioned to a 7 per cent-plus growth as a result of the emerging consumerism of one of the world's youngest population. The broadening and deepening of consumer support, consequent to inclusive politics, should shift the GDP growth dynamic to the upper side of the 7-9 per cent range. The increasingly powerful internal consumption dynamic should ensure robust growth. Superimpose the government-induced growth consequent to inclusive economics requiring rural development, job creation, infrastructure spending, coupled with private investment spending, and we have a tremendous 'opportunity'. It is imperative to ensure 'objective'-based planning, monitoring and accountability; else we are likely to repeat the last 50 years of grand plans and dismal performances. It would be worth discussing a few sub-plots of the future.

Funding

10 per cent growth in GDP would translate (depending on the multiplier used) into credit growth of 25-30 per cent. Funding this growth would require a greater monetisation of the economy. The stock of gold and jewellary in India, approximately $200 billion, is equivalent to half of bank deposits. Deposits represent 60 per cent of GDP compared with 190 per cent in China and 142 per cent in Japan. Corporate banks make up 1 per cent of India's stock of financial assets compared to 10 per cent in Thailand, 20 per cent in Malaysia, and 30 per cent in South Korea, US and Europe.

We clearly need a vibrant debt market and this will require reform in pension and insurance, to create investors, coupled with the introduction of derivatives, to impart liquidity and price discovery. Credit derivatives disperse the risk of the banking system. Simultaneously, the securitisation market must be activated to allow banks to disperse the risk and create funding. Spread of banking is a must. This will require active partnerships among banks, cooperative institutions, post-offices, micro-finance organizations, and so on. We also need to create sustainable livelihoods for the farmer to be able to service his loan and cover disaster risk through insurance.

Demographic Dividend

We are all today enthused by the demographics of our population which will provide us a competitive advantage in the future. However, we need to understand that to reap this advantage, we must create 12-15 million jobs annually and an appropriate skill-set in the population to do the jobs that are created. Otherwise, this demographic dividend will turn into a nightmare. We need to focus on labour-intensive manufacturing and servicing, coupled with revamping of the food chain. Simultaneously, we need to revamp the education system, which continues to produce *'Bhadralok'*-graduates capable of doing clerical jobs whereas the job opportunities in the future will require specific skills.

Two Indias

It is obvious that we need to carry the under-privileged with us. The current system of broad-based subsidies has not helped. We need target/result-oriented subsidies. The success of micro-financing and self-help groups clearly shows what can be achieved with small amounts of money. The employment guarantee scheme should look at creating sustainable employment. Prof. Lawrence Summers, while delivering the L.K. Jha Memorial Lecture, raised some important issues that need to be debated upon, followed by agreed-upon action.

First, the net flow of capital is substantially from developing countries towards the industrialized world, mainly the US. This trend, which has persisted for several years, is based on current projections and is expected to continue. Second, the build-up in US net foreign debt is largely mirrored in reserve accumulation by emerging markets. Third, global reserves of emerging markets are far in excess of any accepted criterion of reserve need for financial protection. Fourth, expected real returns on these reserves are low. Since the reserves are largely invested in the dollar, a return of around 4 per cent would be normal. This presumes no exchange rate adjustment.

The dollar will fall substantially—only the timing is uncertain. The reasons for the expected fall are: First, 7 per cent and growing is an unusually large deficit (in the US). Second, the current account deficit is financing consumption rather that investment as the US net national savings rate is now at a record low of under 2 per cent. Third, investment is tilted towards real-estate and the non-traded goods sector rather than the traded goods sector and away from exportables. Fourth, the net flow of direct investment is out of the US and the flow of incoming capital appears to be of shortening maturity and coming increasingly from official rather than private sources.

Developing countries are paying a high cost of holding reserves beyond what is necessary for financial stability. Excess reserves of various countries defined as reserves in excess of twice short-term debt are given in the Table. Suppose we presume that these reserves could earn between 7 per cent and 10 per cent depending on the countries risk appetite, India could earn (incrementally) annually $3-5 billion while, at the same time, reducing its risk in case of a dollar depreciation.

Excess Reserves Beyond Greenspan—Guidotti Rule

	Excess Reserves (in $ millions, Q3 2005)	*Excess Reserve as a % of 2004 GDP*
China	724,080	41
Taiwan	210,134	69
Korea	136,711	18
Russia	118,154	20
India	107,703	15
Malaysia	58,613	50
Algeria	50,518	60
Mexico	47,083	7
Thailand	35,489	21
Saudi Arabia	73,897	29

Source : LK Jha Memorial Lecture by Prof. Lawrence Summers.

Prof. Summers rightly asked at his lecture: "Spending of what amount of money by the government for uplifting the poor makes headlines or warrants a special mention in the Budget speech." Now, there is the possibility of generating #3-5 billion annually to meet key objectives.

Sustainable Self-Sufficiency

Let's accept it, we cannot have two Indias. The underprivileged have to be helped and quickly. This should create sustainable self-sufficiency. While it is agreed that everybody has to do something, the thought remains in the air because we plead lack of resources. Therefore, it is imperative to examine why this huge amount of revenue for spending cannot be generated. The key questions that need to be debated are:

Who will Decide the Country's Risk Appetite?

Parliament being the representative of the people is the appropriate body to take the decision. This will ensure that the debate brings a convergence between politics and rational economic decision.

Who will Manage the Excess Reserves?

The management should be given, at best, to five fund managers. The mandate should clearly specify the risk appetite. We can start with a few low-risk investments; for example: Buy on standing AAA Indian Paper which now yields 7-8 per cent with a residual maturity of around five years. Fund infrastructure projects with a yield of 7-8 per cent. Balance in a fully diversified equity fund.

Who will be Responsible for any Unforeseen Setbacks?

The fund managers should have a quarter/monthly review with the standing Committee on Finance, which should have experts from the public/private sector for the review.

Infrastructure

We must spend on infrastructure. This cannot wait for the restructuring of the economy. It is imperative to re-examine/ support the Planning Commission Deputy Chairman, Mr. Montek Singh Ahluwalia's proposal for using forex reserves for the development of infrastructure. We should also consider incremental deficit financing as long as it creates productive infrastructure. The recent initiative in terms of right of information and objective-based expenditure evaluation are excellent tools to ensure greater effectiveness in public spending and accountability. This must be backed with appropriate monitoring. India is changing. There is a "can-do attitude" and a confidence. We can match the best in the world. Let's all make sure we reach our rightful place in the world.

13

"Non-Exclusion" to "Inclusive Growth" Strategy : Plan Perspectives

P. Jegadish Gandhi

> "Maximum production and full employment, the attainment of economic equality or social justice. . . . None of these objectives can be pursued to the exclusion of others, a plan of development must place balanced emphasis on all of these".
>
> —*The First Five Year Plan (1951-56)*

"The concept of Development is as old the Old Testament times. The urge for, and urgency of developing a society has been natural phenomenon through the Ages. The conceptualization has been contextualized with the then contemporary motivating and inhibiting factors. 'Development' should, in some sense, be synonymous, or at least identified with, a long-term, sustained process involving improvement or progress. Therefore, the study of this subject is concerned with those changes—social, cultural, political and economic—which contributed to or impede the material progress. The diverse pattern of development of various countries was a product of their peculiar historical, cultural and other circumstances forces.

The nature of economic policies advocated by the Indian national leaders from 1880 to 1905 gave to these years the character of being the period of economic nationalism. Chronologically, not only M.K. Gandhi but also Jawaharlal Nehru was a link in the chain bounding his generation with the past—not only with the distant past, but with the emotional and intellectual urges of the 19th century. The first half of the 20th century before the attainment of Independence, there is no gainsaying the historical fact that Gandhi and Nehru had swayed and shaped the socio-economic thinking in the country. Gandhism between the period of twenty years—1928-48 and the Nehruvism between the period of sixteen years—1948-64. The process was seen at its best in both of them who have left an enduring influence on the economic ideas and institutions of contemporary India. "Gandhi's linkage with the past was most pronounced in his adherence to the concept of swadeshi—the purely constructive and positive elements of swadeshi as a nation-making process, but giving it a new orientation and dimension, bearing in mind the interests of the general masses of the country. There is evidence to show that when Nehru functioned in a free India as Gandhi's heir, he himself felt he had been too optimistic about the possible adaptation of social forces to the remarkable series of economic changes that he set in train to fulfil his dream of democratic socialistic planning by clearing some of the road-blocks on the way, which had appeared formidable before independence.

Gandhi-Nehru Development Model

"The basic objective of the Gandhian model is to raise the material as well as the cultural level of the Indian masses so as to provide a basic standard of life. It aims primarily at improving the economic conditions of all villages of India and therefore, it lays a greatest emphasis on the scientific development of agriculture and rapid growth of cottage and village industries. The Gandhian model of growth hopes to achieve a national minimum level of living within the shortest possible time and aims at removal of concentration of income and wealth and growth with stability. Nehru, the architect of Indian planning, greatly admired the achievements of Soviet planning and so borrowed the concept of socialism from the Russians but, he also regarded the democratic values of the capitalist society as indispensable for the full growth of a just society. Thus, in his endeavour to take advantage of the virtues of the two extreme societies which were themselves also undergoing a transformation, Nehru's vision of the new India was described as "democratic socialism."

It is wrong to indict the Nehru-Mahalanobis model of growth on the ground that it had neglected agriculture and the small sector and that this had resulted in all the economic problems faced by the country, viz. inflationary rise in prices, acute shortages of essential goods, industrial sickness, growing inequalities, mounting poverty, etc. It would be wrong to ignore the development of heavy industry and put all the emphasis on agriculture and the small-scale sector. Let us not forget that it is inadequate investment in the power development programmes and the insufficient generation and distribution of power which has led to the failure in the agricultural sector. In fact there is no conflict between the heavy industry and the agricultural sector in the use of human and material resources. Both can be developed simultaneously. If the approach of balanced growth was valid in 1950's, it is all the more so even now.

Plan-wise Strategies

The basic objectives of our Five-Year Plans were "development along socialist lines to secure rapid economic growth and expansion of employment, reduction of disparities in income and wealth, prevention of concentration of economic power and creation of values and attitudes of a free and equal society." In order to achieve these objectives, the planners formulated a strategy of planned economic development. Nehru-Mahalanobis model of development emerged as the driving force of the strategy of development adopted in the mid-fifties at the time of formulation of the Second Five Year Plan. This strategy has continued right upto the eighties with a short interregnum of about 2-3 years when Janata Party was in power during 1977-80. Nehru-Mahalanobis model was based on long-run development strategy which accorded greater preference to the long-term goals of development.

Since 1951, India has completed ten five-year plans. The guiding principles of India's Five-Year Plans are provided by the basic objectives of growth, employment, self-reliance and social justice. Apart from these basic objectives, each five-year plan takes into account the new constraints and possibilities faced during the period and attempts to make the necessary directional changes and emphasis.

At the time of the *First Five Year Plan (1951-56)* India was faced with three problems-influx of refugees, severe food shortage and mounting inflation. India had also to correct the disequilibrium in the economy caused by the Second World War and the Partition of the country. Simultaneously, the First Plan attempted a process of all-round balanced development which could ensure a rising national income and a steady improvement in the living standards of the people over a period of time.

The Second Plan (1956-61) was conceived in an atmosphere of economic stability. Agricultural targets fixed in the First Plan had been achieved. Price level had registered a fall and, consequently, it was felt that the Indian economy had reached a stage where agriculture could be assigned a lower priority and a forward thrust made in the development of heavy and basic industries of the economy for a more rapid advance in future. The basic philosophy of the Second Plan was, therefore, to give a big push to the economy so that it enters the take-off stage.

Consequently, the *Third Plan (1961-66)* set as its goal the establishment of a *self-reliant and self-generating economy*. But the working of the Second Plan had also shown that the rate of growth of agricultural production was the main limiting factor in India's economic development. The experience of the first two plans suggested that agriculture should be assigned top priority. The Third Plan accordingly gave top priority to agriculture but it also laid adequate emphasis on the development of basic industries, which were vitally necessary for rapid economic development of the country. However, because of India's conflicts with China in 1962 and with Pakistan in 1965, the approach of the Third Plan was later shifted from development to defence and development.

The original draft outline of the *Fourth Plan* prepared in 1966 under the stewardship of Ashok Mehta had to be abandoned on account of the pressure exerted on the economy by two years of drought, devaluation of the rupee and the inflationary recession. Instead, three Annual Plans (1966-69) euphemistically described as "Plan Holiday" were implemented. India learnt a bitter lesson during Indo-Pakistan war when its so-called allies refused to supply essential equipment and raw materials for its economic development. The Fourth Plan (1969-74) set before itself the two principal objectives of *"growth with stability" and progressive achievement of self-reliance"*.

The Fifth Plan (1974-79) was introduced at the time when the country was reeling under a veritable economic crisis arising out of a run-away inflation, fuelled by the hike in oil prices. The final draft of the Fifth Plan prepared and launched by D.P. Dhar proposed to achieve *the two main objectives, viz., removal of poverty and attainment of self-reliance,* through promotion of higher rate of growth, better distribution of income and a very significant step-up in the domestic rate of saving. The Fifth Plan, however, was terminated by the Janata Party at the end of the fourth year of the Plan in March 1978.

There were two *Sixth Plans.* The focus of the Janata Sixth Plan was enlargement of the employment potential in agriculture and allied activities, encouragement to household and small industries producing consumer goods for mass consumption and to raise the incomes of the lowest income classes through a minimum needs programme. When the new Sixth Plan (1980-85) was introduced by the Congress, the Planners rejected the Janata approach and brought back Nehru Model of growth by aiming at a *direct attack on the problem of poverty by creating conditions of an expanding economy.*

The Seventh Plan (1985-90) sought to emphasise policies and programmes which would accelerate the growth in foodgrains production, increase employment opportunities and raise productivity—all these three immediate objectives were regarded central to the achievement of long-term goals determined as far back as the First Plan itself.

The fourth version of the *Eighth Plan (1992-97)* was approved at a time the country was going through a severe economic crisis caused by a balance of payments crisis, a rising debt burden, ever-widening budget deficits, mounting inflation and recession in industry. The Narasimha Rao Government initiated the process of fiscal reforms as also of economic reforms with a view to provide a new dynamism to the economy.

The Ninth Plan (1997-2002) was developed in the context of four important dimensions of state policy, viz. Quality of life, generation of productive employment, regional balance and self-reliance. The Ninth Plan focused on accelerated growth, recognizing a special role for agriculture for its stronger poverty reducing and employment generating effects, which will be carried out over a 15 year period. "The principal task of the Ninth Plan will be to usher in a new era of people-oriented planning, in which not only the governments at the Centre and the States, but the people at large, particularly the poor, can fully participate. A participatory planning process is an essential precondition for ensuring equity as well as accelerating the rate of growth of the economy."

The Tenth Plan (2002-07) was prepared against a backdrop of high expectations arising from some aspects of the recent performance. GDP growth in the post-reforms period improved to an average of about 6.1 per cent in the Eighth and Ninth Plans from an average of about 5.7 per cent in the 1980s, making India one of the ten fastest growing developing countries. Encouraging progress was also made in other dimensions. Although growth has strong direct poverty reducing effects, the frictions and rigidities in the Indian economy can make these processes less effective, and the Tenth Plan must therefore be formulated in a manner which explicitly addresses the need to ensure equity and social justice.

II

DIALECTICS OF INDIAN POLITICAL ECONOMY

1951-1991 : Socialist Pattern of Society

With democratic set-up, the Government of India started towards developing the economy so that people may be assured of a higher level of living. The Congress party Governments, both at the Central and State levels, had an economic model which was based on socialistic pattern of society and aimed at maximum employment, rapid industrialization, reduction of inequalities in income and wealth, alleviation of poverty and self-sustaining growth. The economic blueprint of the Janata Party which emerged on the national scene in March 1977 drew up its policies on a Gandhian approach. The short-spell of the National Front Government under V.P. Singh has opted for indicative planning process in our economy. The Chandrasekhar Government had little *maneuverability* in the planning mechanism due to its political vulnerability. The Janata Party Government had, no doubt, given a new idiom and impulse to the Indian political economy, but it failed to exploit, surplus assets taking advantage of a more conducive socio-economic awakening. The basis of economic policy since the 1980s Indira Gandhi's hesitant liberalization and Rajiv Gandhi's new economic policy has been the reliance on those with resource power to determine the pattern of production within the country. The 1947-91 socio-economic model of India "failed to achieve the primary objective of a rapid growth in real income that was widely shared by the masses of the people. It has left behind a dense tangled undergrowth of institutions, laws, and policies that are inappropriate to a competitive, progressive, and open society in which all would share the benefits of growth".

1991-2006: Globalised Economic Dynamics

The current economic reforms, claimed to be an attempt to alter the basic parameters of economic policies since Independence and to restructure the economy drastically, were launched a few days after a Government under the leadership of P.V. Narasimha Rao was formed at the Centre following the 10th General elections of May-June 1991. The condition of Indian socio-economy was like that of a patient in the intensive care canopy in mid-1991. The economy was best with crippling crises on all fronts—precarious forex position, untamed inflationary pressures, unbridled government expenditure, soaring fiscal deficit, sagging industrial production and, above all, an all-time low of the country's economy standard in the international arena. Against this backdrop of cumulative economic maladies, the launching of a series of structural adjustment programmes of the Narasimha Rao-Manmohan Singh combine had certainly created a new economic environment in the country. In 1999, the BJP-led National Democratic Alliance under the leadership of A.B. Vajpayee has also broadly accepted the supremacy of the globalisation-led open market system. Since 2004 the United Progressive Alliance (UPA) Government led by Manmohan Singh once again has given new impectus to second generation of economic reforms. Sofar the growth pulse is active only in the secondary services sectors dynamics. A decade of globalisation economics revealed the deficiencies of good governance in social sector development. The time has come to humanize the developmental simulation effect through more budgetary allocations for social sectors regeneration.

III

TOWARDS INCLUSIVE GROWTH: THE ELEVENTH PLAN (2007-2012)

The word "inclusive" has become not only fashionable but also quite relevant in our country. The Oxford Dictionary gives four meanings to the word, and the most inclusive meaning is "not excluding any section of society". The Eleventh Plan Approach Paper has the title, "Towards Faster and More Inclusive Growth". A starategy that aims at creating physical assets, human capital and capabilities, and opportunities for productive employment, especially for the lower-middle class and the poor, will help in achieving sustainable and inclusive growth. The recognition of the need for more inclusive growth by our planners is a welcome shift in emphasis from mere increase in growth rates to improvement in standards of living of those below the poverty line through increase in employment opportunities as well as better delivery systems to ensure access to intended benefits by intended beneficiaries.

The economy in 2006-07 appearas to have decidedly 'taken off' and moved from a phase of moderate growth to a new phase of high growth. Achieving the necessary escape velocity to move from tepid growth into sustained high-growth trajectory requires careful consideration of two issues and three priorities. The two issues are: the sustainability of high growth with moderate inflation; and the inclusive nature of such high growth. The three priorities are: rising to the challenge of maintaining and managing high growth; bolstering the twin pillars of growth, namely, fiscal prudence and high investment; and improving the effectiveness of Government intervention in critical areas such as education, health and support for the needy.

On the first issue of sustainability of high growth without running into high inflation, various indicators suggest that the currently growth phase is sustainable. The second issue is about the nature of this high growth in terms of inclusiveness. Putting more people in productive and sustainable jobs lies at the heart of inclusive growth. But such success, primarily, will depend on the success in achieving and maintaining high growth. There cannot be inclusive growth without growth itself. The experience of East Asia clearly reveals how high growth can eliminate poverty and transform a developing country into a developed one. The results of the latest NSSO's 61st Round clearly show how the annual growth rate of employment has not only accelerated from 1.6 per cent during 1993-2000 to 2.5 per cent during 1999-2005, but crossed the 2.1 per cent rate recorded during 1983-94. Unemployment has gone up not because of high growth, but because growth was not high enough. It is important to avoid the misconception that inclusive growth, by necessity, will have to be low growth.

The priority is improving the effectiveness of Government intervention in critical areas especially in the social sector. The goal of inclusive growth can be achieved only through effective government intervention in the areas of education, health and support to the needy. Value for every tax rupee spent has to be ensured by emphasizing the outcomes and avoiding any wastage or leakages in the delivery mechanism of public goods and services. Appropriate design of programmes and placing effective monitors over the programmes are critical in this regard.

The World Bank's India: Development Policy Review (2006) mentions two most pressing challenges for public action in India: institutional reform to enhance the capability of public sector institutions to ensure the effective delivery of core services, and sustaining rapid growth making the process of economic growth more inclusive across sectors across regions, and bringing he benefits of higher incomes and living standards to more people. Economic reforms in India since 1991 and acceleration in the globalisation process in recent years have created new political classes and changed the policy space. The challenge is how to check the temptation for competitive populism in the present day of coalition governments and political myopia.

According to the outlook of *Economic Survey 2006-07* sustained and high levels of economic growth in recent years provide an unique opportunity and momentum for faster social sector development. The buoyant economy should not only generate adequate employment but also provide adequate and need based resources for large interventions in the critical areas of social sector. The recent resurgence of manufacturing also bodes well for employment generation. Availability of resources alone however, will not guarantee faster social sector development. Efficacy of the programmes will depend a lot on the manner in which States implement various social sector programmes, these primarily being in the domain of the States. Time bound achievement of the physical targets will depend a lot on the capacity mobilization of the States at various levels. Accountability and transparency, especially through the PRIs, need to be emphasized to ensure good governance and delivery of quality services through public action for most social sector programmes. Capacity building of PRIs themselves is a critical success factor to achieve these objectives. States must ensure availability of adequate and skilled manpower for PRIs which are crucial for effective implementation of the social sector programmes like the NREGS. Monitoring the progress and effective implementation of the various social sector schemes through the outcome budget along with Right to information Act and decentralization through the PRIs are expected to strengthen the process of inclusive growth.

End Message

We have come a long way of socio-economic development

in the post-Independent era from "non . . . exclusion" emphasis in 1951-56 to "inclusive growth" path in 2007-2012. "The dynamics of policy-making in India should be understood to lie along the divide between inclusion and populism rather than between socialism and 'liberalisation'. . . Inclusion is central to the Indian political process because it is part of the project of nation-building and essential to preserving the national identity and democratic institutions (Ashoka Mody).

Political freedom at midnight on August 15, 1947, put India on a voyage of rediscovery and renewal involving all people for a freer and better life. India in the 60 years (1947-2007) achieved creditable success on many fronts, no doubt, with challenges and crises. The present stage of economic governance in India represents an ambiguous social philosophy which weeps for the woes of poor but sides with the shinny life style of the rich segment. The 60th year of economic independence is best celebrated by a firm solid foundation to build an "inclusive growth" society benefiting all sections. That was what inclusive "Swaraj" was all about!

References

Ashoka Mody (Ed): Inclusive Growth—K.N. Raj on Economic Development, Orient Logman Ltd., Hyderabad (2006).

Nampoothiry, M.M. : "Inclusive Growth", *The Hindu* (December 3, 2006).

Jegadish Gandhi, P. (Ed.): Economic Reforms in India: Mid-way Reflections, IEA Trust for Research & Development, New Delhi (1994).

———, (Ed): Globalised Indian Economy: Contemporary Issues and Perspectives, Deep & Deep Publications (P) Ltd., New Delhi (2003).

———, (Ed.): National and Sub-National Economic Development, Deep & Deep Publications (P) Ltd., New Delhi (2003).

———, "Socio-Economic Thought: An Overview" in *The Socio-Economic Thoughts* of A.P.J. Abdul Kalam, Vellore Institute of Development Studies(VIDS) (2004).

———, (Ed): India and China in the 21st Century: Super Economic Power Dynamics in Asia, Deep & Deep Publications (P) Ltd., New Delhi (2007).

Ruddar Datt and Sundharam, KPM: Indian Economy, S. Chand & Company Ltd., New Delhi (2006).

Economic Survey, 2006-07, Govt. of India.

14

Will the Aim of Inclusive Growth be Achieved?

M.Y. KHAN

INTRODUCTION

The in thing today is inclusive growth, and the United Progressive Alliance Government's main objective of accelerating growth and development of the economy by 'including' the weaker sections is fully reflected in its Budget (2007-08) proposals. Recognising that the crux of the problem is the poor performance of the farm sector, the Budget emphasises agricultural development and rural social infrastructure creation. The indifferent showing on the farm front can be attributed to sluggish investment growth, lack of social infrastructure, including education, health and social security, and rampant corruption.

It is common knowledge that most farmers have no access to adequate credit. The Budget has targeted towards the sector a credit flow of Rs. 22,500 crore compared to Rs. 17,500 crore last year. The other important outlay, of Rs. 22 '52 crore, is on fertilizer subsidy. Interest subvention and insurance outlays will also go a long way in protecting the farmer incomes/cash flows. The Government has not overlooked long-term investment either. For instance, accelerated irrigation, rural infrastructure and road construction have been allocated about Rs. 35,000 crore. Apart from this, Nabard has been permitted to raise funds by issuing bonds so that long-term investment can be financed in rural sector.

Training and Skill Development

Importantly, the Budget has allocated funds for training farmers and factory workers. The training for farmers will cover water management, harvest management, and so on. The Finance Minister has revived the 'training and visit' extension programme, which played an important role in the Green Revolution of the 1960s. It is expected that such training will cover crop-protection, crop-insurance, diversification of crops, warehousing and protection of foodgrains from pests. In a growing economy and given the global competition in the domestic and international markets, it is an urgent necessity that India has a large, well-trained and highly skilled industrial work force. To achieve this, the government has to run education and training programmes on a continuous basis, as the East Asian countries do.

Healthcare

Rapid development and efficient growth require high labour productivity and a hasslefree health environment. In this respect, the Budget has made the right moves in providing higher allocations for drinking water and sanitation, HIV/AIDS prevention, polio and integrated child development services.

For a package of programme under the National Rural Health Mission, the Budget has proposed to increase the funds from Rs. 8,207 crore in 2006-07 to Rs. 9,947 crore in 2007-08. The Government should take this forward by being pro-active in setting up rural hospitals or health centers, staffed by good doctors and equipped with adequate medical equipment and medicines. In the more efficient and productive villages, the private sector may also be persuaded to set-up hospitals and medical centers, for which the Government can offer tax exemptions and other incentives.

Employment

The Government has continued with the National Rural Employment Guarantee Scheme and the Swaran Jayanti Gram Swarozgaar Yojana to provide employment and promote self-employment through Self-Help Groups, respectively. These programmes if pursued without the intervention of vested interests and corrupt officials, will help many families cross the poverty line and lead better lives. However, the Government should have thought of framing self-help schemes that not only give employment but also generate permanent assets. The Government cannot sustain the employment guarantee schemes for long; the right course would be to encourage more people to become self-employed, with the adequate financial support in terms of bank credit.

Eliminating Corruption

The UPA Government has made a sincere effort to offer several benefits to the rural areas and rural poor in terms of investment allocations and schemes. However, their successful implementation will be determined by the extent of corruption among the various authorities down the line and their sense of accountability. Corruption has, over the decades, been the major stumbling block in the path of development. For instance, roads do not last one monsoon, village wells may be dug only on the drawing boards, and schools may provide mid-day meals merely in official documents.

Corruption dogs our day-today-lives, whether it is in the obtaining of a driving licence or receiving subsidized credit. Most often, the poorer sections are the victims of such corruption and seldom the beneficiaries of what they are supposed to receive. And when the poor cannot get medical attention, when they are excluded from potential jobs and bank credit, when they are not paid their due in social assistance because they don't have the support of an influential authority or they cannot pay a bribe, they remain poor. Truly, corruption is the crucial impediment in the path to eliminating poverty. In effect, elimination of corruption should be one of the Budget's chief targets.

Finally, it is advisable to ponder how fast the country can achieve rapid, investment-driven growth with improvement in the quality of the workforce and infrastructure in the rural sector, so that the growth imbalance can be corrected and development is more inclusive.

II

TACKLING PROBLEM OF JOBLESS GROWTH

The Economic Survey, 2006-07 while discussing the issues and priorities in its General Review, argued that the high inclusive growth would mean putting more people in productive and sustainable jobs which can be achieved provided only if the country reaches high growth trajectory. The assumption is that high growth will achieve the goal of generating more productive jobs. A noble perception no doubt, but experience does not provide comfortable evidence of job creation commensurate with economic growth.

Though, the 61st National Sample Survey estimated that employment increased at the rate of 2.48 per cent during 1999-2000 to 2004-05, the unemployment rate was as high as 3.06 per cent of labour force in 2004-05 compared to 2.78 per cent in 1999-2000 and 2.62 per cent in 1993-94. However, this data include disguised employment. The picture of job growth can be drawn on the basis of employment data in the organized sector.

Large Fluctuations

Employment growth in the organized sector has shown large fluctuations. For instance, during 1990-91 to 1995-96 it rose on average at less than 1 per cent, whereas GDP growth was 5.7 per cent per annum. Further, the employment growth rate fell to 0.31 per cent per annum during 1995-96 to 1999-2000 against

GDP growth of 7.5 per cent per annum. The employment growth became negative at –1.33 per cent while GDP growth was 6.7 per cent per annum during 1999-2000 to 2004-05. During the last sub-period, investments had increased substantially to 24.2 per cent of GDP compared to 22 per cent during the preceding period.

Obviously, the economic growth had been jobless. Indeed, in the public sector employment declined by 5-6 lakh persons in absolute term during 1990-2004. Though the private sector generated nearly eight lakh jobs during this period, it was still negligible *vis-a-vis* the working population. The story gets more complicated, with severe disparities emerging in salaries. This may have prompted the Prime Minister to ask the private sector to re-think the salaries paid, but this is difficult in a free market economy.

Lost Share

An analysis of data put out by the Reserve Bank of India on private corporates showed that the quantum of wages and salaries paid *vis-a-vis* the total income of companies declined from 11.1 per cent during 1990-91 to 8.9 per cent in 2003-04. This means the working class has not got its share of corporate income despite the enormous growth in corporate income and retained profits. In many sun rise industries, domestic as well as multinational, salaries have increased multifold for certain levels of employees, while a large has not enjoyed this privilege.

Indeed, neither the GDP growth nor of employment reflects any inclusiveness. With the growth becoming more technology-oriented and capital intensive, its fruits are getting evenly distributed. There is clearly need to focus on common people, their income levels and social reforms, shifting away from high growth and globalisation that has seen reforms in financial as well as real sector.

Unemployment and poverty have high positive correlation. There are 26-28 crore people in India who are poor and without adequate work, especially in rural India where widespread disguised employment gives a misleading picture. This is well reflected in the massive migration of rural youths to the urban areas even for petty jobs.

SEZs, the Way to Go

To tackle the problem of rural unemployment needed are strategies for rural industrialization and large investments in agriculture sector. As for rural industrialization, Special Economic Zones is the answer. Only, the government must ensure that no fertile land is considered for SEZs, as also that the exercise does not end up as a land-grab will leave farmers further impoverished. Only barren land should be used and a condition must be attached that the SEZs should employ as much local people as possible, providing them training, if necessary. The government can pursue corporatisation of already existing rural industrial units by providing them financial incentives and concessions. The utilization of uncultivated land for setting up units to make garments, chemicals, leather goods, agro-products, etc., deserves serious government attention.

15

Strategising "Inclusive Growth"

T.S. PAPOLA

INTRODUCTION

It is well known that the Indian economy has grown at about double the rate in the post-reform period as compared to the decades preceding the reforms. The economy has not only sustained relatively higher growth rate during 1990's, but the growth rate has seen further acceleration in recent years. Growth rate of GDP was estimated to be 5.5 per cent during the 9th Plan (1997-98 to 2002-03) period. According to the latest Economic Survey (2006-07), GDP growth rates were 8.5, 7.5, and 9.0 during 2003-04, 2004-05 and 2005-06 respectively and estimate for 2006-07 are placed at 9.2 per cent.

It is also widely recognized that this shift of the Indian economy from a low growth to a high growth trajectory has been a result of the economic reforms that were initiated partially with the 1980's, but were launched on a much more serious and widespread basis in 1991. Trade liberalization and opening up of the Indian economy, the steps towards its integration into a globalised economic system, have also produced some significant changes in the external sector of the Indian economy. India's foreign trade has grown over five and half times in a period of 15 years. Both imports and exports have increased by that extent during 1990-91 to 2005-06. The external sector of the Indian economy now constitutes about 33 per cent of GDP as compared to 15 per cent in 1990-91. Foreign investment which amounted to a meagre $ 103 million in 1990-91 increased to $ 17224 million in 2005-06. Foreign direct investment increased from $ 97 million in 1990-91 to $ 4730 million in 2005-06, foreign institutional investment, of course, rose much faster: from zero in 1990-91, it reached a figure of $ 9926 million in 2005-06. Foreign exchanges reserves which were hardly enough for import cover of 2.5 months in 1990-91, rose to $ 180 billion as on 31 March, 2006, making for 16 months of a much larger (5.5 times of 1991) import cover.

A high rate of growth of GDP with a decline in the rate of population growth has obviously meant a significant increase in per capita income. If we take the Tenth Plan growth rate to be 7.5 per cent and population growth during 2002-07 as 1.5 per cent, per capita income has grown by about 6 per cent, an increase India has never seen or even envisaged before. Yet, it does not seem to have made a significant dent on poverty. No data on poverty are available exactly corresponding to the period of the Tenth Plan. But if the estimates for the Years 1999-2000 and 2004-05 from the NSSO Surveys are any indicators, the period with probably the highest growth in GDP and per capita income, has been also the one with lowest decline in poverty. Incidence of poverty which is estimated to be 22% during 2004-05, (comparable to 26% in 1999-2000) has declined only by 0.79 per cent per year over the five year period, when GDP growth has averaged at 6.5 per cent and per capita income growth at about 5 per cent.

It is obvious that the growth has been highly iniquitous. High rate of per capita income growth with very little reduction in poverty is in itself a sufficient proof of the iniquitous character of growth. Some recent estimates (by Himanshu and Mahendra Dev and Ravi, *EPW*, February 10, 2007) show that Gini Coefficient of consumption expenditure has increased substantially both in rural and urban areas during 1993-94/.,

Decomposing the change in incidence of poverty during this period, Mahendra Dev finds that in rural India, the growth by itself should have led to about 11 per cent decline in poverty, but increase in inequality adversely affected the impact of growth by about 3 per cent, thus reducing the extent of decline in incidence of poverty to only eight per cent. In urban areas, growth made a positive contribution of 12 per cent but inequality a negative contribution of four per cent, to the decline in poverty.

Inclusive Growth

That the growth has not benefited all sections of population has been recognized by the Prime Minister and the Planning Commission, in their recent emphasis on the need for a more inclusive growth, a term currently in vogue as another, probably more suggestive, expression for 'equitable' growth. The Prime Minister has recognized the need for an 'inclusive growth' in his recent speeches and the Planning Commission has brought it center stage by using it in the title of the Approach Paper for the Eleventh Plan, 'Towards Faster and More Inclusive Growth'. That is implied in this recognition is that a sizeable group of population has not been 'included' in and have, therefore, not benefited from growth. That there has been no 'trickle down' of growth does not seem to be a relevant, let above adequate explanation of this asymmetric process of growth. 'Trickle-down' can take place if the poor are also included in growth process. That is, they are engaged in economic activities that are growing, even though the non-poor may be the main actors and, therefore, main beneficiaries of growth. When certain groups of people are not even 'included' in the growth process, there is no question of the benefits of growth 'trickling-down' to them. In other words, in this situation, the notion of 'trickle-down' is not merely non-operational, it is irrelevant.

Slow Growth of Agriculture

A first step in making economic growth more inclusive is to identify the groups that have been excluded from the past growth and examine why they could not participate in the growth process in the first instance, we need to look at the composition of growth, in terms of sectors and activities. Here, a major reason for the iniquitous and non-inclusive growth is seen in the slow growth of agriculture. While the overall economy has grown at over 7 per cent, average growth of agricultural sector has been only around 1.5 per cent. And agriculture still employs 55 per cent workers and is the major source of livelihood for almost 60 per cent of population. Industry and Service sectors which have experienced much faster growth at around 9 and 10 per cent have not been able to draw many people away from agriculture in their employment and provide them the opportunity for raising their levels of living. As a result of the slow growth of agriculture, the large masses of rural population have remained insulated from the benefits of the high aggregate growth of the economy. Their exclusion has been further reinforced by the fact that urban-centered and high technology-based subsectors in industry and services have been the main engines of recent growth.

Inter-regional Differences

Side by side the rural-urban divide, growth in recent past has also been characterized by vast inter-regional differences in rates of growth. Not ony have the growth rates varied more widely in recent years, but there has been a systematic pattern in this variation: the better off States have experience faster growth while those at the bottom of the ladder of economic development have recorded lower growth. So, the States with high incidence of poverty and low levels of per capita income such as Assam, Bihar, Orissa and Uttar Pradesh registered a growth rate of 4 per cent or lower while Gujarat, Haryana, Maharashtra and Tamil Nadu had a growth rate of over 6 per cent per annum during 1990-2003. Punjab with a relatively low and Rajasthan with high rate of growth have been significant exceptions in this pattern.

Variations of growth rate have led to a widening of disparities in per capita SDP among states. Gini-coefficient of per capita SDP among 14 major states was measured to be 0.152 in 1980-81 and 0.171 in 1990-91, but at a much higher figure of

0.225 in 1997-98 (Ahluwalia, *EPW*, May 6, 2000). Coefficient of variation is measured to have increased from around 31 per cent in early eighties to 38 per cent towards the end of the 1990's. Maximum to minimum ratio has increased from 4.10 to 4.49 during the same period. The negative distance from the national average has increased in the case of the poorest states (Bihar from 60% to 65%, Uttar Pradesh from 29% to 40%, Madhya Pradesh from 31% to 42% and Orissa from 27% to 45%), and the positive distance of the richest states has shown an increase, with the exception of Punjab, Jammu and Kashmir had a per capita income that was 19 per cent higher than the national average in early eighties which had slided down to 28 per cent lower than all-India by the end of 1990's. (These figures are from Ashok Mathur, 'Spatial Income Inequality and Economic Development', paper presented at a Seminar at ISID, New Delhi, September 16-18, 2005).

State disparities in consumption levels are also found to have increased. Growth in per capita consumption expenditure has been less than 4 per cent in Assam, Orissa and West Bengal and over 20 per cent in Delhi, Punjab and Haryana during the seven-year period, 1993-2000. The range of variation in growth is very high: lowest being 1.7 per cent in Assam and highest 30.7 per cent in Delhi. There has been a decline in poverty in all states, but the rate of decline has been lower in states with high incidence and higher in those with low incidence of poverty. For example, Haryana recorded 20%, Punjab 11%, Gujarat and Tamil Nadu 9%, and Maharashtra 8% decline in rural poverty during 1993-94 to 1999-2000, the corresponding figure for Orissa is 0.68%, for Madhya Pradesh 1.49%, for Assam 1.89%, for Uttar Pradesh and West Bengal 4.27% and for Bihar 4.50%. As a result, the share of the six states—Bihar, Uttar Pradesh, Madhya Pradesh, West Bengal, Orissa and Assam—in all India population of rural poor increased from 69 per cent in 1993-94 to 74.4 per cent in 1999-2000 (S. Mahendra Dev, 'Regional Disparities in Poverty and Malnutrition', paper for the Seminar noted earlier).

The relative position in levels of development and SPD growth of different states has in the past closely corresponded to the levels and growth of agriculture, with a very few exceptions. Even with a decline in the contribution of agriculture to GDP to about 30 per cent by early 1990's and less than one fifth now, the importance of agriculture in determining a state's relative position does not seem to have disappeared. There was a highly striking similarity between rankings of states by per capita total and agricultural SDP, in 1992. Thus, Bihar had the lowest rank and Punjab the highest in both these variables. Uttar Pradesh held 14th rank and Haryana second in both and Orissa 16th in total and 15th in agricultural SDP. The symmetry between the ranks by agricultural and total per capita SDP has, however, less striking in 2003 than in early 1990's. Thus in 2003, Gujarat continues to hold 4th position in per capita SDP, but has receded from 5th to 11th position in respect of per capita agricultural SDP; Himachal Pradesh has now one rank lower (7) in total SDP but has slided down from 7th to 13th position in respect of agricultural SDP per capita. J&K had 9th and 10th rank respectively in agricultural and total SDP in 1992, in 2003, the two ranks are 6 and 12, respectively. Yet, Punjab holds first rank both in total and agricultural SDP; and, Haryana second in former and third in the latter. At the lower end, Bihar is at the bottom (17th) and Orissa the next lowest (16th) in both. UP holds 14th rank in both. *(These statements are based on the statistics from Anjani Kumar et al 'Agricultural Growth and Productivity: Inter-State Variations, and B.B. Bhattacharya and S. Shaktivel, 'Growing Apart', papers presented in the seminar noted earlier).*

Such a high symmetry in the two ranks in the case of these states notwithstanding, it can safely be said that over the past decade, agricultural sector is playing a smaller and non-agricultural sector an increasingly larger role in determining the position of a State in comparison to others. Still the contribution of a relatively high rate of agricultural growth has played a significant role in improving their relative position in the case of states like West Bengal, Madhya Pradesh, Karnataka and Maharashtra.

It is well known that relative levels and rates of growth of economic indicators in different states is to a very extent, a function of the levels and quality of infrastructure physical, economic and social. This assumes particular significance in the phase of development where poor states are likely to be able to achieve faster growth and thus bridge the gap with others, only by diversification of their economies, both within agriculture and into non-agricultural sectors. There are large disparities in the levels of physical and economic infrastructure across states. Overall index of infrastructure (comprised of indicators of transport, energy, irrigation, banking, communication, education and health facilities) with all-india as 100 was computed (by Centre for Monitoring Indian Economy) to be as low as 62 for Madhya Pradesh and highest at 207 for Punjab in 1980-81. Minimum to maximum ratio declined to 75 to 191 by 1993-94. Most poorer states, MP, Orissa, UP and Assam have moved closer to national average. Thus, it appears that inter-state disparities in infrastructure, have declined to some extent, though in most poorer states their levels and quality continue to be low. What is, however, particularly encouraging is that the disparities in human development indices are declining. One hopes that in the long-run, this change will contribute towards reduction in regional disparities in economic development as well.

States have large differences in resources endowments and infrastructure and are, therefore, bound to experience varying growth rates. But it is also possible that the liberalized economic policy regime and global orientation of growth, have specially favoured certain sectors, sub-sectors and activities for which larger potential existed in some States than in others. In so far as these sectors were the main contributors to growth, States with no or limited potential for their growth would have got excluded. For example, only a few States had the ready capacity and potential for fast growing sub-sectors like automobile industry and IT and IT enabled services; better developed States and areas are vastly better-off in this respect, and to the extent the new policy regime favoured their fast growth, those poorly endowed in this regard did not benefit from the growth of these sectors.

Towards More Inclusive Growth

After this brief overview of the emerging trends and pattern in inter-state disparities in development, let me raise some questions that I consider of both analytical interest and relevant for policy and strategies to bring about a more regionally balanced and, therefore, more 'inclusive' growth.

1. Is the Indian growth experience over the past two decades in line with the so-called "convergence hypothesis", according to which with an acceleration in the rate of growth, inequalities would initially widen as regions at already higher levels of development with their better endowment in resources, human development and infrastructure would grow faster than others; but after some time, the rates of growth would converge due to setting in of diminishing marginal returns which inturn would reduce the gap between the poorer and the richer regions? Is this sequence inevitable or there are theoretical models and empirical experiences suggesting modifications in it to make the poorer regions also contribute significantly to accelerated growth and thereby achieving a degree of convergence earlier than the eventual decline in marginal productivity of resources in the richer regions?
2. To what extent do the equalizing and inequalising effects of aggregate growth depend on its composition? For example, will the higher growth derived from faster growth in agriculture, rural non-farm sector or decentralized manufacturing be more equalizing than the one derived primarily from the growth of services sector and external trade? Has the growth induced by liberalization and globalisaton, therefore, been inherently inequalising due to their focus on trade and foreign investment?
3. What are the linkages between poverty reducing and employment generating and regionally equalizing characteristics of growth? Does growth that results in larger reduction in poverty and creation of employment also tends to be more equalizing among different states and regions? Also, why similar growth rates often have very different impact on poverty and employment in different states?
4. What are the prospects of a faster market led growth eventually reducing the regional disparities? Is there still need and scope for state initiative in terms

investment in infrastructure and fiscal and credit policies treating the lagging states preferentially?

5. What is the capability of these states to improve their infrastructure and investment climate and markets through public intervention? How have the central transfer of resources through Planning and Finance Commissions helped them to raise their capabilities in this regard? What has been the role of institutional and bank finance in inter-state variations in economic development?
6. In a market led growth process and competitive environment, should not the states, specially the smaller states and those facing special constraints (like the hill states) adopt a growth strategy relying on their comparative advantage, rather than trying to replicate a highly diversified product structure as in larger and better endowed states?
7. How far are the policies of individual poorer states responsible for their slow growth? Are there recent examples of policy reforms and institutional changes that have triggered-off faster growth of some states thus reducing the gap between them and the more advanced states?
8. What is the relationship and sequence in change in disparities in economic indicators and human development indicators? The question assumes particular significance in view of the observation that while inter-state disparity in most economic indicators has increased, that in indicators of human development has declined. In the light of the experience of states like Kerala which earlier was seen as economic laggard though socially advanced, has of late bridged the gap with the national average in economic terms as well, can one expect that a declining trend in disparity in human development indicators will eventually contribute to a convergence of economic growth rate and, therefore, a decline in economic disparity among states?

I also hope that these questions will be taken up by scholars in the field in their future research.

("*Reducing Imbalances in Regional Development: An Essential Ingredient of Strategy for Inclusive Growth*", Inaugural Address at the National Seminar on "Making Growth Inclusive with Special Reference to Imbalances in Regional Development", Department of Economics, University of Jammu, Jammu, 12-13 March 2007).

16

Financial Inclusion

V. JAGAN MOHAN

INTRODUCTION

The following views were voiced recently on financial inclusion and credit penetration in the banking industry.

> There are 93 million mobile users today. The number of mobile phones currently is more than the number of borrowers from the banking system. There is a clear need to increase the outreach and scale up operations at existing outlets.
>
> —*Ms. Usha Thorat, Deputy Governor, RBI at BANKCON.*

> The ratio between banks deposits/accounts operated and total adult population still remained low, even compared to other developing economies. The Indian national average is just 59 per cent compared to 92 per cent in UK. The mere opening of a bank account is not enough. Banks

> should offer all financial services tc those who open accounts. This would wean Rural India away from unorganized sector that charges high rates of interest.
>
> —*Mr. V. Leeladhar, Deputy Governor, RBI, at a meeting on May 21, 2006.*

> The overall percentage of deposit account penetration of 45 per cent for India is misleading as break-up of figures showed that Urban India has penetration of 114 per cent while the figure stood at dismal 19 per cent for Rural India. Interestingly, for 2006, 93 per cent of the borrowers in India borrowed less than Rs. 2 lakh and their share in terms of total outstanding credit was just 18 per cent.
>
> —*Mr. Bhaskar Ghose, MD, IndusInd Bank, at an IBA Seminar.*

> India is practically the only country in Asia with a virtual vacuum in the financial system after the large commercial banks.
>
> —*Mr. Sanjay Sinha, MD, MCRIL, an MFI rating agency, in an article on RRBs.*

The above viewpoints certainly spell out the need for a far deeper perspective on the current status of credit penetration and financial inclusion.

An effort is being made to provide that perspective on the basis of banking figures as on December 31, 2006 and from the growth trends in the years between December 31, 2001 and December 31, 2006 from the date provided by the RBI by various geographical and population segments (See Table 16.1).

The Perspective

The banking industry's size more than doubled, from Rs. 1,605,278 crore to Rs. 4,147,176 crore during last five years with the number of branches growing by 3,757, from 66,261 to 70,018. At the economy growth rate of 9 per cent-plus, the banking industry will double every four years. The share of the

TABLE 16.1

Banking Sector Growth between December 2001 and December 2006

	Number of Branches		Deposits (Rs. Crore)		Credit (Rs. Crore)		Credit/Deposit Ratio (CDR in %)	
	Dec. 2001	Dec. 2006	Dec. 2001	Dec. 2006	Dec. 2001	Dec. 2006	Dec. 2001	Dec. 2006
(1)	(2)	(3)	(4)	(5)	(6)	(7)	(8)	(9)
All India	66,261	70,018	1,021,129	2,367,968	584,149	1,779,208	57	75
Top 6 Metro Centres	5,888 (8.88)*	6,737 -962	356,701 -35	1,072,216 -45	309,730 -53	1,009,905 -56	86	94
Metro Centres	8,627 -13	11438 -16.3	433,347 -42	1,313,471 -55	355,413 -60	1,176,296 -66	82	89
Top 100 Centres (inclusive of metros)	14,867 -22	17,314 -24.7	600,670 -59	1,615,359 -68.2	439,286 -75	1,372,350 -77.1	73	85
Urban Centres (inclusive of Top 100 Centres)	19,133 -29	23,786 -34	670,365 -65	1,791,457 -75	455,997 -78	1,460,657 -82	68	81
Semi-Urban Centres	14,632 (22)	15,646 (22)	201,241 -19	331,280 -16	67,012 -11	173,246 -9.73	33	52
Rural Centres	32,496 -49	30,586 -44	149,522 -14	245,231 -10.3	61,139 -10	145,305 -8.1	41	59

* Figures in brackets indicate relative % share in all India figures.

Source : *RBI Quarterly Bulletin,* December 2006.

top six metros (Mumbai, New Delhi, Chennai, Kolkata, Bangalore and Hyderabad), in total deposits is 45 per cent and in credit 56 per cent.

This segment, with a population of 60 million (2001 Census), represents half the banking industry's size, at Rs. 2,082,121 crore, with 94 per cent CDR. The share of the metro segment, which includes 35 centres with a population of over 1 million, is 55 per cent of deposits and 66 per cent of credit. As many as 2,811 branches were opened in this segment (Rs. 2,489,767 crore or 60 per cent) with an approximate population of 100 million (2001 Census). Excluding the six metros, the remaining 29 metro centers contribute an additional 10 per cent share in deposits and 7 per cent in credit, indicating a lower penetration in these centres, with an approximate population of 40 million.

Other Urban Centres

As for the top 100 urban centres (inclusive of metros), their share is 68.2 per cent of deposits and 77.1 per cent of credit. The remaining 94 centres, with an approximate population of 90 million (excluding the six metros) contribute an additional 12.9 per cent share to deposits, and 10.7 per cent to credit. Assuming urban population of 280 million, as per Census 2001, the branches with a 34 per cent share in this segment contribute a high percentage of deposits and credit. The urban centres (excluding metros) representing a population of around 180 million contribute an additional share of 20 per cent in deposits and 18 per cent in credit.

The share of Semi-Urban Centres has decreased from 19.6 per cent to 14 per cent in deposits and from 11 per cent to 10 per cent in credit, with branch strength remaining at 22 per cent over the five years. The market size in the segment increased from Rs. 268,253 crore to Rs. 504,526 crore. The share of Rural Centres, over the five years, fell from 14.6 per cent to 10.5 per cent in deposits, and from 10.4 per cent to 8.3 per cent in credit. The branch strength declined by 1,910 whereas market size increased from Rs. 210,661 crore to Rs. 390,536 crore.

The Semi-Urban and Rural Centres, covering a population of 780 million, contribute 26.03 per cent of deposits and get

17.83 per cent of credit, with a combined CDR of 55 per cent *vis-a-vis* the national CDR of 75 per cent, Metro CDR of 89 per cent and Urban CDR of 81 per cent.

The Findings

The majority of India's population in the urban, semi-urban and rural areas thus appears to be still underserved by the banking industry, leading to financial exclusion. There are uneven levels of penetration in each population segment, more so at semi-urban and rural segments.

The Bottom of Pyramid (BOP) Financial System is also undergoing tremendous transformation. RRBs are being amalgamated, with consequent organizational, technological and managerial complexities.

The State cooperative banks are being restructured as suggested by the Vaidyanathan Committee recommendations. Urban cooperative banks in the hinterland are on a weak wicket, following the level playing field regulatory norms. Commercial banks are finding it difficult to staff the vacant positions in the rural branches with personnel who have local and rural sensitivities. The BOP of the financial system is not structurally enabled to contribute to the macro-objectives of financial inclusion and credit penetration. The situation certainly calls for some bold out-of-box initiatives.

17

Need for Financial "Deepening"

C.J. PUNNATHARA

INTRODUCTION

There are happy tidings for the country's financial inclusion policy. In a recent speech in London, Ms Usha Thorat, Deputy Governor, Reserve Bank of India, revealed that between March 2006 and 2007 as many as 60 lakh no-frills bank accounts were opened. While this is, no doubt, a creditable achievement for the banks, it is still too early to call for celebrations. There still remains a vast and untapped rural heartland, waiting for financial inclusion.

Financial Deepening

While the no-frills account was perceived as the spring-board for financial inclusion, such inclusiveness is but the stepping-stone to another broader goal—that of financial deepening. For this, the newly empowered bank customers should be enabled to extend their finance activity into an array of products, leading to all round economic development. The endeavour of governments and banks should be to ensure that no-frill accounts are not left idle, but are kept active. Once such customers graduate from a savings bank account to loan products and, later, perhaps to a bouquet of financial products, the country can claim financial deepening. Thus, it is not just the numbers that count, but also the quality of the new no-frills accounts opened. According to disaggregated data, 59 per cent of the country's adult population have bank accounts. But there is a flaw. The percentage is arrived by dividing the total number of bank accounts by the number of adult population and does not take into account the possibility of one person having more than one bank account.

No 'Deepening'

So, the number is likely an inflated one. But it indicates that two in every three adults have a bank account. However, in rural India, the percentage of those without a bank account is 61. An important question is: Are the newly opened no-frills accounts actively operated? Indications are that just a few are active. And even among these, most are proving to be a repository of savings, rather than creating demand for new loans and other products. This is evidenced by the fact that only 14 per cent of the account-holders also have a loan account, while 59 per cent have only savings bank accounts. The picture is bleaker in rural India, where only 9.5 per cent have a loan account.

Though tremendous progress has been achieved, the plight of rural India continues to be alarming as far as financial inclusion and financial deepening are concerned. Of the 203 million households in the country, over 72 per cent numbering 147 million—are in rural India; 89 million are farm households. As many as 73 per cent of these farm households have no access to formal credit. And 51 per cent have no access to any form of credit.

Changing Pattern

According to the All-India Debt and Investment Survey carried out by the National Sample Survey Organisation, there has been a sea change in credit disbursement since Independence. In 1951, non-institutional credit accounted for 92.7 per cent of the total debt. Of this, as much as 69.7 per cent came from money-lenders. By 2002, the share of non-institutional credit fell to 38.9 per cent, with 26.8 per cent still coming from moneylenders.

In 1951, institutional credit comprised a paltry 7.3 per cent, of which 3.3 per cent came from cooperative banks and 0.9 per cent from commercial banks. By 2002, however, institutional credit grew to 61 per cent, of which 30 per cent was from cooperative banks and 26 per cent from commercial banks. Going by these numbers, the country seems to have made marked progress towards financial inclusion. But while the figures might look impressive, the actual number of people who receive credit is still paltry—just 9.5 per cent of the rural population, or 14 per cent of the total population.

Surprisingly, between 1991 and 2002, the extension of institutional credit suffered a setback, falling from 66 per cent to 61 per cent. In its place, non-institutional credit grew from 30 percent (1991) to 39 per cent (2002). And, more significantly, moneylenders seem to have made a comeback, their share growing from 17 per cent to 26 per cent. No doubt, these data are a bit dated. What we need to know is, are non-institutional creditors and moneylenders 're-tightening' their grip of the economy? Preliminary indications are that this may not be so. The growth of 60 lakh no-frills accounts last year is one indicator. Also, evidence comes from the resurgent growth in agricultural credit, by 90 per cent from Rs. 90,541 crore to Rs. 1,72,292 crore between 2004 and 2006.

It is still too early for the financial sector to rest on its laurels. For nurturing greater equity and accelerating economic development, the early gains in inclusion should be transformed into financial deepening as well.

II

BANKING ON A RURAL SHIFT

With banks continuing to veer away from rural to urban India, the number of rural bank branches has shrunk even as urban branches proliferate, and the Government pays lip-service to financial deepening and economic inclusion. As a percentage of the total network, rural branches have shown a perceptible decline over the last seven years. Does this mean the end of the road for financial inclusion? Not necessarily. Even as the number of new bank branches continues to be urban-centric, the smaller numbers that continue to grow in rural pockets are attracting growing business volumes. And there are other dynamics at work that may yet make inclusion a successful proposition.

There can be no doubt that Rural India is still under-represented in the banking industry. While 50 per cent of all commercial bank branches were in rural regions in June 2000, the share declined to 44.2 per cent in June 2006. Rural branch expansion has been far behind the growth in the urban centres.

Not surprisingly, even in absolute numbers, while there were 32,709 rural branches of commercial banks in 2000, the number fell to 30,754 in 2006. Does this imply that banks have been closing rural branches and re-locating to urban India? Given the Government's firm commitment to financial inclusion as well as RBI's strong diktats against rural branch closures, this seems unlikely. Also these numbers run counter to the reports of economic resurgence in rural India, as financial institutions rush to exploit newer economic opportunities.

Getting Reclassified

There are two possible explanations for the decline in the number of rural bank branches. One, that rural pockets are getting subsumed into ever-expanding urban sprawls, or villages are themselves transforming into smaller townships—driven by their inherent economic dynamism.

According to the banking lexicon, bank branches are categorized as 'rural' when they are located in areas with a population of 10,000 or less. As development activities accelerate, attracting a fresh stream of migrant workers, rural pockets graduate into smaller cities and townships—and rural bank branches are automatically re-classified as urban branches. No doubt, the process will accelerate financial deepening.

Therefore, one should use greater discretion when reading of State Bank of India and associate banks' losing 285 rural branches between 2000 and 2006. And of nationalized banks losing 904 branches in the same period. As if to reinforce the point, even regional rural banks, which account for one out of three rural branches, lost 1,030 rural branches. While the penchant among banks to focus on urban India remains as strong as ever, the economic awakening of pastoral India is forcing several of them to sit up and take notice. This is evident in the slow but subtle shifts in the banking sector's credit portfolio. Between March 2004 and 2006, deployment of credit to the farm sector grew 90 per cent, from Rs. 90,541 crore to Rs. 1,72,292 crore.

Viable Activity

This is not only an indicator of greater financial inclusion and deepening, but also that agriculture is no longer taboo to large sections of the banking industry. In effect, agriculture in India is maturing into a viable economic activity and, in several instances, government stipulation is no longer required for extension of credit.

By comparison, the extension of credit to small, medium and large-scale industry in India remains huge, although the growth is at a relatively slower pace. Between 2004 and 2006, credit to industry grew by 75 per cent, from Rs. 3,13,065 crore to Rs. 5,49,057 crore.

Ipso facto, the growing focus on agriculture and allied services by the banking industry is not necessarily a proof of greater financial inclusion. Nor does the falling number of rural branches stand testimony to the reverse. There seems to be inherent merit in the argument that greater numbers are getting into the economic mainstream as rural pockets merge into the urban areas and others upgrade into smaller towns and cities. But there are other dynamics at work in rural India that herald an accelerated pace of economic development. There are clear indicators that, as bank branches proliferate across urban India at the cost of the hinterland, the demand for more rural branches is growing.

In a recent speech, the RBI Deputy Governor, Ms. Usha Thorat, said that from 1991 to 2001 to 2005, the population served by a bank branch grew from 13,711 people to 15,209 and 15,680. Significantly, the growth was even more meteoric in the case of rural branches, where it jumped from 13,462 people to 15,667 to 16,650. The urban branches, meanwhile, showed a decline from 14,484 to 14,137 to 13,619. This is a clear indication that the rural population is growing, leading to increased demand for banking services.

Buoyed by an ebullient rural awakening, savings from rural India surged by 31 per cent. Simultaneously, urban-rural remittances have increased as migrant populations began sending back their earnings to the villages. And in many areas, subsistence agriculture is increasingly giving way to commercial farming, such as horticulture and floriculture—requiring substantial capital infusion, and often technology transfer.

Reflecting on this transformation occurring in rural India, the National Council for Applied Economic Research (NCAER) has said that the low-income population in rural India has come down from around 65 per cent during the early 1990s to 25 per cent now. Meanwhile, middle-income households in rural India have gone up from 33 per cent to 70 per cent. Almost 50 million households have transcended from the low-income to the middle-income bracket in this period.

Affluent Hinterland

This is reflected in a sudden spurt in demand from India's increasingly assertive and affluent hinterland. Rural India now accounts for 53 per cent of the fast moving consumer goods market. Even more telling, close to 59 per cent of demand for consumer durables emanates from rural India. And going by common logic, the rural middle-class population would, rather than approach a moneylender for financing his purchase of a refrigerator, television, two-wheeler or car, prefer going to a bank or an NBFC.

The rural aversion of the banking industry is a historical legacy. Traditionally rural branches were loss-making, poorly run, poorly staffed—in short, an economic liability. That no longer seems to be the case but most banks are yet to lose that inherent aversion. As economic opportunities mushroom across rural India and the banking sector continues to slumber, the non-banking financial companies are awakening to the booming demand from rural households for refrigerators, television sets, air-conditioners, two-wheelers and cars. As the demand arises from deep in the vast hinterland, the NBFCs are making more aggressive inroads into the rural areas.

No doubt, rural banking had a pioneering role to play in sowing the seeds of development in India's agrarian society, but few of those nationalized banks are reaping the rich rewards now. If they do not look smart, they could lose the vital first-mover advantage.

18

The Eleventh Plan and Human Resource Development

BHANOJI RAO

INTRODUCTION

On June 14, 2006 the Planning Commission brought out the 92-page Eleventh Plan Approach Paper. The Paper focuses on achieving high growth and better living standards for the people. The nation can close the books on the Tenth Plan celebrating the achievements on economic growth, savings, investment and foreign exchange reserves. The achievement on economic growth was the result of the joint effort of public and private sectors, with an increasing share of the latter. Post-1991, the share of the private sector in the economy has been growing and now accounts for 70-75 per cent of the total investment. The output share of the private sector is, perhaps, higher, at around 80 per cent, since the government can be presumed to invest in long gestation projects.

11th Plan Targets

The Approach Paper places the economic growth target at 8.5 per cent for the Eleventh Plan with the following growth rates for the key sectors: Agriculture 3.9 per cent; industry 9.9 per cent; and services 9.4 per cent. The Paper correctly notes that the targeted high growth should be accompanied by "a major effort to provide access to basic facilities such as health, education, clean drinking water, etc., to large sections of the population which do not have such access at present".

The seven challenges, according to the Paper, are: Providing essential public services for the poor; regaining agricultural dynamism; increasing manufacturing competitiveness; developing human resource; protecting the environment; improving rehabilitation and resettlement practices; and improving governance.

Human Resource Development (HRD) and improving governance hold the key for all-round progress of the economy and the people and have a direct or indirect bearing on achievements in every economic and social sector.

Human Resource Development

The Paper, in its final form, and the Plan itself, should give particular attention to building world-class schools in the public sector and endowing them with the best teachers. Addressing the drop-out rate in primary schools (around 31 per cent in 2003-04) and meager learning outcomes (55 per cent of children with four years of schooling cannot perform simple division) require concerted action to create attractive school infrastructure and well-paid teachers, the pay being attractive enough to ensure good performance and commitment.

Vast Pool of Trained Human Power

It is a sad commentary on our over five-decade-old socialist ideals that "private aided and unaided schools account for 58 per cent of the total number of secondary schools" and "their proportion is actually increasing at a faster pace than public-funded schools, mainly because State governments have

Macro-economic Performance Indicators

	9th Plan (1997-98 to 2001-02)	Four years of 10th Plan (2002-03 to 2005-06)
GDP growth (%) of which	5.5	7.0
Agriculture	2.0	1.8
Industry	4.6	8.0
Services	8.1	8.9
Gross Domestic Savings as % of GDP	23.1	28.2
Difference (current account balance)	0.7	0.7
Fiscal Deficit of Centre and States as % of GDP	8.8	8.4
Foreign Exchange Reserves (US $ billion) at the beginning of the period	54.2	151.6
Inflation rate (wholesale prices)	4.9	4.8

nearly stopped increasing funding of public secondary schools and aided schools."

It is gratifying that the Eleventh Plan hopes to evolve strategies for secondary schooling that will emphasise the public responsibility. In this context, building first-class standardized school infrastructure and offering good pay for the teachers apply equally well to the secondary education sector. The failings multiply in technical/vocational education. Just about "3 per cent of the rural youth (15-29 years) and 6 per cent of the urban youth have gone through a formal course of vocational training of any kind". Secondary schooling should be integrated with technical/vocational education for ensuring a vast pool of trained manpower. What is needed is a right policy and massive expansion of technical institutions.

Problems in Higher Education

The Approach Paper, thus, identifies the crucial problems

in higher education: First, only about 8 per cent of the relevant age group goes to university compared to 20-25 per cent in many developing countries; second, our institutions are generally not of high standard, though we have islands of excellence; and, third, even the best institutions are finding it difficult to get quality faculty.

The Eleventh Plan objectives and strategies in higher education contained in the Paper can be summarized thus: Setting up new colleges and universities and strengthening existing institutions; encouraging open and distance education; upgrading a few "existing" select universities (at least 20) with "potential for excellence"; increasing enrolment in universities and colleges, especially premier institutions such as the IITs and IIMs; and addressing the problems of varying standards, outdated syllabi, inadequate facilities, and most of all the need to create an environment that will attract top class faculty.

"Achievement of these objectives will require a substantial increase in resources devoted to this sector and successive annual Plans will have to provide rising levels of budgetary support. However, this must be accompanied by internal resource generation by duly and realistically raising fees. Simultaneously, efforts will be made to develop a wider merit-*cum*-means based loan and scholarship programmes through the banking system and other agencies," says the paper.

Creating a Talent Pool

As part of the Eleventh Plan, a bold investment programme is needed to nurture world-class talent pool available for faculty positions, not only in premier institutions but elsewhere too. Ten-thousand fellowships a year with an annual expense of a billion dollars would go a long way in creating a sizeable talent pool. The fellowships must be exclusively for doctoral programmes in top universities in the US and Europe. A minimum six years service in India must be insisted upon of students completing the doctoral programme.

Role of the Private Sector

What is the role of the private sector in higher education?

The Approach Paper bears no mention to this. Away from all existing models of regulation and approvals, the Planning Commission should come up with innovative ideas to ensure an enabling environment with zero corruption for private institutions to thrive in higher education.

Governance

Under the challenge of 'improving governance', it is heartening to read the following: "Corruption is now seen to be endemic in all spheres and this problem needs to be addressed urgently." "Quick and inexpensive dispensation of justice is an aspect of good governance which is of fundamental importance in a successful civil society."

Top priority to corruption control is vital to ensuring private and public sector efficiency for the following reasons: To minimize hidden transaction costs; to ensure that human energy is spent in a value-adding and productive manner; to promote investment from the best and efficient sources rather than those that bribe the authorities; and to promote human development by getting the best from health and educational expenditure by the government and the people.

Part III

ISSUES IN INCLUSIVE GROWTH

19

Can GDP Growth Do Everything?

S. Iyyampillai

INCLUSIVE GROWTH

The concept "Inclusive Growth" (IG) finds place more frequently in the debate and discussion in the Parliament, in the speeches of our political leaders and policy-makers, particularly of our President, Prime Minister [PM] and Finance Minister [FM], more particularly since March 2007. Also varied inclusions such as financial inclusion, social inclusion, educational inclusion, health inclusion, employment inclusion are found in the mass media. Books on "Inclusive Growth" [Ashoka Mody, 2006] are published. It is really a surprise for those who are keenly observing the Indian economy as to how all of sudden the policy-makers have started thinking of including the downtrodden people into the growth process. Two things are clear from this change in the thinking process. One, the increased growth rate of Gross Domestic Product (GDP), which was expected to solve the problems in India, has miserably failed to yield the results desired by the advocates of market-led and private sector-led growth; it is a disappointment. Two, unless something else is done, the higher growth rate of GDP alone cannot solve such problems of the ordinary people as poverty, illiteracy, ill-health, unemployment, social unrest and terrorism; it is a good lesson, though late. The PM of India, Manmohan Singh [MS] himself has accepted the following. United Progressive Alliance [UPA] government aimed at promoting "inclusive growth" as it recognized that high national income growth alone did not address the challenge of employment promotion, poverty reduction and balanced regional development or improving human development [*The Hindu*, 23.5.07, p. 1.].

Ground Realities

The most modest estimate by the Food and Agriculture Organization is that India's army of hungry grew by 13 million between 1995-97 and 2000-02. This constitutes nearly three fourths of the newly hungry across the world. Under this situation, on 6th January 2006, Union Cabinet took a cruel and harsh decision to cut food subsidy under Public Distribution System to the tune of Rs. 4,524 crores per year and to raise the price of grains for Above Poverty Line category. This would further cut present availability of 35 kg. food-grains against the requirement of 60 kg. per family per month. Reduction in per capita food grain consumption has already been reported by many including C.H. Hanumantha Rao, former Member, Union Planning Commission of India. It is estimated that it would affect around 20 crore people [Asad Bin Saif, 2006].

Underlining the importance of agriculture, C. Rangarajan, the Chairman of Prime Minister's Economic Advisory Council has said on June 6th, 2007 that the Indian economy was witnessing "cyclical overheating" but expected the inflation rate to soften in the coming months with good monsoon this year [*The Hindu*, 7.6.2007, p. 17]. Hence, it is the monsoon that determines many things even in the modern (?) India!

Aseem Shrivastava [2007] observes that the present kind of growth can never trickle down. Historically unprecedented economic growth in India during the last decade of reforms will continue to remain exclusive, leave poverty and malnutrition unaffected and lead to growing social tensions unless reshaped by democratic political process. Government should increase allocations for such re-distributive development programmes as the National Rural Employment Guarantee Scheme (whose allocation remains stagnant at a merely Rs. 12,000 crores this year) or the Integrated Child Development Scheme (whose allocation remains miserly at Rs. 4,800 crores. Development must be equitable if it is to be sustainable. Job-destroying growth has to be replaced by job generating growth.

The Trade Policy Review, a 186-page document prepared by the World Trade Organisation (WTO) Secretariat has pointed out the following facts (Moana Bhagabati, 2007). Decline in the share of agriculture and allied activities in India's GDP from 23 per cent in 2000-01 to 18 per cent in 2005-06 and the consequent distress among small and marginal farmers. In agriculture low labour productivity, fragmented landholdings, poor mechanisation, inadequate public investment in infrastructure and research and dependence on rainfall. Stagnant share of 16 per cent of GDP by the manufacturing sector.

The Economic Survey tabled in Parliament on 27th February 2007 has expressed concern over the increasing rate of unemployment, despite the economy expanding rapidly, and asked the government to tap the manufacturing sector for creating more jobs [*The Hindu*, 28.2.2007, 2007]. Jeemol Unni and Raveendran [2007] have reported that over the long-term, employment growth slowed slightly in 1993-2004, compared to 1983-93; the slowdown is quite marked in rural India. . . . There has been a substantial increase in self-employment, much of which is poorly remunerated and for the first time in decades, there has been a decline in the real wage rates of regular salaried workers and urban casual workers.

With published data available from the 61st round [2004-05] of the National Sample Survey [NSS], analysis over the period 1983-2005 shows unambiguously that in spite of higher overall growth, the extent of decline in poverty in the post-reform period [1993-2005] has not been higher than in the pre-reform period [1983-93]. The second clear conclusion is that inequality has increased significantly in the post-reform period and seems to have slowed down the rate of poverty reduction [Mahendra Dev and Ravi, 2007]. To Himanshu [2007], preliminary estimates from the published reports of the 61st round of the NSS suggest that while poverty did reduce during 1993-2005, the annual rate of reduction in this period was lower than that in the 1970s and 1980s.

The present pattern of development in India is bound to increase the number of Indians in the Billionaires Club of the world and also number of people below poverty line. On 11th March 2006 the news papers in the front page carried the report that during the year 2005-06, the number of billionaires in the world rose by 102 to a record 793. Combined wealth of these people grew by 18 per cent to $ 2.6 trillion, which is 3.7 times the GDP of India [John M. Itty, 2006].

The recent experience of failure of the government to control inflation through the traditional fiscal [cut in duties to essential commodities like cement], monetary [revision of repo rate and Cash Reserve Ratio] and trade [cut in import duties] policies only indicate the economic strength enjoyed by the private business persons. It is the corporate sector which does every thing and, the government has almost lost its control on economic activities. In this context, it would be pertinent to quote Patnaik [*The Hindu*, 14.12.2006, p. 4]. Addressing a national seminar on developmental divides organized by the Department of Economics of Stella Maris College in Chennai on 13th December 2006, Prabhat Patnaik explained how international financiers could now dictate fiscal policy by threatening to move money out of a country, precipitating a liquidity crisis, if that country's government failed to curtail its expenditure. "Because financiers are international, while governments are national, they hold the upper hand". This is just opposite to the Keynesian view. According to Keynesian demand management economics, it was interventionist government expenditure that fuelled economic growth and reduced unemployment. However, all over the capitalist world, including India, because of the liberalization of financial flows, governments are forced to cut back on their spending. MS also agrees to this. He says, "In the last year the growth processes we unleashed have put some pressure on prices. We have been faced with galloping demand for many products. This has resulted in inflation becoming a cause for concern, particularly in the case of essential commodities. This has been compounded by a shortfall in production of these commodities" [*The Hindu*, 23.5.07, p. 1.]. In her address, Sonia Gandhi said people in villages were looking to the government to improve their living standards and emphasized that ensuring social and economic justice for all was still a goal to be achieved.

In India, agriculture is the backbone of the livelihood security system for 70 crore of our people and a basic requisite for national sovereignty. However, as Swaminathan [2007] says, "the well-fed individuals in government bhavans" do not recognize this fact. There are hardly any worthwhile steps mentioned in the Report to the People (2004-07) presented by the PM on behalf of the UPA on May 22, 2007, for improving the productivity of small farms, or for generating more income and employment opportunities. On 29th May 2007, at the 53rd meeting of the National Development Council [NDC] the PM acknowledged the following:

(1) Agriculture sector was suffering from a "technology fatigue" for lack of break-through in production.
(2) Small and marginal farming has become an unviable proposition and till we make farming viable, it would be impossible to reduce rural poverty and distress.
(3) To achieve a four per cent annual growth in the farm sector during the 11th Plan, the NDC adopted a resolution that announced a Rs. 25,000 crore additional Central Assistance Scheme over four years to 'incentivise' States to invest more in agriculture [Gargi Parsai, 2007]. If this additional central assistance of Rs. 25,000 crore is worked out per farmer per year it comes around only Rs. 100 which is pea-nut, considering the requirement.

Realisation

In this context it would be pertinent to quote some of the observations made by the leaders-*cum*-policy-makers, in India. Addressing the Business-world-FICCI-SEDF Corporate Social Responsibility awards function, President A.P.J. Abdul Kalam said the following on 7th May 2007 [*The Hindu*, 8.5.2007, p. 16]:

The corporate and industrial houses could make an important contribution by adopting the schools, particularly in rural areas in their region, and providing infrastructure for the schools in the form of clean drinking water, toilet and transportation facilities, building sport complexes and providing computing facilities. He asked the corporate leaders and industrial houses to ensure that the fruits of development and modernization reach those living in rural hinterland. He exhorted the corporate India to understand their responsibility towards children living in rural and semi-urban India and contribute towards their growth and well-being. He hopes that this type of support to government will improve the quality of education to the children in the rural and semi-urban areas, leading to development of enlightened citizens. The support for developing quality human resource with embedded value system is an important social responsibility mission since it creates the human asset for the nation. Kalam is perfectly correct. During the post-budget interaction with members of the Associated Chambers of Commerce and Industry of India, the FM P. Chidambaram [PC] said the following [*The Hindu*, 9.3.07, p. 14]: "When we are promising 1,00,000 jobs to the physically challenged, it is a challenge not only for the Government but also for you. I did not hear any one of you speak about how you will provide jobs to physically challenged persons". The FM is also perfectly correct. But, which corporate sector will do all such non-profit maximizing social service? These are irrational propositions for the corporate sector, as per market economic theories.

During the commemoration of the first War of Independence of 1857 at the historic Central Hall of Parliament on 10th May 2007 [Neena Vyas, 2007], the PM said that it was "our responsibility to ensure that a new prosperous India was inclusive as well as caring". That is, he wants the economically rich to care for the economically poor! But, when the so-called rich always feel greater insecurity and inadequacy of wealth they have amassed, how can they be expected to help the self-contented poor? Rich in India will never reach satiety. So, they cannot be expected to share any thing with anybody, even among their own people; also they will not care anybody nor care for anybody. They are known for all kinds of economic crimes. On 7th March 2007, the FM, PC warned corporate against evasion of excise duty [*The Hindu*, 8.3.2007]. There is another example, female feoticide. Rich are more worried about having a girl child than a poor. That is why, rich states like Punjab and Delhi are having worst sex ratios against female in the country [Anima, 2007].

At a function to mark the completion of three years of UPA government, at the PM's residence, in New Delhi on 22nd May 2007, the PM listed out seven key components in his strategy of "inclusive growth" [*The Hindu*, 23.5.2007, p. 14]. They are:

(1) stepping up investment in rural areas and agriculture;
(2) increasing credit availability to farmers;
(3) increasing rural employment;
(4) increasing public spending on education, health care and strengthening the mid-day meal scheme;
(5) investing in urban renewal;
(6) empowering the Scheduled Caste/Tribes and other backward classes, minorities, women and children socially, economically and educationally; and
(7) ensuring that through public investment the growth process spreads to backward regions and districts.

These are not very new; these are the demands that have been cried for long.

The PM, in the annual session of the Confederation of Indian Industry (CII) on 24th May 2007 cautioned [*The Hindu*, 25.5.2007, p. 1] the corporates against any form of cartelisation, while noting that efforts to maximize profits should be within the bounds of "decency and greed". "The operation of cartels by groups of companies to keep prices high must end. It is unacceptable to obstruct the forces of competition from having freer play. It is even more distressing in a country where the poor are severely affected by rising prices". While attempting to enhance profits, the private sector should show some self-restraint. The business community should resist excessive remuneration to promoters and executives so as to reduce conspicuous consumption, because these aspects could sow the seeds of social unrest. "Even maximization of profit should be within the bounds of decency and greed". Advocating the

"10-point social charter" for sharing the benefits of economic growth with the less privileged and partnering the government to create a humane and just society, the Prime Minister reminded the corporate sector of its social responsibilities to the common man. "Corporate social responsibility must not be defined by tax planning strategies alone". Corporate sector must also facilitate more employment. To be globally competitive, the corporate sector must work in a harmonious environment, an environment in which all citizens feel actually involved in economic growth and in which each citizen sees hope for a better future". Unless workers felt they were cared for, "we can never evolve a national consensus in favour of more flexible labour laws aimed at ensuring that our firms remain globally competitive". Among other things, industry must have a healthy respect for workers, and invest in their welfare, health and their children's education. These alone will result in socially, politically, environmentally and financially sustainable growth.

In sharp reaction to the PM's observations mentioned above, the Confederation of Indian Industry's chief Sunil Mittal on 25th May 2007 [*The Hindu*, 26.5.2007, p.17] expressed his view that the Chief Executive Officers' [CEO] salaries could not be limited. In his response to the observations made by the Prime Minister, who favoured breaks on 'cartelisation' and corporate 'greed' and high salaries of the CEOs, Mittal, asserted that salaries could not be legislated. Mittal also said that there should be a correlation between the size of a company and the salaries to their employees.

Corporate sector's sole aim is maximizing its profit and not serving the poor people. Though corporate sector knows that in the long-run, it cannot survive in the absence of workers and consumers, accumulation of profit by cutting down the wages wherever possible [particularly at the lower strata] is its policy. Many reactions to the PM's observations were recorded. Some of them are: The expenditure incurred on convoys used by Ministers and high officials is also a waste, while at the same time the funds allotted for welfare schemes are not fully utilized, as reported by the Comptroller and Audit General of India. PM's colleagues should be restrained from releasing full-page advertisements even for routine matters. It is his [MS's] government, which has created corporate landlordism by providing facilities and concessions to those industries, which are manufacturing for the rich, thus abetting the vulgar display of wealth.

The FM, PC made the following observations in the annual session of the Confederation of Indian Industry on 24th May 2007 [*The Hindu*, 25.5.2007, p. 16]. Industries should desist from arbitrary hikes in prices by exploiting the prevailing demand-supply mismatch. Pricing power has returned to industry and pricing power is being exercised by industry. We appeal to industry not to exercise pricing powers arbitrarily. Incapacity of the states and administration cannot be a ground to blame growth; if high growth is not inclusive, low growth will be more non-inclusive. Again the FM appears to be very correct in his observations. There is absolutely no problem with higher GDP growth rate. But the problem is this. What are produced? For whom are they produced? Is a vast majority excluded by the market, particularly commodity and labour markets? If so, what is development and for whom? Majority Indians lived as illiterate, sick, unproductive, unemployed and poor; and, they continue to be so irrespective of higher growth rates of GDP. However, the problem with the higher growth rate is increasing chasm of economic inequality, conspicuous consumption, social unrest, terrorism and so on. Market welcomes production of more liquor, drugs, intoxicants, tobacco, weapons for, they could fetch more profit. It is absolutely economically rational. But, will this rational decision help those who cannot earn money, say children and the old people? In this context, the observations made by Prabhat Patnaik, former Professor at Jawaharlal Nehru University and present Vice-Chairperson, Kerala State Planning Commission, while delivering the lecture on "Illusions of Economic Growth" organised by Vichara's School of People's Economics at Kottayam on 14th April, 2007 [Prabhat Patnaik, 2007] are apt.

As per records, during Nehruvian period, nutritional standard of the people was higher when annual average growth rate of GDP was just 3.5 Per cent only than today, when it is 9.2 per cent. Employment was growing when growth rate was 3.5 per cent; it is declining when the latter increases. High growth rate is not a sufficient condition for poverty reduction. Recently along with the growth of GDP, the number of jobless people also increases. As a result, bargaining power of the workers deteriorates with the resulting fall in real wages. When market forces are given a free hand in the decision-making process, technologies that improve per labour productivity by reducing the labour force are introduced. Structural and technological changes followed by neo-liberal policy do not generate demand for employment. As a result, real wage even in the organized sector does not increase in tune with the increase in productivity and consequently unemployment and under-employment increase. Widening of inequality and growing poverty are the net results of this situation.

The following statement made by the Minister of State for Labour and Employment, Oscar Fernandes on 24th May 2007, clearly indicates the least priority given to the social security measures [*The Hindu*, 25.5.2007, p. 1]. Social security for the unorganized sector was a commitment made by the UPA in its National Common Minimum Programme. It was to be introduced in the budget session but this could not be done because Parliament was adjourned earlier than scheduled! God must be thanked.

Why is it so?

How was India able to achieve higher growth rate of GDP within a short span of time, while the same country with almost same government at the centre could not do the same for about 40 years sine 1950? If GDP shows real growth, why did the increased GDP fail to mitigate the problems of ill-health, illiteracy, unemployment, poverty, social unrest and terrorism? Is it true with all the countries or only with India? How the advanced countries could solve their economic problems? Certainly there are some magic with the GDP figures. Those really interested in the people's well-being could easily understand the magic. Production of more weapons, drugs, tobacco and destruction of buildings also increase the GDP.

Amartya Sen has analyzed these issues. Releasing a book, "Locked Homes, Empty Schools: The Impact of Seasonal Migration on the Rural Poor", on 20th December 2006 [*The Hindu*, 21.12.2006, p. 13], Sen said that the market economy was here to stay but could not be relied upon for developmental tasks. He further said that the market economy would neither run the village hostel for children whose parents have to move out of their homes every year to make a living nor would they run schools for their children at the sites where they were employed.

However, Adam Smith in his book, The Wealth of Nations [1776] claimed that in a capitalist system an individual acting on his own good tends also to promote the good of his community. He called this social mechanism "the invisible hand". Nobel laureates Arrow and Debreu in 1952 proved Adam Smith's conjecture that the capitalist form of economic organization, based on competitive markets, is superior to alternative forms of economic organizations is valid only under certain conditions. Economies of scale in production, externalities in production and consumption, presence of public goods and uncertainty can cause "market failures". Can a world of certainty ever exist? It is impossible. Hence market failure is always certain.

In 1936, Keynes argued a case for government intervention to achieve economic stabilization. Welfare economists justify interventionist policies to correct "market failures" and to achieve equity. Adam Smith envisaged only three functions of the state: to protect society from foreign invaders, and every member from oppression and injustice by other members of society, and to provide public goods. These three functions would cause economies of scale in production and create externalities in production and consumption, and hence, would definitely lead to market failures. These market failures would be capitalized by the rich while the poor would fail to do so, resulting in wider economic inequalities and injustice.

Market failure *versus* government failure is a very long debate. The ideological differences go on widening, not shrinking, with the recent experiences in India and elsewhere too. Recently a book "A Journey in Time and Space" edited by Raj Kapila and Uma Kapila was reviewed by C.T. Kurien [2006]. It is a star-studded volume as can be seen from the list of contributors—Jagdish Bhagwati, A. Vaidyanathan, Montek Singh Ahluwalia, Bimal Jalan, V.S. Vyas, C.H. Hanumantha Rao, M.S. Swaminathan, R. Nagaraj, C. Rangarajan, S.S. Tarapore and

Y.V. Reddy and other writers. The PM has praised the book in the following words: "The list of contributors includes some of our most distinguished and eminent economists. Each one of them has contributed immensely to the analysis of India's economic condition and to policy formulation in their respective areas of expertise. . . . I hope these essays will continue to educate and illuminate our thinking on economic policy in India". "But going through the volume", Kurien, one of the few right thinking economists today, writes, "one gets the uncomfortable feeling that the paradox has not been adequately addressed by any of the contributors". This volume has a brilliant collection of essays, however, does not even indicate that there is an important task of including the people who would be excluded by the market forces. Kurien says that the contributors continue to sing the same old song that follows as:

1. "If the economy grows rapidly enough the benefits will reach all sections of the population".
2. "If the state concentrates on public goods such as defence and the administration of justice, if necessary add education and health services, leaving the rest of the economy to the private sector, everybody will find ways of making a living". There is, however, no empirical support so far.
3. "The market forces may tend to increase inequality but can surely wipe out poverty".

Market will function only on the basis of economic power, and, that will lead to economic inequality. If economic power is unequal in an economic system, production will be guided by that inequality. This inequality will exclude those with no economic power from production processes, and, therefore from even a large output. Aggressive market economy will always have exclusionary tendencies. For instance, the aged should get a share in the outcome of the economic activities, but they will be excluded by the market system.

CONCLUSION

The problem with the advocates of market is that they fail to explain as to how the exclusion could be avoided. Exclusion is the built-in strategy in the market economy. Unless the government takes care of the marginalized and left-out people, the exclusion is certain to happen. Corporate sector, by nature, is always in hunger; it cannot understand the needs of the hungry people; it can understand only the conspicuous and ostensible demands of the rich.

References

Anima, P., 2007, "Cell Proposed to Combat Female Foeticide: Sex Selective Abortions Rampant in Delhi", *The Hindu,* Tiruchirapalli edition, May 27, p. 9.

Asad Bin Saif, 2006, "Declining Sensitivity to the Poor", *People's Reporter,* January 25, p. 3.

Aseem Shrivastava, 2007, Why this Growth can never Trickle Down", *The Hindu,* Tiruchirapalli edition, May 20, p. 16.

Ashoka Mody, 2006, "Inclusive Growth", Sameeksha Trust Book, Orient Longman Ltd., Mumbai.

Gargi Parsai, 2007, Tough Decisions Needed to Revive Agriculture: Manmohan", *The Hindu,* Tiruchirapalli edition, May 30, p. 12.

Himanshu, 2007, "Recent Trends in Poverty and Inequality: Some Preliminary Results", *Economic and Political Weekly,* Vol. XLII, No. 6, February 10, p. 497.

The Hindu, 2006, "Call to Reverse Neo-Liberal Financial Policies", December 14, Tiruchirapalli edition, p. 4.

The Hindu, 2006, "Do Not Rely on Market Economy for Development, Says Amartya Sen", Tiruchirapalli edition, December 21, p. 13.

The Hindu, 2007, "Survey Expresses Concern over Rising Unemployment", Tiruchirapalli edition, February 28, p. 14.

The Hindu, 2007, "FM Warns Corporates against Excise Evasion", Tiruchirapalli edition, March 8, p. 19.

The Hindu, 2007, "Put Social Responsibility before Tax Concessions", Tiruchirapalli edition, March 9, p. 14.

The Hindu, 2007, "Inclusive Growth Guiding Principle of Our Policies, Say Manmohan", Tiruchirapalli edition, May 8, p. 14.

The Hindu, 2007, "Kalam Stresses Corporate Social Responsibility", Tiruchirapalli edition, May 8, p. 16.

The Hindu, 2007, "Inflation a Cause for Concern: Manmohan", Tiruchirapalli edition, May 23, p. 1.

The Hindu, 2007, "Share Benefits with Poor, Manmohan Tells Industry", Tiruchirapalli edition, May 25, p. 1.

The Hindu, 2007, "CEOs' Salary cannot be Legislated: CII Chief", Tiruchirapalli edition, May 26, p. 17.

The Hindu, 2007, "Economy Witnessing Cyclical Overheating: Rangarajan", Tiruchirapalli edition, June 7, p. 17.

Jeemol Unni and Raveendran, 2007, "Growth of Employment [1993-94 to 2004-05]: Illusion of Inclusiveness?", *Economic and Political Weekly,* Vol. XLII, No. 3, January 20-26, p. 196.

John M. Itty, 2006, "Growth of the Clubs of Billionaires and the Hungry Billions", *People's Reporter,* March 25, p. 8.

Kurien C.T., 2006, "On the Fast Track, Essays of Distinguished Economists Providing Insights into India's Development Journey", *The Hindu,* Tiruchirapalli edition, December 5, p. 14.

Mahendra Dev S. and C. Ravi, 2007, Poverty and Inequality: All India and States, 1983-2005", *Economic and Political Weekly,* Vol. XLII, No. 6, February 10, p. 509.

Moana Bhagabati, 2007, "A WTO Perspective of Indian Economy", *The Hindu,* Tiruchirapalli edition, June 4, p. 15.

Neena Vyas, 2007, "Manmohan Calls for a New India", *The Hindu,* Tiruchirapalli edition, May 11, p. 1.

Prabhat Patnaik, 2007, "Economic Growth is Good only when it Creates Jobs", *People's Reporter,* Volume 20, No. 8, April 25, p. 1.

Swaminathan M.S., 2007, "Dealing with Agrarian Crisis", *The Hindu,* Tiruchirapalli edition, May 28, p. 10.

20

Inclusive Growth : Is it Achievable?

V. MOHANASUNDARAM

. . . it is an abiding fact of modern civilization that equality is a subject of thoughtful and dedicated interest only to some political activists and fewer philosophers, though unarguably it is the subject of animated discussions at many dinner tables, mainly among right-thinking but not right-leaning people. With the demise of political theory, for example American political science departments, where rational choice theory and formal modeling have preempted any wider concerns with politics, philosophy, and continental traditions of inquiry, one can scarcely expect political scientists to take any interest in the subject. Even the most well-intentioned political scientists, who are demonstrably concerned with issues of equality and inequality, justice and injustice, labour so heavily under the burden of the mathematization of their discipline and its surrender to rampant modeling techniques that they are unable to write discursively or engage with what was once a rich philosophical and political literature on these

> subjects. Economists, with few exceptions, have had little interest in equality, whether as a subject of inquiry or a principle to be striven for: their *raison d'etre*, is to aggravate the conditions of inequality, though if that seems an unusually harsh view of the exponents of the aptly-named dismal science, it will suffice to represent economists as specialists who service the engine of the growth.
>
> —Vinay Lal, Empire of Knowledge

A large number of view points, opinions, comments and observations are available on:

(i) the kind of growth pattern that India has exhibited, so for, [mostly in the form of dichotomous terms: pre and post-independence period, pre and post-reform period (i.e 1991 reforms)];

(ii) the developmental path that India has traversed so far:

- socialistic pattern of society
- mixed economy
- opening of the economy (for private as well as foreign)

(iii) the planning models/strategies adopted to achieve the set targets/goals:

- Public sector dominance
- Two sector model
- Growth with equity
- Balanced regional development
- Target group approach
- Area specific programmes
- Sector-wise initiatives (like Green Revolution)

This brings one to question whether the concept of inclusive growth is all that important or not.

The Concept of Inclusive Growth

Though, for quite sometime, the phrase 'inclusive growth' has been doing rounds in the economic literature, the 11th Five Year Plan's emphasis on it made many to write/quote it very often. One view, as put forward by 11th Plan document, is that, inclusive growth means, "in the process of economic growth, the mass of people are ensured access (equal!) to basic facilities such as health, education, clean drinking water and also employed in adequate income generating activities". For some, it is 'equitable distribution income'. For others, it is 'balanced regional development'. Many emphasize delivery system, i.e. guaranteeing flow of benefits through more employment and income to those sections of society which has been by-passed by higher rates (!) of economic growth. The term is suggestive: treat the rural and less fortunate on par with others in all the endeavours that are being taken up in the economic arena. The term implies, in a pure economic parlance, that in the growth process "the distribution of income moves in favour of the poor". At an higher plane, it is, empowering and creating opportunities for each person. And this is in contrast to the earlier version of inclusive growth namely, "trickle down"—benefits of economic growth percolating down to the downtrodden.

And finally, the first women would be-President of India, Mrs Pratiba Patil observes that economic growth must be all-inclusive benefiting all disadvantaged sections.

The Context of Inclusive Growth

Why there is a sudden upsurge in using the term 'Inclusive Growth' or calling for 'Inclusive Growth'?

The comments are given brackets on every quote to emphasize the point:

(a) The Approach Paper to the 11th Five Year Plan (2007-12) observes that this performance (highest growth rate of 8 per cent during 10th Plan period) reflects the strength of our economy and the dynamism of the private sector in many areas. Yet, it is also true that economic growth has failed to be sufficiently inclusive, particularly after the mid-1990s. (Hence, there is a need for Inclusive Growth).

(b) As the present economic growth of India is commented as "Jobless growth", "Employment–hostile growth" and "Job-destroying growth", there is a need for generation of employment to all. (i.e. including the marginalized and the left over also in the mainstream).

(c) Development must be equitable if it is to be sustainable. (So there is a need for Inclusive Growth).

(d) The growing sectoral imbalances in India, as pointed out by Papola and many others, suggests an inequality in income distribution and its further accentuation will have serious socio-economic consequences (so, be alert, direct the economy towards Inclusive Growth).

(e) "Reforms with Human Pace" (implying that reforms by passing the interest of poor should not be taken up).

(f) From the *rights perspective*: as put forward by Sachs, "Inclusive development calls, first of all, at ensuring the exercise of civil, civic and political rights. . . . All the citizens must have access on equal basis to welfare programmes . . . equitable opportunities of access to public services". By quoting the UN declaration on the *Right to Development*, Sengupta argues that "one of the benefits of using human rights approach to development is that it focuses attention on those who lag behind others in enjoying their rights, and requires that positive action be taken on their behalf".

The Content of Inclusive Growth

As per the 11th Plan Approach Paper, the strategy for inclusive growth must be an all out effort to provide the mass of our people the access to basic facilities such as health, education, clean drinking water, etc. While in the short-run these essential public services impact directly on welfare, in the longer run they determine economic opportunities for the future. It is important to recognize that access to these basic services is not necessarily assured simply by a rise in per capita income. Governments at different levels have to ensure the provision of these services and this must be an essential part of our strategy for inclusive growth. At the same time it is important to recognize the better health and education are the necessary pre-conditions for sustained long-term growth.

Key Challenges in the Path of Inclusive Growth

The President of Asian Development Bank, Haruhiko Kuroda, identified the following as major challenges for India in achieving inclusive growth:

1. Despite strong economic performance, job creation has not kept pace with a growing labour force.
2. Deceleration in agriculture growth.
3. Relatively low employment generation potential of the fast growing services sector.
4. Inequality among states.
5. Pockets of extreme poverty even in the advanced and dynamic states.
6. Finding adequate resources for funding the required infrastructure facilities.

Economic Growth and Inclusive Growth

A lot of analysis and interpretation were done on the growth of Indian economy. Though there is no unanimity about an optimum growth rate to achieve an inclusive growth, many analysts were of the opinion that the current rate of growth (around 8 per cent) is historically higher. There has been many analyses was have done on the rate of growth and its impact on reduction in poverty. One of the studies stated that a ten per cent rate of growth of the economy, will lead to 0.5 per cent rise in employment generation and an associated reduction in poverty rates.

In a working paper published by IGIDR it has been stated that a 20 per cent sustained increase in public sector investment in infrastructure (about Rs. 6900-7500 crores p.a. at 1993-94 prices) will enable the Indian economy to grow at an additional 1.8% and achieve the much debated 10% aggregate real GDP growth per annum in the medium- to long-run. Further, such growth is non-inflationary and welfare improving through higher government revenue and 0.7% reduction in poverty in rural and 0.6% in urban areas. The additional expenditure is about 0.5% of the GDP and 2.7% of the government total revenue in 2002-03. We believe that such investment is quite feasible and cost effective. An alternative simulation wherein the government utilizes accumulated capital inflows instead of borrowing from commercial banks, gave similar results, with few changes in external and monetary sectors. It must be mentioned that the major limitation of the study is its aggregative nature- both sectoral and spatial (all India). A more disaggregated model may give better insights into the process of the working of the Indian economy.

Another two extreme views are related to the economic reforms: one school of thought argues in favour of more reforms (second generation reforms) and further opening of the Indian economy. Another view point is that the reforms should be reversed otherwise it will end in colonization of the economy. Kawadia, on commenting on the Trends and Direction of India's growth process, stated that: ". . . market-oriented economic policies have thrown up more uncertainties for the growth process. Estimates of poverty, consumption expenditure and income inequality clearly indicate that the growth process has failed to trickle down in the economy. There is no indication of convergence in the distribution of gains".

The Way Out

Innumerable suggestions and policy measures are suggested by individuals, intellectuals, institutions—both national and international—to achieve a higher rate of economic growth. At the same time not many concrete policy guidelines are available for an equitable distribution of income and wealth.

The India Development Policy Report (DPR), 2006, of World Bank says that the development process is not simply a measure of aggregate of economic activity but is an assessment of the inclusiveness of economic growth "with emphasis not only on the distribution of economic gains but also on the security, vulnerability, empowerment, and sense of full participation that people may enjoy in social life". Both the goals—improved delivery of core services and more inclusive growth—depend upon empowering and creating opportunities for each person.

The Economic Survey 2006-07 has identified five mantras for achieving high and inclusive economic growth with a view to creating more jobs and eliminating poverty at a faster pace.

1. The government should initiate measures to channelise savings accruing on account of high growth rate coupled with the demographic dividend (a growing proportion of the population in the working age group) for investment.
2. *Secondly*, efficiency improvements in the economy since 1999-2000 will reinforce the country's confidence in the high-growth phase.
3. *Thirdly*, availability of labour at reasonable wages and efficiency improvements will open new avenues in services, including the tourism.
4. As *fourth* step, capacity addition through investments to prevent overheating of the economy as is being feared by some economists.
5. *Fifthly*, the poor infrastructure that constrained growth in the past has started improving and is likely to strengthen further, giving a boost to economic growth.

On his part, Prime Minister Dr Manmohan Singh has put forward some points in the direction of inclusive growth. While talking to people CII, he advocated a 'ten-point social charter' for sharing benefits of economic growth with the less privileged.

1. Corporate social responsibility must not be defined by tax planning strategies alone. Rather, is should be defined within the framework of a corporate philosophy which factors the needs of the community and the regions in which the corporate entity functions,

2. Workers should feel that they are cared for at work,
3. The operation of cartels by groups of companies to keep prices high must end,
4. Creation of an environment that is friendly for the growth of manufacturing industry,
5. The CII should develop the 'codes of conduct' to fight corruption,
6. The industry should gain a competitive edge by investing in R & D and innovation and promoting enterprises,
7. Companies should provide employment opportunities to the socially less privileged and physically less-abled.
8. Excessive remuneration to promoters to be resisted,
9. Allocation of significant resources for skill development, and
10. Work in a harmonious environment, an environment in which all citizens feel actually involved in economic growth and in which each citizen sees hope for a better future.

To achieve the above, in the Indian reality, a lot need to be done in many fields. For example, in the field of governance, a complete over haul is required. Bimal Jalan, has outlined the following as a must for good governance and he has seen commanding heights of the economy in the hands of the public sector. Among others he has suggested the following:

(i) Simplifying Administrative Procedure,
(ii) Managing Fiscal Sector Deficit through Fiscal Policy Changes,
(iii) Ensuring Accountability through legal Reforms,
(iv) Avoiding Bureaucratic Interference, and
(v) Eliminating Administrative Direction.

All these positives indicate the feasibility of achieving inclusive growth. However, caution must be exercised, as populism and symbolism can distort India's recent development agenda.

References

Why this growth can never trickle down, *The Hindu*, June 10, 2007, p. 16.

Jalan, Bimal, "Economics, Politics and Governance", *Vikalpa*, 29 (2), April-June 2004.

Kawadia Ganesh, "Trends and Direction of India's Growth Process (1980-81 to 1999-2000)", *Man and Development*, 24 (1), March 2002, pp. 28-36.

Lal Vinay, *Empire of Knowledge*, Vistaar Publications, New Delhi.

Mody, Ashoka, Quest for Inclusive Growth Continuity and Constraints in Indian Economic Policies, *Economic and Political Weekly*, September 10, 2005, pp. 4052-61.

Murty, K.N. and Soumya, A., *Effects of Public Investment in Infrastructure on Growth and Poverty in India*, Working Paper, IGIDR, Mumbai, October 2006.

Nampoothiry, M.N., Inclusive Growth, *The Hindu*, December 3, 2006, p. 16.

Pant, Devendra Kumar, "Dealing with Disparities", *Margin*, 36 and 37 (4 and 1), July-September and October-December, 2004, pp. 139-56.

Papola, T.S., Emerging Structure of Indian Economy, *The Indian Economic Journal*, 54 (1), Academic Foundation, New Delhi.

Planning Commission, GOI, Towards Faster and More Inclusive Growth—An Approach to the 11th Five Year Plan, December, 2006.

Promoting 'Inclusive Growth'?, *Economic and Political Weekly*, June 2, 2007.

Ramachander, S., Inclusive Growth, *The Hindu Business Line*, June 11, 2007.

Sachs, Ignacy, From Poverty Trap to Inclusive Development in LDCs, *Economic and Political Weekly*, May 1, 2004, pp. 1802-11.

Sengupta, Arjun, "An Essay on the Right to Development", Professor C.N. Vakil Memorial Lecture, 84th Annual Conference of Indian Economic Association, 2001.

21

Inclusiveness and Inequality

RANABIR RAY CHOUDHURY

INTRODUCTION

The United Progressive Alliance (UPA) Government has completed three years of its term and this is the time once more to put its performance under the scanner. Not surprisingly, the views are as numerous as are the commentators. To this writer, however, there are two broad aspects which have received most of the attention, namely, the 'inclusivity' of the growth programmes drawn up and implemented by the Government and whether, and to what extent, 'inequality' has been fuelled by the pursuit of such programme.

In fact, in recent days, the common refrain has been that the UPA's growth programme has increased the content of inequality in Indian society, specifically, that the fruits of growth have till now bypassed *aam aadmi* and to that extent gone against the tenets of the Common Minimum Programme, which is the bedrock of the governance programme of the Manmohan Singh Government. As evidence for this drift away from the

CMP, this school of thought has pointed to the election results in States such as Punjab and Uttar Pradesh, the gist of its argument being that the *aam aadmi* has shied away from the UPA parties because of their failure satisfactorily to attend to his requirements. Furthermore, these parties, especially the Congress, have fared poorly because of the creeping cancer of economic inequality promoted either deliberately or otherwise by the pursuit of the Government's economic policies.

The Tussle

This may or may not be true, but the very basic issue-at least to this writer—is whether one should see the Indian growth experience as a tussle between inclusivity and growing economic inequality or whether one should view the entire exercise as one of registering growth based principally on the principle of inclusivity but which will also exhibit the traits of growing inequality stemming from the link between high-performance and high material recompense.

In other words, it would appear that there is no fundamental conflict between 'inclusiveness' of growth policies and the phenomenon of 'rowing in equality' because the two relate broadly to two different sector of the economy. While the inclusivity of public development programmes is the foremost characteristic (hallmark) of such programmes—meaning that the policies are directed towards the economic betterment of the vast majority of the population—the inequality aspect refers essentially to the non-public sphere of the economy—that is, to employment in the private sector, to the rewards distributed by private sector employers to employees deemed to be specially endowed with talent.

Have the UPA's policies during the first three years of its term been directed to improving the quality of life of the average citizen of the republic? If one has recourse to the foreword by the Prime Minister to the alliance's latest 'Report to the People', one cannot but be impressed by what he has to say on the subject. At a very macro-level, he says: "The main objective of our Government in the past three years has been to ensure that, while sustaining higher rates of economic growth, the improved performance of the economy contributes to employment generation, poverty reduction and human development. In this 60th year of our Independence, the country should have the satisfaction of recording for the fifth year in succession a rate of economic growth of over 8.5 per cent. The recent acceleration of growth to 9 per cent has been made possible by an unprecedented increase in the rate of investment which is at an all-time high of around 35 per cent of national income".

People's Condition

But growth in figures does not automatically imply that the condition of the people at large has improved, as Dr. Manmohan Singh himself says in the document. To quote him: "However, our Government recognizes that high national income growth alone does not address the challenge of employment promotion, poverty reduction and balanced regional development. Nor does growth in itself improve human development. The National Common Minimum Programme is based on the recognition that economic growth must be socially inclusive and regionally balanced. This has been the guiding principle of our Government's policies in the past three years".

In terms of sectoral attainments, he says that the UPA regime "has ensured a massive increase in public investment in the past three years, without reneging on our commitment to fiscal discipline". Thus, Rs. 1,74,000 crore has been invested through Bharat Nirman in rural roads, rural housing, rural drinking water supply, rural electrification and rural telecommunications. The budgetary allocation for education has been increased from Rs. 12,000 crore in 2003-04 to more than Rs. 32,000 crore in 2007-08 (which Dr. Singh describes as 'unprecedented'). The allocation for health and family welfare has been more than doubled, from Rs. 7,620 crore to Rs. 17,560 crore. Investment in agriculture and rural development has risen from around Rs. 20,000 crore to more than Rs. 60,000 crore over the three-year period.

These are impressive increases, and in terms of policy-priorities the UPA cannot be faulted for such action. Of course, it is another thing altogether whether the 'delivery system' has been good enough to translate the promise of such investments into comparable tangible benefits for the beneficiaries concerned. Going by past experience, there is bound to be some leakage, but having said this one must admit that, as far as the evidence on paper is concerned, the Manmohan Singh Government has been quite 'inclusive' in the framing and implementation of its development programmes since 2003-04.

Growing Inequality

Of interest is the fact that, at the same time, there has been growing equality as well if the increase in the general level of salaries is any indication, particularly in some of the so-called sunrise sectors at this point of time. Profits too have soared which, if nothing else, is a direct function of growth in the services, industrial and agro-based sectors. Indeed, it can even be said that the gap between the rich and the poor has increased. This would have been unacceptable if the poor had remained where they were at the beginning of the growth exercise. But then—and this is the crux of the issue—this is not the case.

True, agriculture has lagged behind but, as recent NSSO statistics indicate, demand in the rural areas has increased, which would not have been possible if there was no increase in the wherewithal with which to satisfy rising human aspirations for material well-being.

The point, in short, is that growth is bound to be imperfectly distributed in an economy like India's even if development policy is made as inclusive as possible. Using this yardstick, one would perhaps not be far off the mark in suggesting that the UPA regime has done well till now under the leadership of its economist Prime Minister.

22

Regional Disparities : Need for Social Inclusion

C.J. PUNNATHARA

INTRODUCTION

In its mission to correct regional imbalances and bridge the rural-urban divide, financial inclusion seems to be one of the guiding principles of state policy. Highlighting the need for equitable growth, the Prime Minister, Dr. Manmohan Singh, has often stated that the National Common Minimum Programme aims at economic growth that is socially inclusive and regionally balanced.

Several programmes have been initiated to achieve these goals, and a few have begun to yield results. All indications are that organized bank credit is becoming increasingly accessible, and is being used by the rural people. The incremental capital output ratio is becoming more positive in certain parts of rural India, which are beginning to flaunt their wealth. However, the rural-urban divide and inter-State economic disparities remain as divisive as ever. Spatially, socially and economically, Bharat remains a distant cousin of India.

So much so that the World Bank voiced its concern that "substantial disparities persist within the country." In its *Country Overview 2006*, it pointed out that the reforms process, initiated in the 1990s, was accompanied by visible increase in income inequality – between urban and rural India, between the forward and backward States, as also between skilled and unskilled workers. This all happened even while the country was able to reduce the number of people living in absolute poverty by more than half. The World Bank highlighted that higher-income States have been able to reduce poverty to the levels of some rich Latin American countries. But poverty continues to be endemic and pervasive in such States as Assam, Bihar, Chhattisgarh, Jharkhand, Madhya Pradesh, Orissa, Rajasthan and Uttar Pradesh, it said. And as development process becomes more pronounced, the disparities are set to worsen.

The Disparities

Among the dynamic States, Punjab, Haryana, Maharashtra and Gujarat stood out during the 1980s: the first two primarily spurred by rapid agricultural growth that translated into accelerated industrial production, and the latter two for strong industrial performance. However, with the development paradigm shifting from agriculture to industry, then to services and within it information technology and IT-enabled services, several States have found a shortcut to economic growth.

By 1993-94, Punjab was an economically dynamic State with a per capita net State Domestic Product of Rs. 12,710, followed by Maharashtra (Rs. 12,183), Haryana (Rs. 11,079), Gujarat (Rs. 9,796), Tamil Nadu (Rs. 8,955), Kerala (Rs. 7,983), Himachal Pradesh (Rs. 7,870), Karnataka (Rs. 7,838) and Andhra Pradesh (Rs. 7,416). Bihar, with Rs. 3,037, and Orissa, with Rs. 4,896, were at the bottom of the heap, reflecting the deeply entrenched inter-State disparities.

Over 10 years later, in 2004-05, the same States were still leading the pack, albeit with a minor change of order. Haryana became the leader, with a per capita net domestice product of Rs. 32,712, followed by Maharashtra (Rs. 32,170), Punjab (Rs. 30,701), Gujarat (Rs. 28,355), Himachal Pradesh (Rs. 27,486), Kerala (Rs. 27,048), Tamil Nadu (Rs. 25,965), Karnataka (Rs. 23,945) and Andhra Pradesh (Rs. 23,153).

Though there was all-round growth, the plight of the poorer States worsened. Bihar's per capita income increased to a meagre Rs. 5,772. By contrast, Orissa's per capita surgd 177 per cent to Rs. 13,601: holding out hope for the greater equity.

Driven By ITEs

Several States did not go through the agriculture-industry-services cycle, but directly took the industry-services-IT and ITES path. They have gained substantially in the process, since farm growth was always low, at 4-4.5 per cent. By contrast, industrial growth often ranged between 10 per cent and 20 per cent, the services sector grew 20-30 per cent, and IT and ITES over 30 per cent. The States that drew direct benefits from the industry-services-IT and ITES route directly were able to reap quick and rich rewards.

Himachal Pradesh recorded the top growth of 249 per cent: a State where recent efforts at rapid industrialization and pursuit of IT and ITES (Nasscom Report: *Himachal Pradesh Millennium IT Vision 2010)*, seems to have paid rich dividends. Kerala recorded 239 per cent growth between 1993-94 and 2004-05. But its case is an exception in the development paradigm because of its huge remittance inflows every year.

Andhra Pradesh recorded 212 per cent, followed by Karnataka (205 per cent), Haryana (195 per cent), Tamil Nadu (190 per cent) and Gujarat (189 per cent); all States with proven track records in increased activity in the services sector, IT, ITES and on the industries front. By comparison, Bihar recorded a paltry growth rate of 90 per cent.

While the growth dichotomy is stark among the States, it is even more pronounced between rural and urban India. The hinterland is yet to move away from the low-growth cycle of agriculture. The effort of the Government in setting right the regional imbalances might prove ineffectual, as disparity seems to be an inherent feature of the economic framework. It might be more prudent for the Government to focus on inclusive and equitable growth rather than pursuing the dreams of bridging regional inequalities.

23

In Pursuit of Excellence and Inclusion in Education

P.V. INDIRESAN

INTRODUCTION

The Approach Paper to the Eleventh Plan proposes "expansion, inclusion and excellence" as objectives of education. In his comments of the Approach Paper, the Finance Minister pointedly refers to the folly of throwing more money into poorly managed institutions with little or no accountability. Evidently, he wants expansion and inclusion only when that does not damage excellence. The Approach Paper does express concern about the absence of quality but does not propose any specific scheme for promoting excellence. Collapse of excellence starts at the primary level. The Approach Paper states: "For a large proportion of our children, school is an ill-lit class room with more than one class being taught together by someone who may not have completed her own schooling." As a result, all over the country, richer families, even lower middle-class ones, have opted out of public schools, and send their children to private schools.

Rural education is particularly badly affected because teacher discipline is poor and self-financing schools are unviable As the Sixth Infrastructure Report highlights, very low density of customers per sq km is the basic obstacle to rural development. Rural education can deal with that handicap in two ways: One take a school to every hamlet but cut down the quantity and quality of services to match the small customer size. Two, on the principle if mountain will not go to Mahomet, Mahomet must go to mountain, take children to a central location where schools of good quality can be sustained.

Catch-22 Situation

The Approach Paper endorses the received wisdom "a school that is far away fails to retain students". It says also that students dropout if the school does not function regularly. For rural education, that is a catch-22 situation: If the school is nearby, it is no good: if it is good it has to be far away. We face here the standard dilemma of development: Should we choose a low-cost, low-return option, or should opt for a higher cost, higher return path? Should we invest Rs. 1,000 at one per cent return or should we invest Rs. 2,000 at two per cent return?

Should we be content with low-quality education in every hamlet or should we insist on quality even if that means that every hamlet will not have its own school? That is Issue One. Our education system prescribes syllabi, selects teachers, recognizes schools (or not) but will not accept any responsibility for outcomes. For instance, the accepted principle is (which the Approach Paper endorses) "children must complete eight years of schooling." At the same time, it is the rule that no child should be failed in any class. Hence, the policy is: Children must attend but need not learn. Incidentally, this policy absolves teachers and schools of any responsibility for the outcome.

The Approach Paper does propose setting up national testing standards. What use will they be if the rule is that no child should be failed? As most poorly run schools are under State governments, is not this proposal similar to the idea of belling the cat? That is Issue Two. Many State governments have abrogated their responsibility to provide quality education to the poor, but will not yield their authority to control what private schools can or cannot do. Experience since 1991 has demonstrated that competition (including privatization) is the best guarantor of quality service, even for affordability, for that reason, the Approach Paper lays emhasis on Public-Private Partnership. Then, should not the Plan encourage competition between private and state-run schools/In the true spirit of PPPs, should there not be a plan to help children to study in private schools if they are better than state-run schools?

Stratified Approach

Several private hospitals operate the way the Railways does: Provide different classes of service at different prices. Then, why should private schools not be encouraged to follow suit? For instance, should not private schools be helped to conduct evening classes for poor children by charging marginal costs, or even provide free tuition in English, mathematics, science and computer skills at weekends when school facilities lie idle? That is Issue Three.

Employability is another contentious issue. The Approach Paper starts with the assumption that "education is the most critical input for empowering people to (gain) access to productive employment." Is that always correct? Is it not a fact that school education often increases risks of unemployment for poor children by inducing revulsion against their traditional family occupations and not preparing them for alternative livelihood?

For policy-makers, eight years of compulsory academic education is a settled issue. For many poor families that remains a contentious one. Current policy permits no freedom; insists that the state will have the absolute discretion in dictating what a school should teach, who will teach. Should we pursue that authoritarian policy of straitjacketing education that does not always help the poor to land jobs, or should we offer a choice? That is Issue Four.

Considering that India has entered into global competition and China, our prime rival, is surging by leaps and bounds, can India survive without promoting excellence? If excellence is necessary, can we combine the excellent and the ordinary in one and the same institution, or should we have special institutions for gifted students? That is Issue Five.

Whither Freedom for Schools?

In 1947, India got Independence. In 1991, Indian business got freedom. Even in 2007, schools are yet to get freedom. Parents too have no freedom to decide what kind of education their children should get. In 1991, Indian business was thrown open to competition: even in 2007, for our educators competition is anathema. On the contrary, the state has amended the Constitution to nationalize education.

Even nationalization would not have mattered but for the fact that the education system is peculiarly privileged. For all products and services, consumers can seek legal redress when quality is substandard. Special consumer courts have been set up to simplify the process.

Unfortunately, in the matter of education, consumers have no such protection. No parent or a Public Interest Petitioner can seek legal remedy against bad education. Should education be brought under consumer courts? That is Issue Six. There is a common thread in all six issues raised here: Absence of a realistic, even a theoretical plan for excellence. No doubt, the Approach Paper proposes a programme for preparing standards.

That is unlikely to specify anything higher than minimum tolerable standards. It has no mandate for identifying globally competitive standards of excellence. Should we have a system to identify and propagate globally competitive standards of education? That is Issue Seven.

Expansion, Inclusion and Excellence

Although the Approach Paper has the three objectives of expansion, inclusion and excellence, the Plan itself concentrates on expansion and inclusion with little attention to excellence. Planners face a dilemma: Every child cannot be trained to become an excellent mathematician or a linguist or a musician. Hence, excellence implies selectivity. Inclusion precludes selectivity. We can (and should) think of including every talented child however poor and however remote its residence. That way excellence can be combined with inclusion. That leads us to the final and the most crucial Issue Eight: What is inclusion? Is it for select groups however poorly the child is equipped, or is it for every capable child however poor?

II

To recapitulate: (1) Should we insist on quality even if that means that every hamlet will not have its own school? (2) Is it politically feasible to discipline government schools and expect them to accept outside evaluation? (3) Should we encourage Public-Private Partnership in education? (4) Should school education be academic or should it be job-oriented? (5) Should we have special institutions for gifted students? (6) Should educational institutions be brought under consumer courts? (7) Should we have globally competitive standards of education? (8) Should inclusion be restricted to select castes?

In each of these cases, it is possible to argue both ways. For the present discussion, let us make the following assumptions, which hopefully, will be widely acceptable: (a) multiple choices are needed even at the school level, from job-oriented vocational training at one extreme and global academic standards at the other; (b) Public-Private Partnership is necessary; (c) All children however poor should get good education.

Different Baggage

Unfortunately, the Planning Commission is weighed down by ideological baggage. The words ideological and logical are different. To the extent they refer, what is ideological is not logical. Ideological refers to fixed ideas, which may (or may not) be correct. The Planning Commission is brutally frank in highlighting the flaws in the prevailing education system. Yet it does not have the courage to accept that this sad state of affairs can only be due to faulty ideology. It seeks to merely expand the existing system, not to transform it.

For instance, the Approach Paper says, "often the need for children of poorer families to work also drives them away from school" and on that premise, recommends adding more schools so that no hamlet is without one. All over the world (including India) children happily travel long distances every day to get to school. In truth, it is bad schools (and bad teachers) that drive away children, not distant schools.

Hence, I expand a proposal I have made earlier: Combine the single-teacher schools of adjacent villages to establish one large school with minimum ten teachers. Offer a bus as compensation for each village that surrenders a school on condition it transports its children to the centrally located school. Rest of the time, the village can operate the bus for any commercial purpose. The government can even go to the extent of insisting that the village pays for the cost of transporting the children out of the profits of commercial use of the bus.

Assuming that a bus costs Rs. 15 lakh and has a life of 15 years, the government will then have to allocate Rs. 1 lakh per village per year. That is the cost of hiring a teacher and better than hiring an incompetent teacher who may or may not attend, and even if he (or she) attends, may not be teaching.

Weak on Education PPP

Although the Plan emphasizes Public-Private Partnership, the section on education is particularly weak on that topic. The main reference is to scholarships about which the Approach Paper says: "Scholarships for poor children who complete primary schooling in public schools that would also be valid in unaided private secondary schools which agree to a common fee structure for the scholarship holders." Using the teeth of the 104th Amendment of the Constitution, the Government may force this idea on unaided schools. That is not partnership but an imposition. A partnership should provide mutual benefit.

For that reason, my suggestion is to offer academic autonomy to reputed schools that are willing to provide affordable education to poor students. We could go so far as to institute "autonomous schools" on the lines of autonomous colleges. They will not be constrained by any school board and be free to organize their academic programme independently. Then, the country will enjoy many new experiments and benefit from the innovation and the enterprise such autonomous schools can bring to the education scene. Incidentally, it is easier to enforce accountability in autonomous institutions—they will have no excuses to offer.

Politicians, administrators, educators and courts too are obsessed with fees. The best scheme is the one operated by Harvard University: Admissions are made by a need-blind mechanism. After the selections are made, students are admitted in such a manner that no student pays more than what the family can afford and, further, the total merit of the students admitted is the maximum. Then, a minimum number of rich students are admitted but only for the purpose of maximizing the merit level of the whole class. Harvard has shown that the system is workable and produces high levels of merit.

The Planning Commission (and the UPA Government) has Narcisist fascination with its Sarva Shiksha Abhiyan. That is no different from (in the Finance Minister, Mr. P. Chidambaram's words) increasing the pressure in a leaky pipe. To build a knowledge economy, the country needs a different approach altogether, a Uttama Shiksha Abhiyan, a scheme for superior education for brilliant students.

Better Decentralised

Brilliant students are everywhere but only those in the larger cities get noticed. As the poet said, "full many a gem of the purest ray serene, the dark unfathomed caves of the ocean bear". For that reason, this scheme should not operate nationally as such schemes tend to do, the way the National Talent Search scheme operates. It should be totally decentralized. Selections should be made district-wise, even tehsil-wise to ensure a proper chance for poor children in poor localities.

The government and the educators suffer from yet another ideological hang up: They think ten years of schooling is essential for every child. What use is learning trigonometry and algebra, the names of capitals of distant countries and the like for a child who is utterly poor, and not clever enough to earn a scholarship? Such children are better-off acquiring vocational skills that will provide them with a respectable livelihood.

According to the Approach Paper, India's vocational schools cater to 40 trades; in China, the number is 4000. China is realistic. However carefully chosen (they are not), the 40 trades will not meet the diverse needs of a modern economy. On the other hand, we cannot find enough instructors for 4000 trades. Even if they are found, it will be virtually impossible to support them with up to date equipment, and with materials to offer hands-on experience.

Vocational Training

These problems can be overcome if vocational education is split into two—an academic part teaching measurement and analysis, and a work experience part letting the students learn how to operate machines. The first part can be handled by a school but the second can be managed only in the workplace. Hence, effective vocational education should be a sandwich programme with students alternating between practical training in the workplace and basic instruction in a school.

Inclusion for the Poor

In brief, the Planning Commission should consider (a) bussing rural children to well-equipped schools; (b) organizing a special programme for gifted children and give them free choice to go to private schools; (c) giving autonomy from school boards to outstanding schools (whether private or public) provided they maximize admission to gifted children and accept accountability, and (d) invoking Public-Private Partnership for vocational education. In the matter of education, inclusion should be for the poor, not restricted to the politically privileged.

24

Move Towards an Inclusive Child Health Care System

SHERLY KURIEN

INTRODUCTION

Theoretical work as well as empirical evidence clearly show the positive linkages between good health and economic development. The health status of a population is now considered as an important indicator of development and health is increasingly seen as a development issue, rather than just a medical one. Health has also emerged as a major area of academic interest in the social sciences. With the emergence of human capital economics during the early 1960's, education and health came to be recognized as basic needs along with food, clothing and shelter and it is a precondition for productivity and growth. Health is important for welfare. As a Gujarati poverb says, "the first happiness is health, the second is a full stomach". One cannot enjoy food if one is not healthy. To lead a productive life one needs good health. As Viren (1953) observed, "the first requirements of high labour productivity under modern conditions are that the masses of the population shall be literate, healthy and sufficiently well-fed to be strong and energetic".

Good health is a pre-requisite to human productivity and the "development" process. It is essential as the infrastructure upon which we can build an economically viable society. Improvement in the health status of the people has been one of the major thrust areas for the social development programmes of the country. The idea that governments ought to provide healthcare for their citizens is an international norm. Article 47 of the constitution of India states that, "the state shall regard raising the level of nutrition and standard of living of its people and improvement in public health among its primary duties".

India has made considerable progress in recent decades in several areas. In the field of health India experienced a steady and continuous lowering of mortality rate and a steady increase in life expectancy. We have made dramatic progress in immunization for Polio since 1998, and is about to be wiped out. Similarly small pox is also wiped out. India's per capita-income is much higher and the growth record much better than that of sub-saharan Africa. But it is indeed paradoxical to note that, India still contributes to the majority of the poor of the world with her large population living with poor infrastructure. The proportion of underweight children and the levels of child malnutrition in India are exceptionally high. Inadequate attention has been paid to children with various disabilities. Against this back-drop the current paper makes an attempt to take stock of the state of children in India with focus on nutrition and analyse how far the state has devised measures to protect them.

The Problem of under Nutrition

Children below the age of 18 year 449 million in 2001—account for nearly 44 per cent of India's population. Of these, close to 158 million are extremely vulnerable—between 0-6 years. The average Indian in 2001 near just 23 years old (Sivakumar, 2007).

The nutrition and health status of infants during infancy and child birth depends upon birth weight, adequacy of infant feeding and absence of infection. Breast feeding in the first six months and gradual inclusion of liquids semi-solid foods are the best methods of retaining health and prevention of under nutrition. Infants and children upto a certain age should be given only home made foods. The tin foods available in the market are too costly and unaffordable by the poor. Hence mothers need to be educated to give breast milk and then later on supplement domestic foods. It is computed that exclusive breast feeding and appropriate complementary feeding can lead to 20% reduction in IMR. The nutritional status of pre-school children is a major indicates of community health and nutrition. The inadequate dietary intake of pre-school children is a growing phenomenon in many parts of the country.

Nutritional Status of Rural Households

The NNMB provides the nutritional status of rural households in seven sample states for the periods, 1975-80, 1990-1 and 2000-1. The NNMB classifieds rural children aged 1-5 years into different nutritional grades based on weight for age (Gomez classification). The results show that the percentage of children suffering from severe malnutrition declined from 15 in 1975-9 to 11.1 in 1990-1 and further to 6.4 in 2001-1. If those classified in the moderate and reverse malnutrition ranges are considered together, the percentage of children afflicted by malnutrition declined from 62.5 in 1975-9 to 56.2 in 1990-1 and further to 47.7 in 2001-2. It is thus evident that in spite of some improvement in nutritional status, nearly half of rural children suffer from mal nutrition.

Children of the poor communities suffering from malnutrition not only do not achieve full genetic growth potential and end up as adults with small body size but are also exposed to a greater risk of child mortality. Many studies identified malnutrition as a major cause of death in developing countries. Their result eveal that malnutrition by virtue of its synergistic relationship with infections diseases has a powerful impact on child mortality in India.

There are substantial interstate variations in the levels of malnutrition in children below five. In 2000-1, the percentage of moderately/severally malnourished children varied between 29 in Kerala and 64 in Madhya Pradesh. In terms of nutritional status of children, middle income states such as Kerala, Tamil Nadu and Andhra Pradesh performed better than higher-income states like Gujarat and Maharashtra. Not surprisingly, the poorer states such as Madhya Pradesh and Orissa showed the worst performance. It is noteworthy that despite low food energy intake of children in Kerala and Tamil Nadu, these states could perform better. National Family Healthy Survey (NFHS) data also reveal more or less similar patterns (Parikh and Radhakrishna, 2002).

The preliminary results for 2005-06 from the recently released National Family Health Survey-3 (NFHS-3) confirm the persistent neglect of India's newborn children and pre-school children. The levels of child malnutrition remain unacceptably high and little progress has been made in reducing the proportion of underweight children over the past seven years between NFHS 2 and 3.

According to NFHS-3, in 2005-06, 46 per cent of below three years of age were underweight, 38 per cent were stunted and 19 per cent were wasted. The corresponding levels of child malnutrition are much lower in sub-Saharan Africa where 28 per cent of children below five years are underweight, 37 per cent are stunted and 9 per cent are wasted. In China, only 8 per cent of similar children are underweight and 14 per cent are stunted.

In 2005-06, for instance, only 44 per cent of children of 12-23 months were fully immunized. Despite the importance of breastfeeding and appropriate feeding for preventing malnutrition, only 23 per cent of children under three years were breastfed within one hour of birth and less than half the babies (46 per cent) aged 0-5 months were exclusively breastfed. Equally striking is the low proportion of children of 6-9 months—56 per cent—who received solid or semi-solid food and breast milk. It is well known that frequent illness during early childhood and failing to treat them properly, seriously affects the nutritional well-being of children. Data from NFHS-3 reveal that only 26 per cent of children with diarrhea were given oral rehydration salt (ORS) and barely two-thirds (64 per cent) of children suffering from acute respiratory infection or fever were taken to a health facility. This shows both the poor reach of public health services and also the limited accessibility of such services to children. With only one exception, namely, children aged 0-5 months exclusively breastfed, all other indicators reveal lower reach and access to health services and care in rural than in urban areas. And this explains at least partially the higher levels of under-nourishment in rural than in urban areas.

This survey clearly reveals that progress in reducing under-nourishment in children has been poor and there was only marginal improvement in the reach of basic health services. It is highly unfortunate that we were not able to ensure the right to health for all particularly the children.

Addressing the Needs of Children

India's children bear the burden of multiple disadvantages right from birth in the form of underweight, malnourishment, child labour, child prostitution, child abuse, lack of care and protection and poor living conditions. These and other deprivations stunt the physical and psychological growth of any child. Therefore, the right of every child should be protected and all efforts need to be taken for his well-being and development. The Constitution of India affirms the Indian state's recognition of children as a section of the people deserving of special protection and support.

An examination of present and possible child protection policies, legislation, programmes, investments and outcomes in the context of the potential of the 11th plan must, therefore, begin with an acknowledgement of the real character and dimensions of the protection issues, and therefore of the correctives, safeguards and redressal that could effectively address 'un-protectedness' as it affects children in India. Given the abject situation of millions of children, India stands in urgent need of a radical overhaul of its perception of how children deserve the state's protection. This will obviously imply new and more farsighted measures to actually provide children the protection they need.

Most recently, the new National Plan of Action for Children 2005 (NPA) has affirmed protection to children.

National Plan of Action (NPA) for Children, 2005 (*Excerpts*):

> "All categories of rights apply to all age groups, including before birth. . ."

Guiding Principles

To regard the child as an asset and a person with human rights;
To address issues of discrimination, emanating from biases of gender, class, caste, race, religion and legal status, in order to ensure equality;
To accord utmost priority to the most disadvantaged. . .
To recognize the diverse stages and settings of childhood and to address the needs of each. . .

The 11th Plan Approach Paper clearly states that 'development of children is at the center of the 11th Plan', and outlines commitments to the universalization of ICDS, strengthening of pre-primary schooling, improvement in the quality of education and attention to child mental health. There is also a welcome focus on the most vulnerable children—including street children, trafficked children, victims of sex abuse, differently-abled and HIV affected children and children affected by conflict or natural disasters. Notably, the plan document also recognizes that the demographic profile of India is changing and reflects on the 'talent supply shortages' that indicate that children and young adults will be under-utilized unless provided new like skills. Nurturing the capacities of India's children must, therefore, drive the policy agenda forward.

In India, public health care provision has not been successful in building health security into the lives of the poor. On the one hand, shrinking budgetary support for health care services, inefficiency in public health services and the resultant imposition of rural charges have heightened the concern of the poor and led to a search for alienate financing mechanisms. On the other hand, the belief that the poor are too impoverished to be able to save and contribute towards meeting their health care costs has been questioned in the recent past against this backdrop, health insurance is increasingly being viewed as an important financing tool for improving the access to health services for the poor. There is now a growing realization that even the poor can make small, periodic contributions that can go towards meeting their health care needs. Hence, health insurance for low income groups is emerging in different parts of rural and semi-urban area. Health care provision needs to be strengthened and streamlined if health insurance for the poor is to be developed in a big way. Since health is a state subject involvement of the state government is essential in achieving this. For successfully running health insurance for the poor, co-ordination among multiple agencies is needed.

The US leads the world in health care spending. On a per capita basis, the US spends twice the average expenditure of the OECD countries on health care. Yet its public health indicators are marked by deep inequalities linked to income, health insurance coverage, race, ethnicity, geography and access to health care. For example, the Infant Mortality Rate is now higher for the US than for Malaysia—a country with an average income one quarter of the US. The state of Kerala has an urban infant death rate lower than that African Americans in Washington DC. Inequality in health outcomes are staggering a baby boy from a family in the top 5% of the US income distribution will enjoy a life span 25% longer than a baby boy born in the bottom 5%.

Inadequate public investments are a major factor accounting for the poor reach and quality of basic social services. This is true of health, education, nutrition, water and sanitation. For instance, in 2000, India's public expenditure on health was 0.9% of GDP—among the lowest in the world. (Kumar, 2007).

The approach Paper to the 11th Five Year Plan brought out in December 2006 takes cognizance of several shortcomings and calls for faster and more inclusive growth. It also identified several monitorable socio-economic goals relevant to children that include the following:

- Reduce infant mortality rate to 28 and maternal mortality ratio to 1 per 1000 live births. Reduce malnutrition among children of age group 0-3 to half its present level.

- Reduce anaemia among women and girls by 50% by the end of the 11th Plan.
- Provide clean drinking water for all by 2009. Reduce dropout rates of children from elementary schools from 52.2% in 2003-04 to 2005 by 2011-12.
- Raise the sex ratio for age group 0-6 to 935 by 2011-12 and to 950 by 2016-17.
- Ensure that all children enjoy a safe childhood without any compulsion of work.

The Union Government ministries which have child specific schemes are:

(i) Women and Child Development,
(ii) Human Resource Development,
(iii) Health and Family Welfare,
(iv) Labour and Employment,
(v) Social Justice and Empowerment,
(vi) Tribal Affairs,
(vii) Minority Affairs, and
(viii) Youth Affairs and Sports.

Outlays for child development as a proportion of total outlays by the union government have increased from 0.86% in 2006-07 (BE) to 0.88% in 2007-08 (BE). The union government's outlay for child health as a proportion of its total budget outlay shows a decline from 0.56% in 2006-07 (BE) to 0.52% in 2007-08 (BE). Budgetary provision for child education, as a proportion of total union budget, shows an increase from 3.41% in 2006-07 (BE) to 3.63% in 2007-08 (BE). This increase in the priority accorded to child education in 2007-08 (BE) is mainly on account of a substantial rise in the allocation for the mid-day meal scheme and a near doubling of the allocation for secondary education under the Ministry of Human Resource Development.

Das and Thakur (2007) reiterated the launch of all these schemes as a welcome step, the low magnitude of funds provided. Raises questions over the willingness of the present government to actually implement these schemes in 2007-08.

The total magnitude of resources ear-marked for children in union budget 2007-08, at only 5.08% of the total budget, appears grossly inadequate to address the various problems confronting children in India. Moreover, even within this small quantum of resources earmarked for children, the sectoral composition is heavily distorted. As a result, interventions in important sectors, such as child health and child protection, remain severely under-funded.

Move towards a Healthy System

Providing every family and every child a social safety net that protects their access to quality basic services including clean water, sanitation, nutrition, health and education as well as to the foundations of a reasonable quality life such as decent work and access to justice, is an ideal towards which public policy should strive. The planning process needs to be based on such a vision and support investments and implementation mechanisms that ensure that the vision does not remain at the level of rhetoric. Development planning will also need to focus more sharply on raising the living standards and social status of disadvantaged groups whose experiences reflect histories of neglect.

Every child deserves to have his or her existence acknowledged. This is critical to the protection of his/her civil and political rights—name, identity and nationality. Birth registration is therefore the first protective civil right of every child. India officially claims to have birth registration coverage of 'around 59%'. In 2001, it claimed 'around 54%'. In 2000, it admitted 40% (down from 47% claimed in 1990) in one national report and confessed to 35% in another report. Even the highest figure is nothing to be proud of; the NPA now sets a goal of 100% by 2010.

Malnutrition is a serious problem that India is facing even now inspite of surplus food availability. Recognizing that children are a vulnerable group, special efforts were taken by the government through food supplementation programmes. Data from NNMB reveals that there has been a steady decline in under-nutrition among children. This is mainly attributable to provision of mid-day meals and better access to health care.

However, there are many children who are deprived off many of these facilities. The children who do not come under the umbrella of ICDS appear to be neglected. In this content it would be worthy to note what Jean Oreze has to say.

Nutrition and health education and improved access to health and nutrition care can result in substantial reduction in under-nutrition in children over the next decade.

Another useful test of the government's commitment to "inclusive growth" is the fate of the Integrated Child Development Services (ICDS)—the only major national programme for children under the age of six years. The universalisation of the ICDS is one of the core commitments of the Common Minimum Programme. It is also required for compliance with Supreme Court orders, including the landmark judgment of December 13, 2006, in concrete terms, universalisation involves ensuring that every settlement has a functional Anganwadi (Child care center), and that all ICDS services are extended to all children under six as well as to all eligible women. As things stand, barely one-third of all children under six are covered, and the quality of ICDS services is also far from adequate.

It is startling to find that the budget allocation for the ICDS in 2007-08 is virtually the same as in 2006-07. In fact, it is the same, as a proportion of GDP. This year, the Government of India will be spending less than Rs. 5,000 crore to protect the well-being and rights of 160 million children under six. This compares with Rs. 96,000 crore to be spent on defence—the figures speak for themselves.

ICDS which had been successful in Tamil Nadu and Maharashtra need to be spread on a wider scale to other states too. Budgetary allocation in this regard would be of immense use to the children.

CONCLUSION

Government expenditure affects the welfare of all sections of population, but its effects are not the same for all. Successful measures need to be carried out in a manner that enhances growth and equity. The allocation of resources should favour the poor and vulnerable group and health sector need a complete revamping and greater financial support. As Salam, (2004) pointed out there is need to intensify efforts to increase public as well as private investment and spending on key social services, particularly education, social welfare and Nutrition, water supply, sanitation, housing and urban development and health and family welfare.

Human development which holds the key for all types of development, has to form that core of all development policies and not be pushed to the periphery as the case has been in the past years. This can be done only through more investment in health sector and better health delivery services.

To make India catch-up with the world level the Government needs to pursue policies of doubling resource allocation for public health and this should definitely reach the poor and weaker section of the society. At the state level also there should be more participation in terms of allocation and delivery of health services. Strengthening local institutions and community action are extremely important for accelerating progress for children. Capacity at the community level needs to be augmented so that people can get adequate information, monitor progress and fact in the best interest of the child. This also requires that successful interventions by NGO's and others be assessed and adopted to suit local conditions. Prioritizing for children offers India a unique opportunity to accelerate human development missing this opportunity could prove costly.

References

Kirit, S. Parikh, R. Radhakrishnan, (2002), *India Development Report*, Oxford University Press, New Delhi.

M.D. Abdus Salam, (2004), "Attention Towards Social Section in India", in Ruddar Datt, (Eds.) Deep and Deep Publications (P) Ltd., New Delhi.

Sivakumar, A.K., (2007), "Why are Children Neglected"?, *Seminar*, 574, p. 16.

Sivakumar, A.K., (2007), "Why are Levels of Child Malnutrition not Improving?", *Eonomic and Political Weekly*, 42(5).

Subrat Das and Debdulal Thakur (2007), "Unraveling the Union Budget", *Seminar*, 574, p. 48.

The Hindu, March 9, 2007, p. 12.

Viren, (1953), in *India Development Report* (2002), (Ed): Kirit S. Parikh, R. Radhakrishna, Oxford University Press, New Delhi.

25

Is Inclusive Growth Exclusive of Environment?

G. NARASIMHA RAGHAVAN

"Inclusion is central to the Indian political process because it is part of the project of nation-building and essential to preserving the national identity and democratic institutions".

— *Ashoka Mody*

INTRODUCTION

Not wanting to miss the bandwagon of adjectival-based projection of national policies, India's Planning Commission has supplanted the earlier sacred strategy of 'trickle-down' with the recent strategy of 'inclusive growth'. A word charged with a variety of meanings and denotations, 'inclusive' can refer to a broad-based orientation of state policies. And yet, one would be perplexed to gauge the scope of 'inclusive growth strategy' in its entirety. The 11th Plan's leitmotif of ensuring a comprehensive approach to growth is provoking enough to question whether the former plans were devoid of such a broad approach. This issue apart, the 11th Plan's stratagem, as visualised in the Approach Paper, endeavours to "restructure policies", that aim at "putting the economy on a sustainable growth trajectory". The imperative, then, is on doing away with 'divides' and increasing 'access'. In a similar vein, any reference to environment does not culminate without alluding to the all-powerful concept of 'sustainable development'. The idea, here, is to ensure that the economy does not leave behind 'ecological sustainability' on its way to achieving the mesmerizing growth rate of 10 per cent.

11th Plan and the Environment

The Approach Paper's vision that "The 11th Plan must integrate development planning and environmental concerns", is a statement indicating a focused and decisive direction, but leaves much at the hands of interpreters. Two seemingly dissimilar views crop up when the paper states: "With rapid growth we can have the resources to prevent and deal with environmental problems, but we must also ensure that rapid growth is environmentally benign". The catch here is that the Planning Commission concludes that economic growth and environmental sustainability are poles apart. The most important issues raised by the Approach Paper apropos environment are:

TABLE 25.1
Environmental Concerns in 11th Plan Approach Paper

S. No.	*Environmental Concern*	*Mechanism Remarks*
(1)	*(2)*	*(3)*
1. Air and Water Quality	• Better Monitoring and Pollution Management • Upgrading Technology	Lack of encouragement for developing pollution-free technology
2. Solid Waste Management	• Segregation at source • Maximum Recycling	– No Urban Planning – No effort to check use of hazardous material in production

(*Contd.*)

TABLE 25.1 (Contd.)

S. No.	*Environmental Concern*	*Mechanism Remarks*
(1)	*(2)*	*(3)*
3. Wildlife and Biodiversity	• Maintaining vital database • Inducing voluntary removal of forest dwellers from notified areas	Ignores Biodiversity Act, 2002 and Scheduled Tribes and Other Traditional Forest Dwellers (Recognition of Forest Rights) Act, 2006
4. Increasing Green Cover	• Encouraging Social Forestry • Establishing more Joint Forest Management groups	Encourages Corporate Sector participation, but at what cost?

An area which the government has to tread carefully is the one on 'environmental clearances', which the Commission indicts of propagating "a new licence permit raj system". Evidently, a claim to water down environmental clearance procedures for industries cannot be missed, just as one cannot rue that in certain cases, such clearances do pose a problem—politically and procedurally. In the Deputy Chairman's presentation to the National Development Council, the sticky situation of environmental clearances was left behind to make way for the following assertions:

- Increase forest and tree cover by 5 percentage points.
- Attain WHO standards of air quality in all major cities by 2011-12.
- Treat all urban waste water by 2011-12 to clean river waters.

A Critique

Quite understandably, the Approach Paper's stance is partially pro-environment in aim, albeit not in content. A case in point is the drab treatment of mining activities. Taking up an anthropocentric view, the government aims at maximising investment in exploration and operation of mines, in total disregard to environment. No guidelines or framework to engage in environmental friendly mining operations are outlined, and the conspicuous absence of undertaking Environment Impact Assessment programmes cannot but be noticed. Even a casual reading of the 'Main Recommendations of the High Level Committee on the National Mineral Policy', cited in the Planning Commission's document, makes it hard to miss the lack of 'environment conscious' approach to mineral excavations. Another missed opportunity is the flagrant non-attendance to energy-environment linkages. There is also the criticism that the Planning Commission has attempted to rely heavily on market mechanism to solve environmental problems. Still further, operational environmental management plans are non-existent.

Environmentally Sustainable Inclusive Growth Strategy

Including environment in a national level policy has to be accompanied by pointers that would help in integrating environment into mainstream growth process, as represented in Figure 25.1.

As can be deciphered, the agenda is clear, the process executable and the target achievable. It would do one good to take a cue from the former Deputy Chairman of the Planning Commission, Mohan Dharia: "*. . . India needs growth coupled with social justice and due care of environment*". One without the other is an insincere gesture to national development agenda.

FIG. 25.1

Achieving Pro-Environmental Inclusive Growth

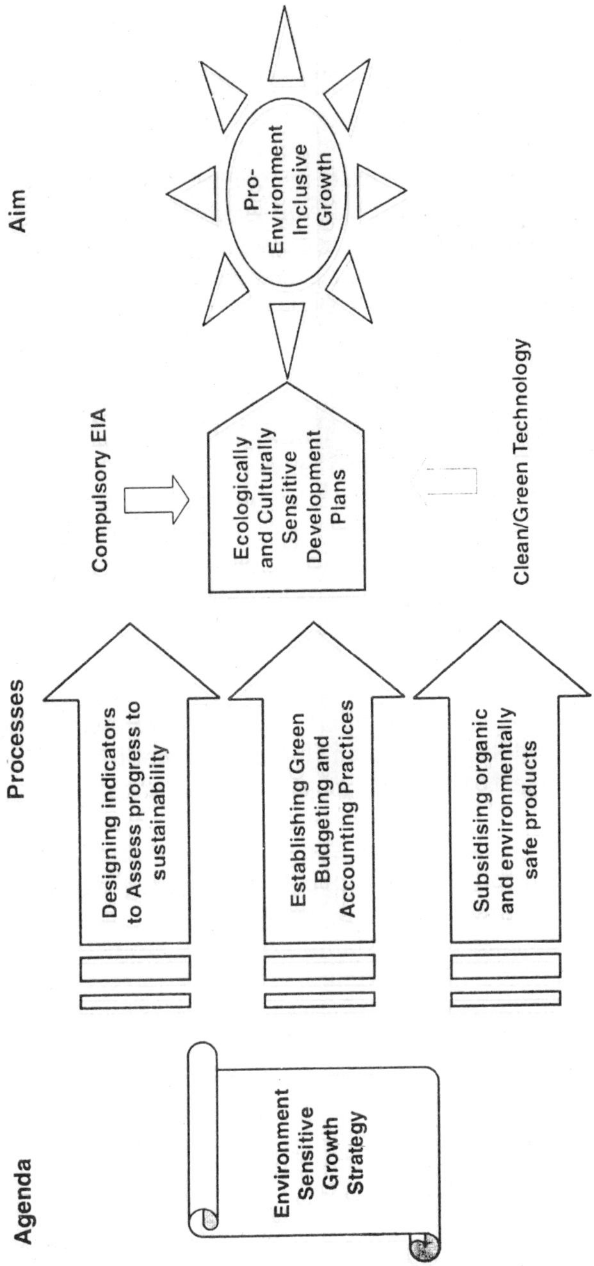

Note : EIA – Environment Impact Assessment.

Source : Based on Kothari, Ashish, "No Sign of Green", *Frontline*, 24(7), April 07-20, 2007.

References

"Quest for Inclusive Growth: Continuity and Constraints in Indian Economic Policies", *Economic and Political Weekly,* September 10, 2005, pp. 4052-61.

Planning Commission, *Towards Faster and More Inclusive Growth,* December 2006.

"Monitorable Socio-Economic Targets: 11th Plan", *Yojana,* Vol. 51, April 2007.

"CPI(M). Comments on the Approach Paper to the Eleventh Five Year Plan-II", *People's Democracy,* Vol. XXX, No. 31, July 30, 2006.

Himanshu Thakkar, "Any hopes for a People Friendly 11th Plan?", South Asia Network on Dams, Rivers and People, July 2006.

"Approach to Eleventh Five Year Plan", *Yojana,* Vol. 51, April 2007, pp. 23-25.

26

Inclusive Need for the Interlinking of Rivers

R. CHRISTOPHER RAJKUMAR

INTRODUCTION

21st Century is marked by the development and progress based on modern Science and Technology. But this neo-development and neo-economic policies do not allow the people to drink Water from the springs. The river-water polluted by the industrial waste, de-forestation and global-warming result in the ground water table being disturbed. Above all the media of today is encouraging (forcing) us to drink water from the 'packed bottle'. The increased privatization and commoditization is so severe that we depend on the market even for our basic needs like water. Water scarcity is one of the major problems in India. Water resources are privatized and have become an expensive commodity. In this context, it is important to affirm that "Water as Life: Water as

Right". Water is a God given gift and it should be accessible to the entire creation.

August 25th 2005 was a black day in India's environmental life, because the first agreement on the inter-linking of rivers was signed between the Governments of Madhya Pradesh and Utter Pradesh along with the Cabinet Minister for Water Resources, in the presence of the Prime Minister of India at Delhi. The rational behind this project is to make use of the surplus water of *'Khen'* River by linking with 'Petwa' River by which both the governments foresee better Development. The former Prime Minster Vajpayee describes this event as historical. And further the Minister for Water Resources said, the project proposal for inter-linking of 14 rivers in South India is ready and that will be implemented soon. Now the entire economy of the nation depends on the 'water-business'.

BRIEF HISTORY OF INTERLINKING OF RIVERS (ILR)

The Government of India claims that the IRL Project proposal is in its infancy. But the historical reading of this project tells us that, it is not at all a new project. In 1881, Arthur Cotton proposed an idea of 'linking of inter-basin water to the linking of rivers and canals to then the British rulers. It was under consideration for a while and then it was rejected. The British regime continued for another 66 years in India, but they had never reviewed this Cotton's Proposal. In 1975, Dr. K.L. Rao suggested a similar proposal. The idea was similar to Cotton but it was about the inter-basin transfer of water through *Ganga-Cauvery* and Bramaputra-Ganges link canals. Capt. Dinshaw Dastur forwarded a proposal to make a canal link between the *Himalayan* and Peninsular components with two pipelines in 1980. These two proposals were also rejected under technical and financial grounds. The National Water Development Agency was established in 1982, to explore the feasibilities of inter-basin transfer of water. There was an objection in regard to link the *Bramaputhra-Ganga* basin to the river basins in the rest of the country. Then in 2002 the New Water Policy was proposed and adopted. The country was divided in to several water-zones keeping in mind both the surplus and deficit regions. On the eve of Independence Day 2002, the President of India urged for the ILR to combat flood and drought.[1] With reference to this President's address, the apex court and the division bench headed by the Chief Justice, Kirpal gave the landmark judgment on Oct. 31, 2002, asking the Central Government to 'complete' the ILR project by the end of 2016. Accordingly the Government formed a task force headed by the Chairmanship of Mr. Suresh Prabhu, who was then the Minister of Power in the Union Cabinet, to do the needful. This task force is supposed to explore the possible means to execute this huge project estimated as INR. 5,60,000 crores.[2]

CONCEPTUAL ISSUES IN THE ILR PROJECT

1. There are few pivotal questions before the ILR Project. These are—

   (a) Is there a grave necessity for such a huge or mega project?
   (b) Can the Project fit well with in our National Planning Process and the Budget?
   (c) Where will the money come from?
   (d) Will this Project yield the desired benefit to the whole country?
   (e) Is it mean to be seen as a Human Right problem or Basic need?
   (f) Do we have any right to restrict the flow of water?

2. Social issues in the ILR Project.

(a) Environmental Concerns

Though this ILR Project proposes to bring the adequate sharing of controlled water management system, it denies and ignores the fundamental ecological principal that there is no component in nature which is either excess or wasted. The ecological cost for the interlinking of rivers is immense and the whole exercise depends upon the prediction of regular monsoons. The natural habitat of several species of birds and animals, which survive in certain geographical area, is also indeed a matter of concern. The effect of human intervention is beyond our calculation.[3]

(b) Displacement of People

There are no words to describe the displacement problems if this project is implemented. Construction of dams and reservoirs effectively results in a direct assault of the country's tribal population as it has affected the '*Narmada*' Valley.

(c) Drought Resistance

Certainly not the ILR Project is an adequate solution to resist the drought, because transfer of water to one river to another place might be possible only if some additional water exist in this area. Even then, transfer of water can only help the low level drought prone areas that are small part of land compared with large acute drought prone areas.[4] On the other hand the 'rainwater harvest' is an effective method available. But the Government assumed that the project would lead to a permanent drought proofing of the country by raising the irrigation potential. But the environmentalists oppose that it is not practically a viable project.

(d) Flood Control

The primary justification for IRL project, propounded is flood control. Contrary to this rationale, the water resource engineers argue that the idea of flood control would be made possible only through the launch out of particular projects in specific locations and not through the ILR.[5] ILR is certainly not the solution for flood control, when 1,400 cu.m could be discharged through canals. Various studies were done during the flooded time in *Ganga* at *Farakka* and *Bramaputhra* at *Pandu, and it is found that the* discharge of water was 75,900 cu.m. It is just withdrawal of 1,400 cu.m would not make much of a difference logically and then that there lies no justification for inter-linking of rivers.

(e) Drinking Water

ILR plans to bring the drinking water facility to 101 districts and 5 metropolitan cities.[6] It is doubtful if the river link would be the solution, when there are possible local water source management systems such as local ponds, lakes and common wells. Safeguarding the lakes and ponds and constructing the check dams in the traditional way could solve almost 90% of our drinking water problems.

(f) Ecological Impact

A complete study on the ecological impact has not made yet, but it is estimated that around 79,292 hectares of prime forest might be submerged under the reservoir scheme can be estimated. A large number of people would be displaced, but the official document determines only 4.5 lakh people.[7] Another expressed concern is the present polluted rivers. If the toxic streams are interlinked, will it not affect the available fresh water in other areas? And also what will happen to the species of that particular area? The third and important area is 'death of oceans'. If all the rivers streams area interlinked to the land, who will feed the seas and oceans? What will happen to the species of the sea? In a poetical reflection Dr. M.J. Joseph writes,

> "O man! Respect the freedom of the rivers to take their own course
> You may harness the power from its course
> You may allow the little creatures to live in them
> *Wants all to live in the fullness of life....*"[8]
> Is it not a genuine tone?

(g) Other Related issues

(i) North-South link of the project seems to be an impossible task as the '*Vindhya*' Range of hills stands tall in the Indian topographical structure. Canalizing the water through '*Vindhya*' hills is not as easy as fixing the railway tracks. It is to generate 34 Million KW, but did not take into consideration that power required lifting the water across the topographical barriers. In fact, we need more power then what we produce now.

(ii) It is estimated that the project would cost INR 5,60,000 crores. This estimate was prepared by the existing value of the raw materials and other accessories. This could possibly rise up between 2 and 3 times of estimated cost in every year. If it is happened we may not able to complete the project within the time frame and unable to mobilize the resources.

(iii) The estimated cost of this ILR project is INR 5, 60, 000 crores, twice the annual revenues of the Government By the time we may expect 200%to 300% raise in the expenditure. So the ultimate cost would escalate the GDP of the country and financial management would be impossible.[9]

(iv) The average efficiency of the existing dam-canal is 38%-40% only. The water holding capacity in the entire reservoir is diminishing faster than anticipated. According to a study in 1991 about 3.30 million hectares of land being affected by water logging and Salinization. More new canals will aggravate further interruption.[10]

(v) Several water borne diseases are caused due to the water logging and sanitation. This will make the ordinary people to suffer further.

(vi) The ILR Project involves in acquisition of about 8000 sq. km. of land. This would cause the people to be landless.

(h) Neighbourhood Relations

A. The Nepalese experts say that, more then 75% of the Ganges water during the dry season flows from Nepal. If ILR project worked out Nepal has to take a permission to construct a dam or to implement a similar project like this.

B. Thus, it is imperative for the Bangladesh Government to turn its attention to the ILR project before India gets the chance to build and operate it to make it into a fait accompli like Farraka barrage. Bangladesh government should get its act together with no loss of time to do all things that must be done to nip this project in the bud. Specially, opposition to it must be built among the donors, which India would be requesting for resources to implement the project. On the other hand, the donors are likely to have a rethink and withhold assistance to the project if Bangladesh can convince them enough about its disastrous impact on Bangladesh and show to them how international law is completely on the side of Bangladesh in relation to this Issue.

In Short, we have to ask two basic questions with regard to ILR project.

(i) Will the project be actually implemented with given economic and political constrains?
(ii) If the ILR Projects were implemented, what are the ecological catastrophes that we would encounter?

As citizens we are obligated to the following :

(a) Mobilize the masses with hope against the private entrepreneurs and Government officials.
(b) Any small initiative from our part (hopefully through this study conference) could go a long way.
(c) In this context we have to pledge to strive to save our rivers and to sow the seeds of development with our resources in a self-reliant way.
(d) Like any other human rights issue this 'Right to Water' is also 'respected'.
(e) Water and its sources (Local) are to be protected from the third parties.
(f) The possible means are to be facilitated in assisting the locals in water management.
(g) The access to water is to be ensured, i.e. physical access, equal distribution and local monitoring and evaluation.
(h) The local panchayats to be empowered in managing the local water resources.

Above all, our response to this ILR should be spelt through actions towards 'just' and 'equitous water management' which is not the farcical solution of ILR offered to us in a glossy and glaring present form.

NOTES AND REFERENCES

1. 2002 was the Year of Drought when there was a Great-less Rain Falls in the Country.
2. The Hindu. "Interlinking Problems", in Suresh Prabhu on River Linking (11.08.2003).
3. Statement of the Seminar on "Interlinking of Rivers", ECC News, The Ecumenical Christian Centre, 2004, p. 20.
4. Ramaswamy, R. Iyer, "River-Linking Project: Many Questions' in Medha Patkar (ed.) *River Linking: A Millennium Folly?* National Alliance of People's Movement, Mumbai, 2004, p. 13ff.
5. *Ibid.*
6. The Hindu, *op. cit.*
7. Manas Das Gupta, "*Experts Raise Doubts about River-linking Project*". Retrieved from URL: http://www.hinduonnet.com/thehindu/2003/01/31/stories.
8. M.J. Joseph, Boasting of Rivers, "One in Many: Many in One", CSS, Thiruvalla, 2005, p. 249.
9. ECC News, *op. cit.*, p. 20.
10. Sudhirendar Sharma, The Hidden Impact of River Linking: Widespread Water logging and Salinity, Retrieved from URL: http//www.infochangeindia.org/features/(2003).

27

Inclusive Growth in the Globalised India : A Critique

G.M. BHAT AND SHABIR AHMAD PADDER

INTRODUCTION

The approach paper of Eleventh Five Year Plan comes at a time when the Indian Economy has come on cross roads. There are inter-personal and inter-regional disparities. The differences across states have long been a cause of concern but increasingly there is a recognition of the problem of severe imbalances within states. Backward districts of otherwise well performing states, present a dismal picture of intra-state imbalance and neglect. There are gaps between different social groups in India, more glaring in case of SCs/STs and minorities. There are excluded groups in our society such as SCs, STs and OBCs and some minorities who continue to lag behind the rest. Another important divide in gender discrimination. The divide between urban and rural India has become a truism of our times.

The last three plans beginning from the 8th through the 10th Five Year Plan has seen tremendous economic growth under the New Economic Policy. But the economic growth has been mainly steered by the services sector followed by the manufacturing sector. The agricultural sector has seen large fluctuations and its average growth rate has been barely around 2 percent. It is notable that agricultural sector provides livelihood to around 60 percent of India's population. The New Economic Policy has remained confined mainly to urban areas and the rural areas have got a very miniscule share in development. It is in view of all these, the eleventh five year's main thrust is on inclusive growth. The Planning Commission approved the Approach paper to the Eleventh Five-Year Plan (2007-12) on October 18, 2006. The Prime Minister, Dr. Manmohan Singh, rooted for a growth rate of 10 percent in the final years of the Plan in order to be in "the front ranks of fast growing development countries". Presiding over the full Plan panel meet, Dr Singh said that by ensuring inclusive growth, the Eleventh Plan would set "our economy on a growth path, which would finally liberate millions of our countrymen from the perennial scourges of poverty, ignorance and disease". What is implied in this recognition is that a sizable group of population has not been "included" in and have, therefore, not benefited from growth. Trickledown can take place if the poor are also included in the growth process that is they are engaged in economic activities that are growing, even though the non-poor may be the main actors and, therefore main beneficiaries of growth. When certain groups of people are not even "included" in the growth process, there is no question of the benefits of growth "trickling-down" to them. Thus the notion of "trickledown" is not merely non-operational, it is irrelevant (Papola, 2007)

The Approach Paper to eleventh five year plan starts with the assertion that the Indian economy on the eve of the 11th Plan is in a much stronger position than it was a few years ago. After slowing down to an average growth rate of about 5.5% in the Ninth Plan period (1997-98 to 2001-02), it has accelerated in recent years and the average growth rate in the Tenth Plan period (2002-03 to 2006-07) is likely to be about 7%. This is below the Tenth Plan target of 8%, but it is the highest growth rate achieved in any plan period. While this performance reflects the strength of the economy in many areas, it is also true that large parts of our population are still to experience a decisive improvement in their standard of living. The percentage of the population below the poverty line is declining, but only at a modest pace. Far too many people still lack access to basic services such as health, education, clean drinking water and sanitation facilities without which they cannot be empowered to claim their share in the benefits of growth. These problems are more severe in some states than in others, and in general they are especially severe in rural areas.

INFRASTRUCTURAL DISPARITIES

The Eleventh Finance Commission devised an infrastructure index for the states for the year 1999. The index brings out a composite comparative profile of the availability of physical, social and institutional infrastructure in the states.

Amongst all the states that existed in 1999, Goa had the highest infrastructure index, i.e., it was the best placed state in terms of infrastructure facilities while Arunachal Pradesh had the lowest infrastructure index.

TABLE 27.1

Index of Social and Economic Infrastructure, 1991 (Arranged in Increasing Order)

Sl. No.	States	Index
(1)	(2)	(3)
1.	Arunachal Pradesh	69.71
2.	Jammu & Kashmir	71.46
3.	Tripura	74.87
4.	Manipur	75.39
5.	Meghalaya	75.49

(Contd.)

TABLE 27.1 (Contd.)

(1)	(2)	(3)
6.	Rajasthan	75.86
7.	Nagaland	76.14
8.	Madhya Pradesh	76.79
9.	Assam	77.72
10.	Orissa	81.00
11.	Bihar	81.33
12.	Mizoram	82.13
13.	Himachal Pradesh	95.03
14.	Uttar Pradesh	101.23
15.	Andhra Pradesh	103.30
16.	Karnataka	104.88
17.	Sikkim	108.99
18.	West Bengal	111.25
19.	Maharashtra	112.80
20.	Gujarat	124.31
21.	Haryana	137.54
22.	Tamil Nadu	149.10
23.	Kerala	178.68
24.	Punjab	187.57
25.	Goa	200.57

Source : Eleventh Finance Commission Report, 2000.

DISPARITIES IN THE GROWTH OF GROSS STATE DOMESTIC PRODUCT

Mr. Montek S. Ahluwalia, in his paper 'Economic Performance of the States in the Post-Reforms Period' has analysed the disparities in the growth performance of different states.

The accompanying table presents the estimated growth rates of SDP in the 14 major states in the pre-reform period 1980-81 to 1990-91 and in the post-reform period 1991-92 to 1997-98.

TABLE 27.2
Annual Rates of Growth of Gross State Domestic Product (SDP)

States	*1980-81 to 1990-91 % p.a.*	*1991-92 to 1997-98 % p.a.*	
1. Bihar	4.66	2.69	↓
2. Rajasthan	6.60	6.54	↓
3. Uttar Pradesh	4.95	3.58	↓
4. Orissa	4.29	3.25	↓
5. Madhya Pradesh	4.56	6.17	↑
6. Andhra Pradesh	5.65	5.03	↓
7. Tamil Nadu	5.38	6.22	↑
8. Kerala	3.57	5.81	↑
9. Karnataka	5.29	5.29	—
10. West Bengal	4.71	6.91	↑
11. Gujarat	5.08	9.57	↑
12. Haryana	6.43	5.02	↓
13. Maharashtra	6.02	8.01	↑
14. Punjab	5.32	4.71	↓
Combined SDP of 14 States	5.24	5.94	↑

The following conclusions can be drawn from the growth performance of the states.

1. The growth rate of the combined SDP of all the 14 states taken together has increased from 5.2 percent in the pre-reform period to 5.9 percent in the post-reform period.
2. The disparities between the performances of individuals states have increased significantly in the 1990s. The range of variation in the growth rate of SDP in the 1980s was from a low of 3.6 percent per year in Kerala to a high of 6.6 per cent in Rajasthan—a factor of less than two. In the 1990s the variation was much larger, from a low of 2.7 percent a year in Bihar to a high of 9.6 percent for Gujarat—a factor exceeding 3.5.

3. The differences in performance across states become even more marked when we evaluate the performance in terms of growth rates of per capita SDP. The variation in growth rates in the 1980s ranged from a low of 2.1 per cent for Madhya Pradesh to a high of 4.0 for Rajasthan, a factor of 1:2. In the 1990s it ranged from a low of 1.1 percent year in Bihar and 1.2 percent in Uttar Pradesh, to a high of 7.6 percent per year in Gujarat, with Maharashtra coming next at 6.1 percent. The ratio between the lowest (Bihar) and the highest (Gujarat) is as much as 1:7.
4. In the 1990s while the growth accelerated for the economy as a whole, it actually decelerated sharply in Bihar, Uttar Pradesh and Orissa all of which had relatively low rates of growth to begin with and were also the poorest states. These three states together also account for over a third of the population of our country. There was also a deceleration in Haryana and Punjab, but the deceleration was from relatively higher levels of growth in the 1980s, and these states were also the richest.
5. Six states of the country showed acceleration in growth of SDP in the 1990s. The acceleration was particularly marked in Maharashtra and Gujarat, both of which were among the richer states, but there was also an acceleration in West Bengal, Kerala, Tamil Nadu and Madhya Pradesh belonging to the middle group of states in terms of per capita SDP.
6. Another point to be noted is that the high growth performers in the 1990s were not concentrated in one part of the country. The six states with growth rates of SDP above 6 percent per year in the 1990s are fairly well-distributed regionally, i.e., Gujarat (9.6 percent) and Maharashtra (8.0 percent) in the west, West Bengal (6.9 percent) in the east, Tamil Nadu (6.2 percent) in the south and Madhya Pradesh (6.2 percent) and Rajasthan (6.5 percent) in the north.

An interesting feature of the performance in the 1990s is that the so-called grouping of BIMARU states (Bihar, Madhya

Pradesh, Rajasthan and Uttar Pradesh) as poor performers does not hold true in case of economic performance. Though Bihar and Uttar Pradesh performed poorly, growing more slowly than the average, the other two members of this group, Rajasthan and Madhya Pradesh, have performed reasonably well. In the 1990s Rajasthan grew at a rate marginally lower than its average in 1980s, but nevertheless remained a strong performer. Madhya Pradesh's growth in the 1980s was below the average of the 14 states but it accelerated significantly in the 1990s.

Similarly, the perception that coastal states or the southern states have all done well in the period of liberalization is not valid. Orissa being a coastal state has not done well whereas Rajasthan and Madhya Pradesh are heartland states and have performed reasonably well. The southern states as a group have done well, but they have not been the only beneficiaries of growth in the 1990s. In fact, Tamil Nadu is the only southern state in the top six best performers.

The performance of Kerala in the sphere of human development has been commendable. Its economic performance in the 1990s showed a marked improvement compared with the 1980s. Because of low population growth, its per capita income was more than the average for the 14 states.

In conclusion, the superior performance of Gujarat and Maharashtra must be attributed to the fact that the states were able to provide an environment most conducive to benefiting from the new policies of the 1990s. The key ingredients of success in these states should be identified and emulated by other states. Simultaneously the basic factors hindering the growth of the poor performers should be tackled at the earliest.

IMPLICATIONS OF INTER-STATE INEQUALITY

Montek Singh Ahluwalia has estimated Gini coefficient measuring inter-State inequality for 18 years from 1980-81 to 1998-99. His estimates confirm the common perception that inter-State inequality in the decades of 1980s and 1990s has increased. Gini coefficient measuring Inter-State inequality is 0.225 for 1997-98 as against 0.175 for 1989-90 and 0.152 in 1980-81. His estimates of Gini coefficient, measuring inter-State inequality for 18 years from 1980-81 to 1998-99 are reproduced in Table 27.3

TABLE 27.3
Trends in Gini Coefficient Measuring Inter-State Inequality

1980-81	0.152
1981-82	0.152
1982-83	0.152
1983-84	0.151
1984-85	0.154
1985-86	0.159
1986-87	0.157
1987-88	0.161
1988-89	0.158
1989-90	0.175
1990-91	0.171
1991-92	0.175
1992-93	0.199
1993-94	0.207
1994-95	0.206
1995-96	0.230
1996-97	0.222
1997-98	0.235
1998-99	0.233

According to Montek Singh Ahluwalia, these estimates do not suggest that the rich States got richer and poor States got poorer. This inference is based on the following results:

1. Punjab and Haryana were the two richest States but their growth rates fell below the national average.
2. Performance of four middle income States West Bengal, Kerala, Tamil Nadu and Karnataka was above the national average. In fact, West Bengal registered very steady growth.

3. Bihar, Uttar Pradesh and Orissa the poorest States performed very poorly in the 1990s.

INCIDENCE OF POVERTY

Poverty in any society is considered an important indicator of economic backwardness. In India, poor are to be found everywhere, but the percentage of population below poverty line is not the same in the States. The Planning Commission's latest estimates of incidence of poverty in different States 1999-2000 are shown in Table 27.4.

TABLE 27.4
Incidence of Poverty

States		*1993-94 Poverty Ratio (Per cent)*	*1999-2000 Poverty Ratio (Per cent)*
1.	Andhra Pradesh	22.2	15.8
2.	Assam	40.9	36.1
3.	Bihar	55.0	42.6
4.	Gujarat	24.2	14.1
5.	Haryana	25.1	8.7
6.	Himachal Pradesh	28.4	7.6
7.	Karnataka	33.2	20.04
8.	Kerala	25.4	12.7
9.	Madhya Pradesh	42.5	37.4
10.	Maharashtra	36.9	25.0
11.	Orissa	48.6	47.2
12.	Punjab	11.8	6.2 A
13.	Rajasthan	27.4	15.3
14.	Tamil Nadu	35.0	21.1
15.	Uttar Pradesh	40.9	31.2
16.	West Bengal	35.7	27.0
	All-India	36.0	26.1

Source : Tata Services Ltd., *Statistical Outline of India*, 2005-06, (Mumbai, 2006), Table 166, p. 150.

According to the Planning Commission's estimates of the incidence of poverty around 26.1 per cent of the population of India was below the poverty line in 1999-2000. However, certain States, the incidence of poverty was much less. For instance, population below the poverty line was 6.2 per cent in Punjab, 15.8 per cent in Andhra Pradesh, 14.1 per cent in Gujarat, 8.7 per cent in Haryana are 12.7 per cent in Kerala. It is interesting to note that Andhra Pradesh and Kerala are middle income States and yet in these States incidence of poverty is far less than Maharashtra which is a high income State. As against this, incidence of poverty was as high as 42.6 per cent in Bihar, 47.2 per cent in Orissa, 37.4 per cent in Madhya Pradesh, 36.1 per cent in Assam and 31.2 per cent in Uttar Pradesh. Hence, in 1999-2000 out of 260.3 million poor in India, 135.2 million were in these five States. Bihar, Uttar Pradesh and Madhya Pradesh are big States. In 1999-2000, these three States together accounted for 42.0 per cent of the total number of poor in the country. This implies that there was concentration of poverty in economically back ward big States.

DISPARITIES IN HUMAN RESOURCE DEVELOPMENT

Infant mortality rate and literacy rate are two very good indices of physical quality of life. Infant mortality rate shows a tendency to decline with economic and social development. From this point of view Kerala is far ahead of other States. In 2002 infant mortality rate in Kerala was 10 per 1,000 live births as against the national infant mortality rate of 63 per 1,000 live births. Punjab, Maharashtra, West Bengal and Tamil Nadu had infant mortality rates in the range of 44 to 51. The States registering high infant mortality rates in 2002 were Orissa (87), Madhya Pradesh (85), Uttar Pradesh (80), Rajasthan (78), Assam (70) and Haryana (62). Even on other criteria most of these States have been found to be extremely backward.

Literacy rate in general and female literacy rate in particular are regarded as good indicators of development. On these criteria Kerala (the first ranked State) has done extremely well *vis-a-vis* other States. According to 2001 census, the overall literacy rate in Kerala was 90.9 per cent, as against the national average of 65.4 per cent. Even the female literacy rate in Kerala was as high as 87.9 per cent. In the States of Bihar, Rajasthan and Uttar Pradesh the literacy rates ranged between 47.5 and 61.0 per cent. In these States the female literacy rate ranged from 33.8 to 44.3 per cent. Interestingly in Haryana, the third ranked State in terms of per capita income both overall literacy rate and the female literacy rate were more or less the same as all-India rates. This perhaps is due to the low priority given to education in patriarchal agrarian societies.

DISPARITIES IN INDUSTRIAL GROWTH

The initial distribution of industries in India was determined by the historical processes of growth in the interests of the British rulers. As a result, most of the industries got concentrated at a few centres. This pattern continued in the post-Independence period as well. For instance, a study of 28 large-scale manufacturing industries in India in 1950 showed the dominance of the Western region and West Bengal in the regional distribution of industries. Thus, 34.60 per cent of total productive capital was concentrated in Western region while 24.65 per cent was concentrated in West Bengal, their combined share being as much as 59.25 per cent. Taken together, the Western region and West Bengal accounted for 63.03 per cent of total persons employed, 60.41 per cent of gross ex-factory value of output, and 63.95 per cent of value added by manufacture.

This pattern of concentration has not changed substantially during the planning period despite all attempts made at regional dispersal of industries. For instance, as late as 2002-03 the two States of Maharashtra and Tamil Nadu accounted for 28.9 per cent of factory employment, 28.5 per cent of invested capital, 28.8 per cent of gross output and 29.1 per cent of value added by manufacture. If the three industrially advanced States of Maharashtra, Gujarat and Tamil Nadu are considered together, the true picture of regional concentration of industries is explicitly brought into prominence. In 2002-03 these three States together (having 20.4 per cent of total population according to 2001 census) accounted for 45.0 per cent of gross output, 42.4 per cent of value added, 45.7 per cent of total invested capital, and 37.9 per cent of employment in factory sector. The mere fact that more than two fifths of the total output, value added and fixed capital and a little less than two-fifths of total employment in factory sector is found in these three States alone while the remaining States and Union Territories contribute only a little more than half of total value added and total output is a proof of substantial regional concentration of industries in the three industrially advanced States of Maharashtra, Gujarat and Tamil Nadu.

DISPARITIES IN AGRICULTURAL DEVELOPMENT

As far as the agricultural sector is concerned, regional disparities have increased over time with the States of Punjab and Haryana and parts of Uttar Pradesh pushing well ahead of others. This is due to the reason that the success of the programme of High Yielding Varieties of seeds (known as HYVP or New Agricultural Strategy) was largely limited to wheat growing areas. In fact, due to HYVP, the combined share of Punjab and Haryana in total output of foodgrains rose from 7.5 per cent in 1964-65 to 20.16 per cent in 2003-04 while these States account for a mere 4.4 per cent of the country's population (as per 2001 census). In 2002-03, per capita output of foodgrains was 964.3 kgs. in Punjab which was more than five and a half times the national per capita output (the national per capita output of foodgrains in 2002-03 being 169.3 kgs). The per capita output of foodgrains in Haryana was 583.4 kgs. which was about three and a half times the national per capita output. The position of these States *vis-a-vis* other States would be clear from the fact that the per capita output of foodgrains in Uttar Pradesh (which ranked third in 2002-03) was 218.4 kgs. and in West Bengal (which ranked fourth in 2002-03) was 193.6 kgs. Thus the per capita output of foodgrains in Punjab was more than four and a half times the per capita output in the third ranked State. The prosperity of agriculture in Punjab and Haryana is largely due to irrigation facilities and high fertiliser consumption per hectare of cropped area. In Punjab and Haryana, in 1999-2000 gross irrigated area as percentage of gross cropped area was 90.9 per cent and 85.0 per cent respectively, as against all India average of 40.2 per cent. Likewise, fertiliser consumption per hectare of cropped area was 184.0 kgs. in Punjab and 167.1 kgs. in Haryana in 2003-04, as against the national average of 89.8 kgs. in the same year.

SOME MAJOR CHALLENGES

Some of the major challenges the 11th Five Year Plan's approach paper points out are:

(a) Providing Essential Public Services for the Poor

The most important challenge is how to provide essential public services such as education and health to large parts of our population who are denied these services at present.

(b) Regaining Agricultural Dynamism

One of the major challenges of the 11th Plan must be to reverse the deceleration in agricultural growth from 3.2% observed between 1980 and 1996-97 to a trend average of only 1.5% subsequently. This deceleration is undoubtedly at the root of the problem of rural distress that has surfaced in many parts of the country. A second Green Revolution is urgently needed to raise the growth rate of agricultural GDP to around 4%.

(c) Increasing Manufacturing Competitiveness

The manufacturing sector has also not grown as rapidly as might have been expected. The average growth rate of this sector has accelerated compared to the Ninth Plan but is unlikely to exceed 8% in the 10th Plan. It should be targeted to grow at around 12% or so if we want to achieve a GDP growth of between 8 and 9%. The most important constraint in achieving a faster growth of manufacturing is the fact that infrastructure, consisting of roads, railway, ports, airports communication and electric power, is not up to the standards prevalent in our competitor countries. This must be substantially rectified within the next 5-10 years if our enterprises are to compete effectively.

(d) Developing Human Resource

To ensure a continuous and growing supply of quality investments in public sector institutions of higher learning combined with fundamental reforms of the curriculum and also service conditions to attract high quality faculty. The scope for expanding capacity through private sector initiatives in higher learning must also be fully exploited, while also ensuring that quality standards are not diluted. Unless this is done on an urgent basis, we will fail to attain global standards.

(e) Protecting the Environment

Environmental concerns are growing globally as well as within the country. Neglect of environmental considerations can lead to adverse effects very quickly. The threat of climate change also poses real challenge to the well-being of future generations which we can ill afford to ignore. Our development at strategy has to be sensitive to these growing concerns and should ensure that these threats and trade-offs are appropriately evaluated.

References

Planning Commission, (October 2006), *Approach Paper to the Eleventh Five Year Plan (2007-12)*, Govt. of India, New Delhi.

S. Mahendra Dev, "Regional Disparities in Poverty and Malnutrition", paper presented at a Seminar at ISID, New Delhi, September 16-18, 2005.

Papola, T.S., *Reducing Imbalances in Regional Development: An Essential Ingredient of Strategy for "Inclusive Growth"*, Inaugural address at the National Seminar on "Making Growth Inclusive with Special Reference to Imbalances in Regional Development", Department of Economics, University of Jammu, Jammu, 12-13 March, 2007.

Rajaram, K. and Singh, S.N., Indian Economy, Spectrum Books Pvt. Ltd., New Delhi, 2005.

Misra, S.K. and Puri, V.K. (2006), Economics of Development and Planning, Himalaya Publishing House, New Delhi.

APPENDIX

TOWARDS FASTER AND MORE INCLUSIVE GROWTH

OBJECTIVES AND CHALLENGES

Indian on the eve of the 11th Plan is in a much stronger position than it was a few years ago. After slowing down to an average growth rate of about 5.5% in the 9th Plan period (1997-98 to 2001-02), it has accelerated significantly in recent years. The average growth rate in the last four years of 10th Plan period (2003-04 to 2006-07) is likely to be a little over 8%, making the growth rate 7.2% for the entire 10th Plan period. Though, this is below the 10th Plan target of 8%, it is the highest growth rate achieved in any plan period.

This performance reflects the strength of our economy and the dynamism of the private sector in many areas. Yet, it is also true that economic growth has failed to be sufficiently inclusive, particularly after the mid-1990s. Agriculture lost its growth momentum from that point on and subsequently entered a near crisis situation. Jobs in the organized sector have not increased despite faster growth. The percentage of our population below the poverty line is declining but only at a modest pace. Malnutrition levels also appear to be declining, but the magnitude of the problem continues to be very high. Far too many people still lack access to basic services such as health, education, clean drinking water and sanitation facilities without which they cannot claim their share in the benefits of growth. Women have increased their participation in the labour force as individuals, but continue to face discrimination and are subject to increasing violence, one stark example of which is the declining child sex ratio.

Despite these problems, most of the ordinary people have tried to cope with their livelihood issues. Many have participated in collective action to try to improve their social and economic conditions. Empowerment of Panchayati Raj Institutions (PRIs) is ongoing but much remains to be done. Civil Society Organizations have gained strength and are trying new experiments to reach the unreached, often in partnership with PRIs. Women are participating in PRIs and leading group action for a better life.

1.1 A Vision for the 11th Plan

The 11th Plan provides an opportunity to restructure policies to achieve a new vision based on faster, more broad-based and inclusive growth. It is designed to reduce poverty and focus on bridging the various divides that continue to fragment our society. The 11th Plan must aim at putting the economy on a sustainable growth trajectory with a growth rate of approximately 10 per cent by the end of the Plan period. It will create productive employment at a faster pace than before, and target robust agriculture growth at 4% per year.

The first steps in this direction were initiated in the middle of the 10th Plan based on the National Common Minimum Programme adopted by the government. These steps must be further strengthened and consolidated into a strategy for the 11th Plan.

Rapid growth is an essential part of our strategy for two reasons. Firstly, it is only in a rapidly growing economy that we can expect to sufficiently raise the incomes of the mass of our population to bring about a general improvement in living conditions. Secondly, rapid growth is necessary to generate the resources needed to provide basic services to all. Work done within the Planning Commission and elsewhere suggests that the economy can accelerate from 8 per cent per year to an average of around 9% over the 11th Plan period, provided appropriate policies are put in place. With population growing at 1.5% per year, 9% growth in GDP would double the real per capita income in 10 years. This must be combined with policies

whereas in industrialized countries and even in China it is rising. The presence of a skilled young population in an environment where investment is expanding and the industrial world is ageing could be a major advantage. It is important to realize however that we can only reap this demographic dividend if we invest on human resource development and skill formation in a massive way and create productive employment for our relatively young working population.

1.3 Some Major Challenges

The strengths enumerated above are real and provide a sound base on which the 11th Plan can build. Yet several challenges remain.

(a) Agricultural Crisis: Regaining Agricultural Dynamism

One of the major challenges of the 11th Plan will be to reverse the deceleration in agricultural growth from 3.2% observed between 1980 and 1996-97 to a trend average of around 2.0% subsequently. This deceleration is the root cause of the problem of rural distress that has surfaced in many parts of the country and reached crisis levels in some. Low farm incomes due to inadequate productivity growth have often combined with low prices of output and with lack of credit at reasonable rates, to push many farmers into crippling debt. Even otherwise, uncertainties seem to have increased (regarding prices, quality of inputs, and also weather and pests) which, coupled with unavailability of proper extension and risk insurance have led farmers to despair. This has also led to widespread distress migration, a rise in the number of female headed households in rural areas and a general increase in women's work burden and vulnerability. In 2004-05, women accounted for 34% of principal and 89% of subsidiary workers in agriculture, higher than in any previous round of the National Sample Survey.

The crisis of agriculture is not a purely distributional one that arises out of the special problems of small and marginal farmers and landless labour. In fact, agricultural deceleration is affecting farms of all sizes. To reverse this trend, corrective policies must not only focus on the small and marginal farmers who continue to deserve special attention, but on middle and large farmers too who suffer from productivity stagnation arising from a variety of constraints.

It is vital to increase agricultural incomes as this sector still employs nearly 60% of our labour force. A measure of self-sufficiency is also critical for ensuring food security. A second green revolution is urgently needed to raise the growth rate of agricultural GDP to around 4%. This is not an easy task since actual growth of agricultural GDP, including forestry and fishing, is likely to be below 2% during the 10th Plan period. The challenge therefore is to at least double the rate of agricultural growth and to do so recognize demographic realities—particularly the increasing role of women.

(b) Changing Employment Patterns

Doubling the growth of agricultural GDP to 4% per annum will improve rural employment conditions by raising real wages and reducing underemployment. However, even if this is attained, an *overall* growth of 9% will further increase income disparity between agricultural and non-agricultural households unless around 10 million workers currently in agriculture find remunerative non-agricultural employment. To make this possible, and absorb all new entrants into the labour force, non-agricultural employment would need to increase at over 6% per annum during 11th Plan. This poses a major challenge not only in terms of generating non-agricultural employment but also in matching its required location and type. Care has to be taken to manage the resulting livelihood changes and to ensure that employment is generated at all levels of skill in non-agricultural sector. The inadequacy of widely dispersed and sustainable off-farm productive employment opportunities is a basic cause of most divides and disparities. Growth without jobs can neither be inclusive nor can it bridge divides. All avenues for increasing employment opportunities, including those that can be provided by micro and small enterprises need to be explored. If we fail to do so, the demographic dividend can turn into a demographic nightmare. Thus employment creation and raising employability is another major challenge for the 11th Plan.

(c) Providing Essential Public Services to the Poor

A key element of 11th Plan strategy should be to provide essential education and health services to those large parts of our population who are still excluded from these. Education is the critical factor that empowers participation in the growth process, but our performance has been less than satisfactory, both overall and in bridging gender and other divides. Overall literacy is still less than 70% and rural female literacy less than 50% with corresponding rates even lower among the marginalized groups and minorities. While the *Sarva Shiksha Abhiyan* has expanded primary school enrolment, it is far from providing quality education. Looking ahead, we cannot be satisfied with only universal primary education; we must move towards universal secondary education too as quickly as possible. In the area of health, there continue to be large gaps in the most basic services such as mother and child care, clean drinking water, and access to basic sanitation facilities. The poor do not have even minimum access.

While both education and curative health services are available for those who can afford to pay, quality service is beyond the reach of the common people. Other privately provided services are of highly variable quality. In this situation, access to essential services can only be through public financing. In most cases this means public provision or partnership with non-profit and civil society organisations.

A major institutional challenge is that even where service providers exist, the quality of delivery 7 is poor and those responsible for delivering the services cannot be held accountable. Unless such accountability is established and cutting edge service providers trained, it will be difficult to ensure significant improvement in delivery even if large resources are made available.

(d) Increasing Manufacturing Competitiveness

Although growth in manufacturing sector has accelerated compared to the 9th Plan, it is unlikely to exceed 8% in the 10th Plan. This is unacceptably low. If we want our GDP to grow at 9%, we have to target a 12% growth rate for this sector.

Our remarkable success in IT enabled services (ITES) has prompted some observers to conclude that China has a comparative advantage in manufacturing while India in services. It has thus been suggested that we should concentrate on growth of high value services. This approach is simplistic. India's performance in IT enabled and other high end services is clearly a source of strength that must be built upon. However, India cannot afford to neglect manufacturing. We meet most of the requirements for attaining a double digit growth rate in this sector. We have a dynamic entrepreneurial class that has gained confidence in its ability to compete. We have skilled labour and excellent management capability although this is an area where supply constraints will soon emerge. There are, however, some important constraints which limit our competitiveness, especially in labour intensive manufacturing, and the 11th Plan must address these on a priority basis.

A major constraint in achieving faster growth in manufacturing that needs immediate attention, is the inadequacy of our physical infrastructure. Our roads, railways, ports, airports, communication, and above all power supply, are not comparable to the standards prevalent in our competitor countries. This gap must be filled within the next 5-10 years if our enterprises are to compete effectively. In the increasingly open trading environment that we face today, our producers must compete aggressively not just to win export markets, but also to retain domestic markets against competition from imports. Indian industry recognizes this and no longer expects to survive on protection. But they do expect a level playing field in terms of quality infrastructure. Development of infrastructure is therefore to be accorded high priority in the 11th Plan.

(e) Developing Human Resources

Decades ago we had emphasized on quality higher education by setting up IITs and other premier educational institutions. This has paid us rich dividends. However, there are emerging signs that rapid growth can result in shortage of high quality skills needed in knowledge intensive industries. One area of concern is that we are losing our edge on the tracking of pure sciences. To continue our competitive advantage and ensure a continuous supply of quality manpower, we need large investments in public sector institutions of higher learning. This should be accompanied by fundamental reform of the curriculum as well as service conditions to attract a dedicated and qualified faculty. Expanding capacity through private sector initiatives in higher learning needs to be explored while maintaining quality standards.

At the present pace of economic development, the country cannot train everyone to become skilled professionals. Even university level education to all cannot be ensured. But our industries require skills in specific trades, and India has historically lagged behind in the area of technical/vocational training. Even today enrolment rates in Industrial Training Institutes.

(ITIs) and other vocational institutes, including nursing and computer training schools, are only about a third of that in higher education. This is quite the opposite of other Asian countries which have performed better than us in labour intensive manufactures. Vocational training institutes need to be substantially expanded not only in terms of the persons they train but also in the number of different skills and trades for meeting industry requirements as well as creating opportunities for self-employment.

(f) Protecting the Environment

Our concern for environmental issues is growing along the lines of global concern. While in the short-run there may seem to be a trade-off between environmental sustainability and economic growth, we must in the longer run, take recourse to the complementarities between environmental sustainability and human well-being. We have already seen that neglect of environmental considerations. For example, profligate use of water or deforestation has devastating effects. The threat of climate change poses a real challenge to future generations. Our development strategy therefore, has to be sensitive to these concerns and should ensure that threats and trade-offs are appropriately evaluated.

(g) Improving Rehabilitation and Resettlement Practices

Our practices regarding rehabilitation of those displaced from their land because of development projects, conflicts, or calamities are very deficient. These have caused many people to feel vulnerable and there is anger because of forced exclusion and marginalisation. In particular, the costs of displacement borne by our tribal population. have been unduly high. Compensation has been tardy and inadequate, leading to unrest and insurgency in many regions. This discontent is likely to grow exponentially if the benefits from enforced land acquisition are seen accruing to private interests, or even to the state at the cost of those displaced. To give displaced people especially women, their due rights, it is necessary to frame a transparent set of policy rules that address compensation, proper resettlement, and rehabilitation and also gives project affected persons a permanent stake in project benefits. Moreover, these rules need to be given a legal format in terms of the rights of the displaced

(h) Improving Governance

Good governance and transparency should be ensured in the implementation of public programmes and also in government's interaction with the ordinary citizens. Corruption is now seen to be endemic in all spheres of life. Better design of projects, implementation mechanisms, and procedures can reduce the scope for corruption. Much more needs to be done by both the Centre and the states to lessen the discretionary power of government, ensure greater transparency and accountability, and create awareness among citizens. The Right to Information (RTI) Act empowers people to demand improved governance, and as government we must be ready to respond to this demand.

Justice delayed is justice denied. Quick and inexpensive dispensation of justice is an aspect of good governance which is of fundamental importance in a successful society. India's legal system is respected for its independence and fairness but it suffers from notorious delays in dispensing justice. The poor cannot access justice because delays cost money. Fundamental reforms are needed to give justice two essential attributes: speed and affordability.

1.4 Disparities and Divides.

Even as we address the specific challenges listed above, we must deal with the perception that development has failed to bridge the divides that 9 afflict our country and may even have sharpened some of them. Some of these perceptions may be exaggerated, but they exist nonetheless. The 11th Plan must, seek to bridge these divides as an overarching priority.

There are many divides. Foremost among these is the divide between the rich and the poor. As explained in Chapter 5, poverty is declining, but only at a pace which is no longer acceptable given the minimalist level at which the poverty line is fixed. There is also a divide between those who have access to essential services such as health, education, drinking water, sanitation, etc., and those who do not. Groups which have hitherto been excluded from our society such as SCs, STs and some minorities and OBCs, continue to lag behind the rest.

Another important divide relates to gender. It begins with the declining sex ratio, goes on to literacy differential between girls and boys and culminates in the high rate of maternal mortality. The extent of bias is self evident. The statistics given in Table 2 are reflective of the trend but do not tell the whole story. Differentials in educational status and economic empowerment are heavily biased against women. Special, focused efforts should be made to purge society of this malaise by creating an enabling environment for women to become economically, politically, and socially empowered. Measures to ensure that society recognizes women's economic and social worth, and accounts for the worth of women's unpaid work, will be a concomitant of this.

The divide between urban and rural India has become a truism of our times. The central government has already adopted a multi-pronged strategy to reduce this divide in its various dimensions. For example, the Bharat Nirman programme addresses gaps in rural infrastructure and covers

TABLE 2

Status of Some Socio-economic Indicators

Average/All India Best State Worst State

Around Recent Recent Recent

1990 Year Year Year

Per Capita Net National Product : 7321 **11799** 16679 3557

(Rs. per person at 1993-94 Prices)1

Consumption Poverty: 36.0 **27.8** 5.2 46.5

Head Count Ratio (%)2

Literacy (age 7+) Male:3 64.1 **75.3** 94.2 59.7

Literacy (age 7+) Female: 3 39.3 **53.7** 87.7 33.1

Attending Elementary Schools 55.3 **71.1** 103.1 55.8

(6-14 years)3

Child Sex Ratio (0-6 year olds): 945 **927** 975 793

(females/1000 males)3

Infant Mortality Rate: (2003) 80 **60** 11 83

(Per 1000 live births)4

Maternal Mortality Rate: (1997) **4**

(Per 1000 live births)4

Undernourished Children: (1998-99)5

Weight-for-age **47.0** 20.6 55.7

Height-for-age **45.5** 18.1 55.5

Weight-for-height **15.5** 4.8 24.3

1. For the years 1990-91 and 2003-04
2. The poverty estimates given are for 1993-94 and the latest estimates based on the NSS 2004-05

   survey which is comparable with 1993-94.
3. Calculated from information based on Census 1991 and 2001
4. Based on SRS
5. Percentage below 2 standard deviation from the mean of an international reference population.

irrigation, road connectivity, housing, water supply, electrification, and telephony; the National Rural Employment Guarantee Act (NREGA) attempts to ensures a social safety net as it provides guaranteed employment in rural areas and at the same time has the capacity to build rural infrastructure especially if resources from other programmes are pooled in; the Sarva Shiksha Abhiyan and National Rural Health Mission are ambitious programmes for providing elementary education and primary health services respectively. All these programmes indicate the priority being given by the Government to Rural Development and are meant to give a new hope to rural India. While making these provisions for rural India, the 11th Plan must also provide basic amenities to the growing number of poor in urban areas.

Regional backwardness is another important issue. Differences across states have always been a cause of concern but there exists imbalances within states as well. Backward districts of otherwise well performing states, present a dismal picture of intra-state imbalance and neglect. The Centre and the states will together have to deal with this problem on a priority basis otherwise discontent, injustice and frustration will only breed extremism. The spread of Naxalite movement to more than hundred districts in the country is a warning sign. There is anger and frustration where communalism has left scars. This is the direct fallout of the failures of the state apparatus to create an environment where the bulk of the people reap the benefits of development.

Special efforts must be made to give the people a sense of fairness, dignity and hope. The Backward Regions Grant Fund is meant to address the problem of regional imbalance so that the growth momentum is maintained.

Source : Approach Paper to 11th Plan, Planning Commission, Government of India.

Index